LITERARY FORMS
IN THE NEW TESTAMENT

LITERARY FORMS

in the

NEW TESTAMENT

A HANDBOOK

JAMES L. BAILEY
and
LYLE D. VANDER BROEK

Westminster/John Knox Press
Louisville, Kentucky

Book design by Gene Harris

First edition

Published by Westminster/John Knox Press
Louisville, Kentucky

This book is printed on acid-free paper that meets the American National Standards Institute Z39.48 standard. ∞

PRINTED IN THE UNITED STATES OF AMERICA

9 8 7 6 5 4 3 2 1

Library of Congress Cataloging-in-Publication Data

Bailey, James L., 1938–
    Literary forms in the New Testament : a handbook / James L. Bailey and Lyle D. Vander Broek. — 1st ed.
        p.   cm.
    Includes bibliographical references and index.
    ISBN 0-664-25154-4
    1. Bible. N.T.—Language, Style.   I. Vander Broek, Lyle D.   II. Title.
BS2361.2.B25 1992
225.6′6—dc20   91-37586

To

Judy

and

Rachel

CONTENTS

THE GOSPELS AND ACTS   89

OTHER NEW TESTAMENT WRITINGS   189

INDEX OF SCRIPTURE REFERENCES   211

PREFACE

Although we wrote most of this volume during our recent sabbaticals, we realize that it is also the product of years of teaching exegesis to seminary students. Researching and writing this book have increased and deepened our knowledge of literary forms in the New Testament, and we hope that the published results of our efforts will make the examination of literary forms a more productive part of the exegetical process, whether in the seminary classroom or the parish.

It has been our intent to avoid sexist language, even though such is not always possible in quoted material. To this end we have used the New Revised Standard Version of the Bible. Where indicated, we offer our own translations of the text. In some instances, our own translations vary from the New Revised Standard Version only for a word or phrase in order to reveal more exactly the meaning of the Greek language.

This has been very much a joint effort, and each of us claims responsibility for the whole. Nevertheless, Professor Vander Broek has had primary responsibility for the research and writing of the material published in the sections "The Pauline Tradition" and "Other New Testament Writings," and Professor Bailey has had primary responsibility for the section "The Gospels and Acts."

We want to express our appreciation to the University of Dubuque Theological Seminary and Wartburg Theological Seminary for granting us sabbaticals during the 1990/91 academic year, thus making the writing of this volume possible. We are grateful to the Lutheran Brotherhood for the generous grant awarded Professor Bailey, allowing him to spend the year studying at Columbia Theological Seminary, the Candler School of Theology at Emory University, and the Interdenominational Theological Center in the Atlanta area.

Our thanks also extend to various individuals who directly participated in this project: to Richard Drummond, Vernon Robbins, Stanley Saunders, and Howard Wallace, who read the manuscript and offered numerous suggestions for improvement in its substance and style; to the librarians of the various institutions, especially Patrick Graham, reference librarian at Pitts Theological Library, Emory University, who provided helpful bibliographical suggestions and generally made our research work easier; to Judith Bailey, Douglas Bailey, Rhonda Hanisch, Mary Rowland, Rachel Vander Broek, and Nancy Wiesner, who proofread the manuscript and suggested changes designed to increase its clarity and readability; to Jeffrey Ruetten, who prepared the scripture index; to our typist Mary Trannel, whose patience in typing and retyping far exceeded the call of duty; to John Gibbs, who greatly encouraged us in the early stages of the project; to editors Jeff Hamilton and Cynthia Thompson of Westminster/John Knox Press for their thoughtful guidance and assistance throughout.

We are particularly appreciative to our colleagues and friends at Wartburg Theological Seminary and the University of Dubuque Theological Seminary for their friendship and support, and our families, whose patience and love undergird all that we do.

JAMES L. BAILEY

LYLE D. VANDER BROEK

INTRODUCTION

The impulse for writing this book comes primarily from our seminary teaching. As teachers of the Bible, we seek to help incoming students practice interpretive procedures that will allow them to grapple responsibly with New Testament texts. One of the exegetical steps that is consistently problematic for our students deals with literary form. Inexperienced interpreters, we have discovered, often exhibit little or no awareness of how a text communicates its message because they do not understand the nature and function of the passage's literary form. We live in a society that has little knowledge of the workings of literary forms, even though there is no such thing as "formless" speech or writing in the contemporary world. When someone greets us with the words "How are you doin'?" we usually respond in a way that is consistent with the form ("Okay" or "Fine"), although such responses may not reflect the true state of our health. The form molds our speech in a powerful way, yet it has become so commonplace that we are not normally conscious of its role in communication. Or when reading a newspaper, we unconsciously discern the differences between the editorial or feature story or obituary and interpret accordingly, yet few people are cognizant of the literary forms of these pieces and how they relate to what is being communicated.

If most people have little awareness of the oral and literary forms used for communicating in the present environment, it is

not surprising that entering seminarians often know little or
nothing about the specific literary forms that were used in the
first-century world and now appear in the New Testament. Of
course, this lack of knowledge about ancient forms represents a
serious problem for the New Testament interpreter. Although
we might be able to intuit the formal characteristics of contemporary literary forms and interpret accordingly, such is hardly
possible with forms that are not used in our society. Moreover,
even after students become aware of certain New Testament
forms, they still might have difficulty in understanding how
knowledge of a specific form is helpful in the interpretive process. As teachers interested in cultivating seminarians' sensitivity to New Testament literary forms, we have noted a lack of
appropriate resources for the beginning student. While the more
common forms confronted, such as Gospel, parable, and letter,
are discussed in the introductory literature, many forms that the
student learns about in commentaries and monographs are defined only in rather specialized and often hard-to-find articles.
More often than not, these scholarly treatments have little to say
about the significance of the literary form for the exegetical task
engaged in by the seminary student or pastor.

This volume attempts to address these concerns. Each article
defines a common New Testament literary form, gives numerous
examples, suggests ways in which knowledge of the form is
helpful in interpretation, and offers an annotated bibliography
for the specific form discussed. There is a decidedly exegetical
emphasis throughout. We try to pose and to some extent answer
questions the exegete is confronted with as she or he interprets
a literary form in preparation for proclamation and teaching.
The book's comprehensive nature (over thirty forms are discussed) and its exegetical focus encourage us to hope that it will
have an ongoing value as a reference tool for those engaged in
biblical interpretation.

Exactly what is a literary form, and how does a knowledge of
the literary forms in the New Testament help the interpreter?
Our definition of literary form has two components. First, literary form refers primarily to the structure or organization of a
literary unit or passage, although elements such as style, content, and function might also have to be noted when defining a
particular literary form. The form we call "chiasm" serves as a
helpful example. Note the structure found in Rom. 10:19 (here
Paul is quoting Deut. 32:21):

    A. I will make you jealous
        B. of those who are not a nation;
        B'. with a foolish nation
    A'. I will make you angry.

Both A and A' and B and B' are parallel in terms of aural effect, meaning, and word order. Statements in the first part of the verse (A, B) are paralleled with statements in the second part (B', A'), although they are given in reverse order. This reverse parallelism certainly represents an identifiable structure.

Second, a literary form exhibits a structure that is commonly used, one that is found elsewhere in the literature of the period. It is helpful at this point to distinguish between "conventional" form and "organic" form (see Holman, 192, for further definitions of these terms). Organic form refers to a unique structure or organization of a piece of literature, that which is invented or fashioned by the author to best communicate the desired meaning. In organic form, the structures are as diverse as the ideas expressed, as diverse as the author's whims. Almost every piece of literature has some structure, some organic form that the reader can discern. Conventional form, on the other hand, refers to standard, widely recognized, and repeatable structures. Certain forms are commonly used in a society, and an author employs them, whether consciously or unconsciously, because their structure is widely understood and is appropriate to a certain content. A literary form, as we define it, is a conventional form. Again, the chiasm serves as a useful example. The structure we identified in Rom. 10:19 is not an isolated one. Reverse parallelism is common in Jewish and Hellenistic literature during the first century. The very fact that this structure has been named (chiasm) indicates its widespread use. The value of our study relates in a large part to the conventional nature of literary forms; the identification of a literary form in a particular instance will enable the interpreter to identify and understand the form when it occurs elsewhere in the New Testament.

There has been considerable scholarly discussion about the definition of literary form in relationship to what is called "genre." This is an important question for exegetes because several longer literary units in the New Testament—Gospel, letter, apocalypse, and perhaps midrash—are often labeled genres. Genres are usually distinguished from literary forms on the basis of length and complexity. Whereas literary forms can be short and structurally simple, the Gospels, the letters, and the one apocalypse (Revelation) in the New Testament are longer pieces that may themselves contain a number of shorter literary forms. Moreover, genres are often defined in terms of content, function, and technique, as well as structure. Certainly the differences between literary form and genre must be kept in mind. Our treatments of the genres Gospel, letter, and apocalypse are longer articles that recognize their complexity. But there must not be, in our opinion, a hard and fast distinction between literary form and genre, as if they were completely different categories. The genres listed above do exhibit "a coherent and recurring configuration of literary features" (Aune, 13), but so do the shorter literary forms. And some of the shorter literary forms in the New Testament are extremely complex and beg to be defined in terms of content and function as well as structure, like the so-called genres. It is perhaps best to see literary form as an umbrella under which the continuum from complex (including genres) to simple forms can be found.

It is important for interpreters of the New Testament to understand the literary forms found there because there is almost always a relationship between a literary form and the meaning conveyed. Consider a modern example: a sonnet, with its fourteen metrical lines and two-part progression, communicates a type of meaning and is received by its hearers in a way that is quite different from the impact created by the extended narrative of a novel. Although the exact relationship between literary form and meaning is unique for each form, it is possible to point out certain common ways in which literary forms influence meaning. For example, the structure of a literary form often dictates to a large extent both what is communicated and how interpretation is to proceed. The reverse parallelism of the chiasm, for instance, imposes significant restrictions upon both writer/speaker and interpreter. The writer of a chiasm cannot simply proceed haphazardly; each part in the first half of the chiasm must have a parallel in the second. The person attuned to this structure hears a series of statements that are in some way amplified or further defined by their parallel parts. The interpreter must note the parallel parts and try to understand their relationship. If the chiasm has a component at its center (A B C B' A'), the interpreter also learns to recognize this central element as the place of emphasis. In the chiasm there can be little doubt that what is stated and how it is heard is significantly shaped by the structure itself. Structure and meaning are inseparably linked.

In other cases, literary form is related to meaning on the basis of the audience's expectations and the form's typical function. The conventional nature of literary forms may mean that they are used in certain typical ways of which the interpreter must be aware. The diatribe, for instance, was normally used by teachers to instruct students about some error or problem. Although the structure of the diatribe is well-defined and important relative to meaning, the structure itself does not necessarily point to this function. That information must be gleaned from a study of the form's typical use in Greco-Roman literature. Another helpful example is the household code, a form that often had an apologetic function. The structure of the code—a listing of the duties of wives, children, and slaves, and masters overseeing them—shows no obvious links with tactics of defense. In order to understand the household code, the interpreter must be aware of how the form was typically employed and thus how a first-century audience would have understood it. Literary form and meaning are related on the basis of conventional use.

Certainly the relationship between literary form and meaning is also influenced by the way the author uses the form. The writer's employment of a form may reflect its conventional structure and function, or it may indicate a novel adaptation of the form. Paul's use of the letter form, for example, is in many ways consistent with its use in the Hellenistic world. Yet there are times when he feels free to deviate from the normal letter structure; these alterations of a standard form can be very telling indeed, as, for example, in Galatians when he omits the thanksgiving section of the letter. The Gospels provide another example of this creative adaptation of existing literary forms. Rather than follow the pattern of one literary type, the evangelists apparently adopt for their purposes elements of both biblical history and Greco-Roman biography. Thus the Gospel is a "mixed genre" that does not simply repeat old literary forms but offers a new way of using them to present the story of Jesus.

There are countless other ways in which literary form and meaning are related, but the above gives some indication of the value of the study of literary forms. Gaining knowledge about a literary form is not an academic exercise devoid of practical use. The individual literary forms examined in this volume illustrate over and over again the necessity of this kind of formal awareness. Modern interpreters must not be blind to the literary forms that ancient writers and audiences considered so important.

Although this volume examines literary forms in the New Testament, it should be underscored that our study is not simply an exercise in form criticism, at least as that term has usually been defined in biblical studies. Our concern is not limited to those forms that arose in the oral tradition, nor are we especially intent to explain the use of the forms in their original social settings (in German, *Sitz im Leben*), an important task of the early form critics. Forms that began orally are treated (e.g., aphorism, miracle story, and creed), but so are ones that originated as literary compositions (e.g., genres such as letter, Gospel, and apocalypse). Moreover, it should be noted that we include articles on forms of argumentation and articles that describe how rhetorical argumentation, known and practiced in the Hellenistic world, has influenced certain forms (e.g., letter, speech, and pronouncement story).

This rather inclusive understanding of literary form reflects current trends in biblical scholarship, especially the impact literary criticism and rhetorical criticism have had upon formal studies (see Robbins). Literary criticism of the New Testament, or what has sometimes been termed "aesthetic criticism," has to a large extent built on the contributions of the form critics. Using a number of methods, literary criticism endeavors to understand the biblical unit—whether it be a parable or an entire Gospel— as a literary work in its present form, much the same way that one understands a work of art that takes on a life of its own. As part of this interpretive process, literary critics focus on aspects of style and overall structure that are important to the form-critical investigation of texts. But literary critics are not concerned simply with identifying general characteristics of literary forms. They also try to determine how a particular literary text functions with its audience and, in the case of the New Testament, how it functions as a religious text. This is why literary criticism considers as well the dynamics of language, imagery, and metaphor, and the hermeneutics of understanding. Although in this volume we have not sought to take into account the numerous and variegated contributions of literary critics, it is obvious that articles on certain forms benefit from literary analysis; for example, chiasm, poetry and hymn, aphorism, parable, miracle story.

In recent decades, traditional form criticism has also been modified by rhetorical criticism. Vernon Robbins identifies three modes of rhetorical criticism affecting current scholarship. Some scholars (e.g., Amos Wilder and Robert Tannehill) have used what might be called a "rhetorical form criticism" with an emphasis on the aesthetic study of forms such as parable, sayings, and pronouncement story. They seek to demonstrate how the literary characteristics of the textual unit exercise their rhetorical effect on the audience. Others (e.g., Hans Dieter Betz) now use knowledge of the forms and patterns of Hellenistic rhetoric to analyze forms in the New Testament, on the assumption that these rhetorical patterns were influential in first century c.e. Jewish and Christian circles. A third type of rhetorical form criticism is represented by the work of the German scholar Klaus Berger, who draws on Hellenistic rhetoric but is concerned as well with social analysis. As one might expect in an introductory work such as our own, we refer at times to all these approaches. Our basic purpose is to illustrate how the strategies and structures of ancient rhetoric have influenced the New Testament, even to the extent that common Greco-Roman rhetorical forms can be found there.

One's definition of a literary form will depend largely upon the structural criteria used to identify that form. We understand literary form to be an inclusive term encompassing conventional forms determined by various criteria. In a document like the New Testament, which has diverse origins and which is studied through various modern methodologies, the interpreter must be aware of the multiplicity of formal criteria. A good part of the New Testament circulated orally before it was collected and put in written form. It was influenced by various Jewish and Hellenistic traditions. As we have noted, rhetoric was important in the ancient world, and elements of the speechmakers' art can be detected there. Recent scholarship has reminded us again that the New Testament documents were meant to be read aloud and heard by a community of people. Such an oral presentation of the text clearly makes rhetorical argumentation very important. Yet at the same time, the New Testament is very much a collection of written documents that assumed their final form through conscious literary construction and editing. At times, the structures of New Testament passages were perceived aurally by listening audiences, whereas at other times they were perceived visually by those who read them. In light of the differing criteria used for classification, we have seen how one passage might be described as exhibiting various literary forms. First Corinthians 13 is a prime example of this. Various interpreters have labeled it poetry, chiasm, or encomium (a rhetorical form). In a similar way, various scholars have classified Luke 5:1–11 as a miracle story, a commissioning story, and a story about Jesus.

Our broad definition of literary form accounts for the great variety of entries in this volume. The actual selection of forms is based especially on what we think is their helpfulness for the beginning interpreter of the New Testament. Literary forms most commonly referred to in the introductions and commentaries used by our seminary students are largely the focus. Some might argue that it would be wiser to deal only with oral forms or Jewish forms or rhetorical forms. But as persons who teach exegesis, we know how helpful a wide-ranging handbook would be. There is great value in having in one book definitions of forms referred to in various works and in various methodologies. Our definitions, though brief, should help the biblical interpreters identify forms they had not noticed before. It is our hope that interpreters will not only study our article on a specific form but will select materials in the bibliography for further reading about that form and the criteria by which its structure has been described.

Above all, we hope to encourage our readers to wrestle with the relationship between literary form and interpretation. Exactly how does knowledge of a literary form inform the exegetical process; what is the relationship between form and meaning? This is no easy task. At times, the relationship may not be so obvious. It is quite possible that the author/speaker may use a conventional form to communicate in ways not normally associated with that form. Of course, the socio-historical and literary contexts for the passage are also critically important to any interpretation. When we offer interpretive suggestions for any particular form, it must not be assumed that we are presenting a never-fail formula for discovering meaning. Rather, our interpretive remarks are meant to be illustrative and suggestive, designed to encourage our readers to begin the process of pondering how the meaning of a text results from the effect of its content and form on the audience. To engage in this interpretive process is most challenging and exciting, and at times, extremely difficult. But the difficulty of the task affirms its importance. For this reason, providing students of the New Testament a foundation for understanding the movement from form to interpretation is no insignificant matter.

A glance at the table of contents will alert readers regarding the chosen order for the articles. We begin with forms and patterns found in the Pauline tradition, including ones in the later deutero-Pauline letters. Then we proceed to a consideration of literary forms that occur in the Gospels and Acts, and conclude with those that appear in other and often considered later documents of the New Testament, that is, Hebrews, James, First and Second Peter, Jude, and Revelation. The scripture index should be helpful for those who sense that a particular passage follows a certain form or pattern but are unable to label that form. It is our hope that this handbook will provide considerable help to interpreters who wish to take more seriously the literary form of New Testament texts.

Selected Bibliography

Aune, David E. 1987. *The New Testament in Its Literary Environment*. Philadelphia: Westminster Press. This book discusses the major genres (Gospel, letter, and apocalypse) in detail.

Berger, Klaus. 1984. "Hellenistische Gattungen im Neuen Testament." In *Aufstieg und Niedergang der römischen Welt*, 1031–1432, II.25,2. Berlin & New York: Walter de Gruyter. For those who read German, this section represents an indispensable resource.

Holman, Hugh C. 1980. *A Handbook to Literature*. Indianapolis: Bobbs-Merrill Educational Publishing. This handbook is a helpful resource for defining such terms as form and genre, especially as they are used in reference to nonbiblical material.

Robbins, Vernon K. 199?. "Form Criticism: New Testament." In *Anchor Bible Dictionary*, edited by D. N. Freedman. Garden City, N.Y.: Doubleday & Co. This article, which describes the development of form criticism and its recent modifications by literary and rhetorical criticism, is forthcoming as an entry in this new Bible dictionary.

THE PAULINE
TRADITION

THE PAULINE LETTER

Definition of the Form

All the material we have from Paul comes to us in the form of letters. In addition to the correspondence known to have been written by Paul (Rom.; 1, 2 Cor.; Gal.; Phil.; 1 Thess.; Philemon), the letter form occurs in material where Pauline authorship is debated (Col.; Eph.; 2 Thess.) or even unlikely (the Pastorals: 1, 2 Tim.; Titus). Later N.T. writers also pen letters or at least borrow some of the letter's elements (Heb.; James; 1, 2 Peter; 1, 2, 3 John; Jude; Rev.), making it the most common literary genre in the N.T. Based upon a letter's purpose and the type of audience addressed, scholars have identified various types of letters in the Hellenistic world: personal letters, business and official letters, public letters (open letters addressing public issues), pseudonymous or fictitious letters (letters written in another person's name or using an imagined situation), and essay letters (essays or academic treatises using the letter form; see Doty, 4–8). Although Paul writes a personal letter (Philemon) and a letter that in some ways resembles an essay (Rom.), most of his letters fall somewhere between the private and the academic. He addresses specific situations and people with whom he has personal relations, but it is also true that he writes as an apostle (as an authoritative representative of the church) to communities of faith. Paul expects his letters to be read aloud to the assembled body so that he might instruct the life of the church (see 1 Thess. 5:27; Col. 4:16). In terms of form, letters in the Hellenistic era exhibit a three-part structure: an opening, a body, and a closing. Paul always follows this general structure, although he freely modifies the individual parts to meet his needs.

The Opening

The opening section in Paul's letters consists of three subparts: a statement of sender and recipient, a salutation, and a thanksgiving. Following the Hellenistic form, Paul's letters begin with a statement of sender and recipient: "Paul, to the church of God that is in Corinth." Actually, Paul's initial words in 1 Corinthians are much more involved and give us some insight into his modification of the form:

23

> Paul, called to be an apostle of Jesus Christ by the will of God, and our brother Sosthenes, to the church of God that is in Corinth, to those who are sanctified in Christ Jesus, called to be saints, together with all those who in every place call on the name of our Lord Jesus Christ, both their Lord and ours.

Paul not only gives his name, but mentions his call and authority as an apostle, certainly an appropriate introduction for a letter in which he intends to teach and reprove a Christian community. Notice also that Paul refers to Sosthenes, a co-sender (his secretary?) who, as a common acquaintance with the Corinthians, would give Paul's letter added authority. Even the recipients are not simply listed but are described, perhaps as Paul hopes they might be! This embellishment of what is usually a very succinct part of Hellenistic letters can be an important exegetical clue. Paul often expands his sender/recipient statements in a way that foreshadows the content of his letters and explains the situation he is addressing (see Gal. 1:1–2; 2 Cor. 1:1; Rom. 1:1–7a).

After the statement of sender/recipient, the typical Hellenistic letter simply declares "Greetings!" Again, Paul modifies the form. Instead of greetings (in the Greek, *chairein*), Paul writes a salutation: "Grace to you and peace." The use of "grace" (*charis*) certainly reflects Paul's theology and may even have been used because of its linguistic similarity to the typical greeting (*chairein*). Paul's use of "peace" may indicate his dependence upon the Jewish letter form, which often had a prayer for peace instead of a greeting. Although the salutation in Paul's letters is usually a simple request for God's grace and peace upon the recipients, it too can be embellished (see Gal. 1:1–5).

The openings of Paul's letters conclude with statements of thanksgiving. Rather than thanking the gods for saving the sender or recipient from some danger, as is typically the case in Hellenistic letters, Paul's thanksgivings especially give thanks for the faithful Christian witness of the congregation to whom he is writing. Perhaps because the thanksgiving is the last subsection before the body of the letter, Paul may use it to telegraph the main themes to be pursued later (see 1 Cor. 1:7, for instance, where Paul mentions two major themes in the letter, spiritual gifts and eschatology). At times, Paul can lengthen a thanksgiving for emphasis (see 1 Thess.) or omit it altogether (Gal.).

The Body

It is the purpose of the body of the letter to communicate its central message. Formal analysis of the body of Paul's letters has been a difficult task, however, because they often appear to be shaped more by content or Paul's concerns than by a typical structure. Many literary and rhetorical forms have been identified within the bodies of Paul's letters (see sections on *Chiasm, Poetry and Hymn, The Diatribe, Paraenesis/Topoi, Vice and Virtue Lists,* and so on), but most of these are not inherent to the Hellenistic letter.

A few formal characteristics do appear regularly and are worth noting. Certain introductory or transition formulas, found also in Hellenistic letters, are often used to introduce important themes in the body of the letter. Phrases such as "I want you to know that . . ." (Phil. 1:12; 1 Thess. 2:1; Gal. 1:11), "I appeal to you . . ." or "I urge you . . ." (1 Cor. 1:10; 4:16; Philemon 9; 1 Thess. 4:1–2, 10b), and "I do not want you to be ignorant . . ." (1 Thess. 4:13; 2 Cor. 1:18) may be significant clues concerning structure and thought.

As one might expect in communication between two parties, Paul's letters contain several themes or topics common in Hellenistic letters: the health of the sender or recipient (2 Cor. 1:8–11; Phil. 2:25–30; Eph. 6:21–22), business matters (2 Cor. 8, 9; Phil. 4:14–18), and talk of a future visit (Rom. 15:14–33; 1 Cor. 4:14–21; 16:1–11; Gal. 4:20; Phil. 2:19–30; 1 Thess. 2:17–3:13). The latter usually conclude the body of the letter and are especially noteworthy because they attest to the importance of Paul's personal and apostolic presence for the communities he is addressing (Funk, 263ff.). Another standard theme found in Paul, the autobiographical statement, is interesting because Paul appears to follow the typical rhetorical structure of Greco-Roman autobiography. George Lyons finds the conventional structure in Gal. 1, 2: 1:10–12, *prooimion,* or introduction concerning Paul's divine gospel; 1:13–17, a statement of *ethos,* or character, both as persecutor and preacher; 1:18–2:10, *praxeis,* or description of Paul's conduct; 2:11–21, *synkrisis,* or comparison of Paul and his "opponents"; 2:21, *epilogue,* or Paul's conclusion that he does not nullify God's grace (cf. the form in 1 Thess. 1:2–2:13; Phil. 1:12–26; 2 Cor. 1:12–2:17; 7:5–16; Lyons, 135). Because this form is used in various types of speeches to affirm the character of the speaker, Lyons challenges the commonly held assumption that Paul's autobiographical statements must have an apologetic function. It is more likely, according to Lyons, that Paul uses such autobiography to define himself as one whom *God* has used and thus as a disciple whose life can serve as an edifying example (223–227). The autobiographical statements in Paul usually occur at the beginning of the body of the letter.

The bodies of Paul's letters also contain paraenesis (ethical exhortation), and several conclude with a paraenetical section (Gal. 5:1–6:10; Rom. 12:1–15:13; 1 Thess. 4:1ff.). Placing these hortatory statements toward the end of the letter is a logical way for Paul to apply the theological truths he has been emphasizing and stress in another way his authority over and responsibility for the churches he had founded. Paul readily uses and adapts the standard paraenetical forms (see *Paraenesis/Topoi, Vice and Virtue Lists*).

One productive area in the analysis of the bodies of Paul's letters has come through comparison with specialized types of ancient letters. Hellenistic epistolographers enumerate various types of letters based upon rhetorical form and function. Some of these types appear to be helpful in explaining the form of Paul's letters. George Kennedy, for instance, calls Romans an epideictic letter, a type of speech in which the author eulogizes or recommends something or someone (see *Forms of Argumentation* for further definition of this and other rhetorical terms). According to Kennedy, both the intent (Paul wishes to recommend his gospel to a church he had not founded) and the structure of Romans (1:8–15, proem or introduction; 1:16–17, proposition or statement of theme; 1:18–11:36, proof or support for the proposition; 12:1–15:13, practical concerns; 15:14–33, epilogue or conclusion) are consistent with epideictic speech (152–156). Most of 2 Corinthians falls into the category of judicial speech, which is typical of the apology subtype; Paul defends himself against his opponents using a standard structure (Kennedy, 86–96). Scholars continue to debate whether Galatians is to be seen as a judicial letter (apology or defense; see Betz, introduction) or a deliberative letter, a form of speech in which Paul is trying to convince his hearers as he might in an assembly (Lyons, 170–176; cf. J. Smit, "The Letter of Paul to the Galatians: A Deliberative Speech," *New Testament Studies* 35, 1–26). Some types of ancient letters that do not readily fit into the typical rhetorical categories have also been helpful in classifying Paul's letters (see Stowers, 49–166). First Thessalonians, for instance, has the form and function of a paraenetical letter

(Stowers, 94ff.). Philemon can be compared to Hellenistic letters of recommendation (Aune, 211).

Of course, an awareness of Greco-Roman rhetoric is also valuable in that it helps the interpreter identify rhetorical forms or units within the bodies of the letters (see *Forms of Argumentation*). Shorter, individual arguments of Paul often follow a standard rhetorical format as well. Paul's persuasion is proving to be less haphazard than earlier scholars had believed. The interpretive methodology called rhetorical criticism represents the new frontier for analysis of the bodies of Paul's letters.

The Closing

Paul uses considerable freedom in his closings. The typical Hellenistic letter in Paul's day contained a final greeting, a final wish for good health, and a farewell. The most important element in Paul's closings, on the other hand, is the grace benediction ("Grace be with you . . ."), which almost always comes at the very end (see, however, 1 Cor.). This is usually accompanied by a peace wish (Phil. 4:9; Gal. 6:16; 2 Cor. 13:11) and, in two cases, by a doxology (Rom. 16:27; Phil. 4:20). Additional common elements include autobiographical greetings (like many Hellenistic letter writers, Paul probably used a secretary; see 1 Cor. 16:21; Gal. 6:11), the holy kiss (1 Thess. 5:26; Rom. 16:16; 1 Cor. 16:20; 2 Cor. 13:12), and final greetings and greetings from people other than Paul (Rom. 16:3ff., 21ff.; Philemon 23, 24; 1 Cor. 16:19). Even editorial comments relating to the theme of the letter find their way into the closings (see Gal. 6:12ff.; 1 Cor. 16:22).

The Value for Interpretation

Among the almost endless implications of the study of the letter form for exegesis, the following are especially important. An understanding of the opening of the letter (and to a lesser degree, the closing) can be particularly helpful because the way Paul alters or emphasizes parts of the opening can signal issues he will pursue later in the letter. In the sender/recipient statement in Galatians, for instance, Paul adds a clause about his authority in Jesus Christ that relates directly to the issue he is confronting in that community ("Paul an apostle—sent neither by human commission nor from human authorities, but through Jesus Christ and God the Father, who raised him from the dead—"; cf. 2 Cor. 1:1; Rom. 1:1–7a). In this same letter, Paul actually omits the thanksgiving, a key indication of his mood and intentions (cf. how the thanksgiving in 1 Cor. 1:4–9, especially vs. 7, 8, points to themes he will discuss later). None of these uses and modifications is theologically innocent. The exegete must be attuned to Paul's creative alteration of a form that was very familiar to him and his hearers.

Paul's train of thought can be ambiguous, and scholars often disagree about what the main sections of his letters are. Insights into the literary and rhetorical components of the body of the letter can be helpful in that they provide clues to the structure of Paul's thought. These components include not only those discussed in this section, but also the forms to be dealt with later. The possible examples are infinite. The student who is aware of Paul's transition formulas will immediately note the signaled transition in Rom. 12:1 ("I appeal to you therefore . . .), perhaps even before he or she discovers the shift to the imperative mood and paraenesis. Of course, paraenesis itself is a significant structural feature in the bodies of Paul's letters (see 1 Thess. 4:1ff.; Gal. 5:1ff.; in addition to Rom.). The exegete who is aware of Paul's use of "visit plans" will realize that the form often indicates the conclusion of the body. The identification of a literary form in Paul is always structurally significant because, at the very least, it helps define a unit of thought. Rhetorical criticism has proven to be especially important in terms of overall structure because it points not only to individual rhetorical forms but also to larger structures and strategies of persuasion. As has been pointed out, entire letters can fall into one of the speech types; how one outlines a letter may relate directly to the rhetorical structure identified (see Kennedy and his outline of Rom., above).

An awareness of structural issues in the letters may also cue the interpreter to what appears to be a later joining of independent fragments of Paul's letters. Many scholars feel that 2 Corinthians and Philippians are compilations. Even a cursory reading of 2 Corinthians suggests that 2 Cor. 6:14–7:1 is an interpolation and that chs. 8 and 9 are independent statements on the same theme. In terms of rhetorical type, chs. 1–7 (minus 6:14–7:1, which is formally distinct) are judicial, whereas chs. 8 and 9 are deliberative. Chapters 10–13 are also judicial, but they appear to be independent of the rhetorical unit in chs. 1–7. In Philippians, note the rough seam in 3:2 and the awkward exhortations *after* what looks like a closing benediction in 4:7. It is difficult, perhaps impossible, to interpret properly these letters without some knowledge of how the diverse parts have been joined together. An understanding of the formal characteristics of Paul's letters provides the foundation for this analysis.

It is often said that Paul's letters are one half of a dialogue. Paul is responding to the needs and requests of specific Christian communities. His letters are "situational"; they are real letters written to real churches. Certainly Paul's use of the letter form supports this view. He alters his sender/recipient statements and thanksgivings in a way that indicates his awareness of the community and situation being addressed. Paul includes in his openings and closings elements associated with worship (the salutation, the prayerlike thanksgiving, the grace benediction, the peace wish, the holy kiss), affirming his role as spiritual leader. The autobiographical and visit statements point to his intimate and authoritative relationship with his hearers. Paul's paraenesis is usually directed toward specific situations. Above all, knowledge of Paul's use of the letter form tells the exegete that she or he must attempt to hear both halves of the dialogue represented by the letter. The letter, perhaps even more than the other longer literary forms found in the N.T. (i.e., Gospel, apocalypse), demands that the exegete seek to understand the situation and community being addressed. What was the community like? What were its problems? What questions had they asked of Paul in their own correspondence (see 1 Cor. 7:1)? What theological and pastoral issues is Paul trying to address? These are difficult questions, to be sure. Yet this understanding of the situational nature of Paul's correspondence lies at the heart of the exegetical task.

It is important to realize, however, that not all of the N.T. letters lend themselves easily to this situational interpretation. In the Pastorals, for instance, aspects of style, content, and vocabulary indicate that they were most certainly not written by Paul to Timothy and Titus. They are pseudonymous both in terms of author and recipient (Meade). In this case, the interpreter should not take the letter form and what it indicates about a situation at face value. Nor can one assume that the other letters found in the N.T. are essentially like Paul's. Some are addressed not to a particular congregational setting but to a wider audience (e.g., 1 Peter; James; see *General Letters*), whereas others borrow some of the formal characteristics of the letter but are in reality different literary forms altogether (see *Apocalypse; The Sermon*). As standard as the letter form is in the N.T., it does not always indicate a personal and apostolic relationship between stated sender and recipient. The implications of the letter form must be studied anew for each N.T. writer.

Selected Bibliography

Aune, David E. 1987. *The New Testament in Its Literary Environment*. Philadelphia: Westminster Press. See Chapters 5 and 6, which are very helpful in comparing early Christian letters with the rhetorical styles and letter types in the ancient world.

Betz, Hans Dieter. 1979. *Galatians: A Commentary on Paul's Letter to the Churches in Galatia. Hermeneia*. Philadelphia: Fortress Press. See especially Betz's introduction concerning the rhetorical structure of Galatians.

Doty, William G. 1973. *Letters in Primitive Christianity*. Philadelphia: Fortress Press. This older book is still perhaps the best introduction to the subject.

Funk, Robert W. 1967. "The Apostolic *Parousia:* Form and Significance." In *Christian History and Interpretation: Studies Presented to John Knox*, edited by W. R. Farmer, C. F. D. Moule, R. R. Niebuhr, 249–268. Cambridge: Cambridge University Press. This study of Paul's "visit plan" statements is helpful in terms of what it says about Paul's apostolic presence.

Kennedy, George A. 1984. *New Testament Interpretation Through Rhetorical Criticism*. Chapel Hill: University of North Carolina Press. This book is one of the best introductions to rhetorical criticism.

Lyons, George. 1985. *Pauline Autobiography: Towards a New Understanding*. SBL Dissertation Series No. 73. Atlanta: Scholars Press. Lyons defines autobiography as a rhetorical form and shows how its use in Paul need not have an apologetic function.

Meade, David G. 1986. *Pseudonymity and Canon*. Grand Rapids: Wm. B. Eerdmans. Meade discusses the reasons for the widespread use of pseudonymity in the N.T. writings.

Stowers, Stanley K. 1986. *Letter Writing in the Greco-Roman World*. Philadelphia: Westminster Press. Stowers illustrates the various types of Greco-Roman letters and suggests N.T. parallels.

White, John L. 1988. "Ancient Greek Letters." In *Greco-Roman Literature and the New Testament*. SBL Sources for Biblical Study No. 21, edited by David E. Aune, 85–105. Atlanta: Scholars Press. This helpful introduction shows the influence of Greek letter writing upon N.T. letters.

FORMS OF ARGUMENTATION

Definition of the Form

Modern readers may be surprised to discover that arguments or various types of persuasion can have standard forms. This surprise is in part because of our lack of contact with a discipline called rhetoric, an area of study that seeks to understand how language becomes persuasive. During the last two decades, biblical scholars have begun to rediscover how the theory and practice of classical rhetoric, that is, Greco-Roman rhetoric, has influenced the material now found in the New Testament. The biblical discipline that pursues this rhetorical analysis is commonly called rhetorical criticism.

Rhetoric was an important part of the curriculum in Greek and Roman schools. It dealt with a whole range of topics concerning effective persuasion, including aspects called *invention* (how a subject and proofs are chosen), *arrangement* (ordering properly the material in the argument), *style, memory,* and *delivery.* Theories of persuasion were developed under the headings *ethos* (how the speaker establishes himself or herself as being trustworthy), *pathos* (knowledge of the audience and how they could be motivated), and *logos* (the content and logic of the speech). Of course, rhetoric concerned itself with far more than simply matters of style (a modern misconception); it was an expansive field covering everything from details of oral delivery to the philosophy of communication.

In the construction of a specific argument, classical rhetoric was more concerned with strategies of persuasion than with the necessity of using rigidly defined structures. Various formal possibilities might exist, depending on the subject matter being pursued and the types of support or proof available. Nevertheless, it is legitimate to point out certain common structural features that are characteristic of the most typical forms of argumentation.

These structural features are related in part to the type of
rhetorical speech in which they are found. Three types of speech
were usually identified: the *judicial*, the *deliberative*, and the
epideictic. Each type was defined in various ways, but the occasion of the speech and its positive and negative subtypes are
especially helpful in definition. Thus the occasion for a judicial
speech would be a courtroom setting (or some similar setting
where a past action is to be judged); its contrasting subtypes
would be speeches of accusation and defense. The occasion for
the deliberative speech would be the assembly (or some setting
where the appropriateness of a future action is considered); its
contrasting subtypes are persuasion and dissuasion. Epideictic
speech has as its occasion a setting in which someone or something is honored or blamed; hence praise (the positive epideictic
speech is called an encomium) and blame are its subtypes
(Kennedy, 19).

Judicial and deliberative arguments usually exhibit similar
essential forms. They often begin with what is called a *proem* or
exordium, an introduction acknowledging the audience and the
situation at hand. The *narration* and/or *proposition* follow; the
narration gives appropriate background material, and the proposition succinctly states the main point of the argument. Next
comes the *proof*, the body of the argument in which support for
the proposition is given. An *epilogue* concludes the unit; it summarizes and often encourages the audience to agree with the
speaker's position in the argument. A common variation in the
judicial speech is the presence of a *refutation* section (following
the proof) in which the speaker anticipates and negates opposing
points of view. Deliberative persuasion is less likely to have a
narration section (Mack, 41f.; Kennedy, 23f.).

Epideictic speeches usually exhibit a simpler form. The body
of the speech (after the proem, before the epilogue) often consists of a series of colorful laudatory statements that praise the
person or topic being discussed (the "praise" subtype is more
common than the "blame" subtype).

As important as these basic forms are, it is vital to realize that
the speakers were expected to exercise creativity within the
various sections in order to make them effective. The rhetorical
subunits (some of which have their own distinct forms) and
stylistic devices available were almost endless. Speakers could
garner support by arguing "the opposite" (showing the absurdity of the opposing point of view), "from the lesser" (showing
how, if something is true concerning an insignificant issue, it is

certainly true relative to the more significant issue being discussed), and by using historical examples, written authorities, analogies, and fables (Mack, 40). They could employ hyperbole, alliteration, the repetition of words, rhetorical questions, emotional appeals, and so forth (Kennedy, 26f.). A successful argument used the conventional form, but also creatively employed proof and aspects of style to address the situation at hand.

All of the above is a rather lengthy yet necessary introduction to our understanding of Paul's arguments. Rhetorical criticism has made significant discoveries about Paul's use of persuasion and how it reflects classical rhetoric. While rhetorical criticism has analyzed various parts of the N.T., studies in Paul have been especially productive. Paul's letters often resemble speech material, not only because they were intended to persuade an audience relative to a specific situation, but also because they were usually read aloud in the churches. Although they are written documents, Paul's letters often have important aural qualities.

Examples of the three types of persuasion can readily be found in Paul's writings. Burton Mack offers a helpful outline of 1 Cor. 15:1–58 as, essentially, a deliberative argument (56ff.).

Proem: Vs. 1–2. Paul personally addresses his audience and reminds them of the foundation of their faith.

Narration and Proposition: Vs. 3–20. The narration itself (vs. 3–11) gives the background about the church's reception of the resurrection of Christ. The proposition states the issue being challenged (some say the dead are not raised, v. 12), shows the absurdity of rejecting the resurrection of Christ (vs. 13–19), and clearly states the thesis of the entire argument (since Christ has been raised, believers are also raised, v. 20).

The Proof: Vs. 21–50. A wide variety of proofs are used, with varying effectiveness. Verses 21–28 are a paradigm contrasting Christ and Adam, especially emphasizing the eschatological order brought about through Christ (vs. 23–28). Verses 29–33 contain three examples: baptizing on behalf of the dead (v. 29), dying daily (vs. 30, 31), and enduring persecution (vs. 32, 33). Verses 35–44 explain the nature of the resurrected body through analogies about seeds (vs. 36–38) and the various kinds of body (vs. 39–44). An authoritative O.T. citation and its implications conclude the proof (vs. 45–50).

Epilogue: Vs. 51–58. Paul motivates the audience to agree
with his thesis by using an eschatological scene about resurrection (vs. 51, 52) that builds to a crescendo around O.T.
references concerning death (vs. 53, 56), and by using a
thanksgiving (v. 57) and an exhortation (v. 58).

In this case, the form of the argument sends mixed signals
about its type. The presence of what appear to be refutations
(vs. 12f., 35f.) might indicate that it is a judicial speech. It is
perhaps best to label this a deliberative speech, however, not
simply because of the form, but also because of the author's
intention and the situation being addressed. The Corinthian
community is being persuaded to accept fully what they know
concerning their own future resurrections (see vs. 1, 2). Identification of the basic form of the argument is certainly helpful in
defining Paul's unit of thought and in understanding his intentions in each of the sections of the form.

Note how Paul creatively develops the basic sections of the
argument through rhetorical devices and forms. Verses 12–19
are a series of overlapping phrases, repeating the final words of
one statement in the first part of the next and relying on the
"if-then" logic to show the absurdity of denying the resurrection
of Christ. Verses 23–28 have a similar form, although the orga-
nizing theme is eschatology. Both forms would have had a significant aural impact through the repetition of sounds and ideas
and because of their strong conclusions (vs. 18, 28). The rhetorical crescendo Paul develops in vs. 51–57 makes the epilogue
powerful indeed, moving as it does from a tone of eschatological
mystery (v. 51) through anticipated scriptural fulfillment (vs. 54,
55) to thanksgiving (v. 57) and exhortation (v. 58). The climax
Paul offers in these verses signals clearly that the argument has
concluded (cf. Rom. 8:31–39; 11:25–36).

As one might expect in the writings of a person often forced
to defend himself or his teachings, judicial speech (of the defense or apology subtype) abounds. George Kennedy's understanding of the structure of 2 Cor. 1–7 is instructive (87ff.).

Proem: 1:3–7. Paul reestablishes his relationship with the
congregation.
Narration: 1:8–2:13. Paul not only relates recent events in his
life, but indicates the point of contention (the letter he
wrote, 1:13; 2:3f.) and begins to make his defense (see
1:15ff.; 2:1f.; 2:4, etc.).
Proposition: 2:14–17. Paul uses a metaphor (he is the aroma

of Christ, vs. 14, 15) and succinctly states three elements ("people of sincerity," "commissioned by God," "in the sight of God we speak in Christ," v. 17) upon which he will base his defense.

The Proof: 3:1–6:13. After an interlude in which Paul describes the Corinthians as his character witness (3:1–3), he builds his proof on the three elements given in the proposition.

> 3:4–4:1. "Commissioned by God."
> 4:2–6. "People of sincerity."
> 4:7–12. "Commissioned by God."
> 4:13–5:10. "People of sincerity."
> 5:11–6:13. "In the sight of God we speak in Christ."

Epilogue: 7:2–16. (6:14–7:1 is most certainly a non-Pauline interpolation.) Paul concludes his speech by reiterating his defense (7:2ff.) and recent experiences (7:5ff.), and by making an emotional appeal to the Corinthians (7:8–16).

Again, the typical form is obvious. The references to the point of conflict and Paul's defense make it clear that this speech is of the judicial type. Note especially Paul's creativity in his ordering of the key elements of his defense in the proof section and his highly effective personal appeal in the epilogue. Kennedy's assessment of 2 Cor. 1–7 as a complete unit supports rhetorically the understanding that 2 Corinthians is a compilation of letters (usually ch. 8, ch. 9, and chs. 10–13 are seen as independent parts).

The interpreter must realize that the three main types of persuasion described above are found not only in shorter units within letters but also comprise entire letters (see Additional Examples, below). It should further be noted that a great many rhetorical subforms exist, forms that have their own standard structure and that are often employed within the three basic types. Examples in Paul include autobiography (see *The Pauline Letter;* Lyons), the diatribe, topoi, and chiasm (see respective sections).

The Value for Interpretation

Scholars of rhetoric have rightly emphasized the value of identifying rhetorical units. Knowing the forms of argumentation gives the exegete yet another way of ascertaining where Paul begins and ends a unit of thought. Even more, knowledge of these forms gives the interpreter a concrete tool by which he or she can analyze Paul's train of thought. Identifying the main sections of an argument should help the interpreter grasp Paul's intentions in each of those sections. If one can positively identify a narration or epilogue, for instance, that information about the form gives the exegete a great advantage over someone who can do no more than identify the body of a letter.

Insight into Paul's train of thought is furthered if one uses the tools of rhetorical criticism to discover exactly what forms and devices Paul employs in each of the sections to persuade his audience. Why, for instance, is a certain proof section effective? What specific arguments or stylistic devices does he use? First Corinthians 15:1–58, analyzed above, is a graphic example. The power and logic of Paul's argument there is significantly enhanced if the hearer can appreciate the crispness of his thesis (v. 20), the overlapping style of his arguments (vs. 12–19, 23–28), the vividness of his analogies (vs. 36–44), and the emotional appeal of his final crescendo (vs. 51–58). A thorough knowledge of the rhetorical forms and devices helps the interpreter more fully value Paul's rhetorical activity and perhaps even anticipate how the persuasion might proceed.

It should always be kept in mind that in Greco-Roman rhetoric an effective argument is one that wisely uses available evidence and the many rhetorical tools to convince an audience; it is not necessarily one that strictly follows an established form. Significant variation in form is possible, and the interpreter must be attuned to this possibility. Even the length of the argument can vary greatly. In Paul, arguments can be relatively short (as we have seen, above) or can encompass an entire book. As helpful as the identification of the forms of argumentation can be, the serious exegete of the N.T. is also encouraged to delve into the world of ancient rhetoric in order to understand what an effective argument is and how it is constructed. An awareness of the forms of argumentation should lead the interpreter into the discipline called rhetorical criticism (see the Selected Bibliography).

It should also be stated that these rhetorical forms remind the interpreter that he or she is dealing with a type of communication that can best be understood when the situation addressed is understood. Both proem and epilogue reflect a social context, a relationship with the parties being addressed. The narration section of an argument often recounts events important to both speaker and hearer. The proof, to be effective, must convince the audience. Rhetorical criticism properly stresses the necessity of grasping the social context of any given argument. As in the case of the letter form, and others as well, interpretation can take place only when both speaker and audience are considered (see Stowers).

Additional Examples

Deliberative: 1 Cor. 1; 2 Cor. 8, 9; Galatians (according to Kennedy, 144–152; Smit); 1 Thessalonians. Judicial: 1 Cor. 9; 2 Cor. 10–13; Galatians (according to Betz, introduction). Epideictic: Romans; 1 Cor. 13.

Selected Bibliography

Betz, Hans Dieter. 1979. *Galatians: A Commentary on Paul's Letter to the Churches in Galatia. Hermeneia.* Philadelphia: Fortress Press. See especially his introduction, where Betz outlines Galatians as an apology or judicial type of speech.

Kennedy, George A. 1984. *New Testament Interpretation Through Rhetorical Criticism.* Chapel Hill: University of North Carolina Press. This book is an excellent introduction by a student of classical rhetoric.

Lyons, George. 1985. *Pauline Autobiography: Toward a New Understanding.* SBL Dissertation Series No. 73. Atlanta: Scholars Press. Lyons defines autobiography as a rhetorical form and illustrates its use in Galatians and 1 Thessalonians.

Mack, Burton L. 1990. *Rhetoric and the New Testament.* Minneapolis: Fortress Press. This very helpful introduction to rhetorical criticism contains many useful N.T. examples.

Smit, Joop. 1989. "The Letter of Paul to the Galatians: A Deliberative Speech." *New Testament Studies* 35, 1–26. Smit argues, in contrast to Betz, that Galatians is deliberative.

Stowers, Stanley K. 1984. "Social Status, Public Speaking and Private Teaching: The Circumstances of Paul's Preaching Activity." *Novum Testamentum* 26, 59–82. Stowers offers helpful insights about the social context of Paul's rhetorical activity.

Wuellner, Wilhelm. 1979. "Greek Rhetoric and Pauline Argumentation." In *Early Christian Literature and the Classical Tradition,* edited by William R. Schoedel and Robert L. Wilken, 177–188. Paris: Éditions Beauchisne. This chapter is a seminal early essay on rhetoric in Paul.

THE DIATRIBE

Definition of the Form

The diatribe (from the Greek *diatribē*, often defined as "dialogue" or "lengthy address") is a form in which the speaker confronts and debates with an imaginary addressee in order to instruct his audience. Both the form and its implications for New Testament interpretation have been widely recognized since the research of Rudolf Bultmann (1910), but a recent study by Stanley Stowers has sharpened our understanding of the diatribe's structure and function.

Although several of Paul's letters contain a sampling of the elements found in the diatribe (i.e., rhetorical questions and false conclusions; see 1 Cor. 15:29–41; Gal. 3:1–9, 19–22), only in Romans do we have what approximates a complete form. Stowers identifies two common subforms of the diatribe in Rom. 1–11. The first he labels "address to the imaginary interlocutor" (79–118). Of the several examples of this subform found in Romans (see 2:17–24; 9:19–21; 11:17–24; 14:4, 10), 2:1–5 is typical. It displays many of the characteristics found in Greco-Roman diatribes:

1. A larger context in which there is an indictment against arrogant or pretentious people. Romans 1:18–32 and 2:6ff. give this context for 2:1–5, here in terms of those who are arrogant concerning God.
2. A sudden turning to and an indictment of the "interlocutor." In 2:1 there is a shift to the second person ("*you* have no excuse") and the use of *anthrōpe* (the Greek word for "human being" put in the case of direct address; see also the use of *anthrōpe* in v. 3).
3. Indicting questions addressed to the interlocutor. These occur in 2:3, 4. Further typical features include a verb of thinking used to show the incorrect views of the interlocutor (v. 3) and a question about his lack of perception (v. 4).
4. A list of vices. In Romans the list occurs before the address to the interlocutor (1:29–32).

It should be noted that in Rom. 2:1–5 there are also features not typical of the Greco-Roman diatribe: the use of *pas* ("all") to generalize the address in v. 1 (hence applying to everyone); the use of the participle form of the verb to describe the interlocutor (vs. 1, 3); the use of the first person plural ("we know," v. 2, emphasizing Paul's relationship with his audience; Stowers, 93f.). Paul puts his own stamp upon the form, reflecting his situation and theology. Still, the form displayed in Rom. 2:1–5 shows great similarity to those found in Hellenistic literature.

Stowers labels the second subform "objections and false conclusions" (119–154). Of the many examples found in Romans (see 3:1–9; 3:31–4:2a; 6:15, 16; 7:7, 13–14; 9:14–15, 19–20; 11:1–3, 11, 19–20), 6:1–3 has the typical form:

1. The form usually occurs when the context demands either a pointed reaction to what has been said or a transition to a new level of thought. In 6:1–3 we find a reaction to 5:20 and also a transition to another level of the argument (6:4ff.).
2. An exclamation. In 6:1 it is "what then shall we say?" (cf. 3:5; 6:15; 7:7; 9:14).
3. A rhetorical question giving a false conclusion. The false conclusion in 6:1b is in the first-person plural ("are *we* to continue in sin that grace may abound?"), typical of Paul, but unusual in the Greco-Roman diatribe.
4. A rejection. In 6:2a the rejection is *mē genoito* ("by no means!"), common in Paul (but see 3:9) as well as in classical literature.
5. Reasons for the rejection. In 6:2–3 they come in the form of rhetorical questions, as is often the case. In the Hellenistic diatribe, these reasons may take several forms, such as examples, stories, analogies, sayings, and quotations. Paul especially likes to quote scripture to make his point (see 3:4, 9; 4:3ff., 9–15). In 3:1–9 and 3:31–4:2 Paul uses dialogue to develop the subform (Stowers, 155–174).

The Value for Interpretation

Even though he has personalized it in some ways, Paul is clearly using the diatribe form in Rom. 1–11. How does knowledge of Paul's use of the form facilitate interpretation? Stower's research has been helpful in that it has clarified the use of the diatribe in relationship to its literary context. The larger context of the first subform, "address to the imaginary interlocutor," often has the theme of indictment against the arrogant person. This means, for instance, that Rom. 2:1–5 should probably be closely linked with the indictment against the arrogant toward God found in 1:18–32, especially because a vice list, usually connected with the form, is found in vs. 29–32. Such an insight is valuable because scholars have often felt that 2:1ff. is part of a new section in which Paul begins to address the Jews (as opposed to a Gentile audience in 1:18–32). Stowers concludes that the address to the interlocutor in 2:1–5 is a dramatic way of speaking to the same audience and issue Paul has had in mind since 1:18 (i.e., either Gentiles or all people), not a means of shifting to a new audience (112–117). Not until 2:17ff. is the interlocutor called a Jew.

The subform "false conclusions" is also closely linked to its context. The false conclusion given in 6:1 (with the rejection and reasons for the rejection that follow, 6:2ff.), for instance, is a reaction to a proposition stated in 5:20f.—that where sin increases, grace abounds. This subform of the diatribe is perfectly suited to bringing out a possible misinterpretation of an important point and dealing with it in a decisive way. As further examples, notice how 3:1 reacts to 2:28–29, how 3:31f. reacts to 3:30, how 6:15 reacts to 6:14, how 7:7 reacts to 6:5–6 (Stowers, 149f.). It is important to realize that the rejection of false conclusions in Paul's diatribes may also lead to new developments in his argument, as is the case in 6:4ff.

The various parts of the diatribe combine to give a decidedly dramatic impact. A sudden turning to an imaginary interlocutor, indictments, rhetorical questions, exclamations, strong statements of rejection—these are powerful literary and rhetorical tools! Why does Paul use the diatribe, and what does its use tell us about his relationship with the Roman church? One of the most helpful aspects of Stower's study has been his research into the intention and use of the Greco-Roman diatribe. Bultmann had concluded, based upon a limited number of sources, that the diatribe was primarily a tool of polemic used by the Cynic/Stoic philosophers as they "preached" to the common people. More extensive research into the use of the diatribe, however, indicates that it was most commonly used in philosophical schools as a means of instructing students. Teachers used the device of the imaginary interlocutor, not to devastate opponents, but to enlighten their students about typical errors and pitfalls.

Certainly this understanding of the diatribe relates to Paul's employment of the device in Romans. Paul is not engaged in a polemic against certain groups in Rome (thus the book is quite unlike 2 Cor. and Gal.), but rather he uses the diatribe as a teacher would—to point out possible inconsistencies in the thought of his students. The diatribe is perfectly suited to a situation in which the teacher knows something about his audience and feels he can best instruct them by dialoguing with an imaginary addressee as representative of the typical error. Paul had never been to Rome, although the greetings in ch. 16 and the topoi in 13:1–7 and 14:1–23 (see *Paraenesis/Topoi*) may indicate that he had some knowledge of the church's situation. The diatribe is used by Paul to instruct the church in an indirect way and also to give them a sampling of his teaching style in preparation for his imminent visit (Rom. 15:22ff.; see Stowers, 175–184).

While Paul's use of the diatribe may not settle the issue about how knowledgeable he is concerning the church at Rome (see the debate as outlined by Donfried), its use does help the interpreter understand the apostle's intentions as a teacher of the gospel. Its presence in Romans also emphasizes the uniqueness of that letter and encourages the interpreter to continue to think about the form in relationship to the letter's setting in Rome.

Selected Bibliography

Bultmann, Rudolf. 1910. *Der Stil der paulinischen Predigt und die kynischstoische Diatribe*. Göttingen: Vandenhoeck & Ruprecht. This is a key work, especially because it was Bultmann's conclusions about the diatribe that influenced scholarship in Romans for so many years.

Donfried, Karl P. 1977. "False Presuppositions in the Study of Romans." In *The Romans Debate*, edited by Karl P. Donfried, 120–148. Minneapolis: Augsburg Publishing House. This helpful "pre-Stowers" essay discusses Paul's knowledge of the Roman church in relationship to his use of the diatribe.

Malherbe, Abraham J. 1980. "*Mē Genoito* in the Diatribe and Paul." *Harvard Theological Review* 73, 231–240. Through a study of Paul's use of *mē genoito* the author affirms the schoolroom setting for the diatribe.

Stowers, Stanley K. 1981. *The Diatribe and Paul's Letter to the Romans*. SBL Dissertation Series No. 57. Chico, Calif.: Scholars Press.

This very insightful study, which carefully defines the form and purpose of the classical diatribe, shows how Paul uses the diatribe in Romans.

MIDRASH

Definition of the Form

Midrash is a Hebrew term meaning "inquiry" or "interpretation." Although scholarship has given the word various technical definitions relative to the interpretation of scripture, it is legitimate to define midrash as a literary genre. Gary Porton, speaking about rabbinic midrashim, gives the following helpful definition (62):

> I would like to define *midrash* as a type of literature, oral or written, which stands in direct relationship to a fixed canonical text, considered to be authoritative and the revealed word of God by the midrashist and his audience, in which this canonical text is explicitly cited or alluded to.

Porton's definition indicates that midrash assumes a hermeneutical stance—the authority and relevance of scripture—that will issue forth in various exegetical approaches. As such, midrash might be seen as an interpretive methodology, but this fact need not detract from the assertion that midrash is a distinct type of literature that has an identifiable structure and various common subforms. In the Pauline literature, there are no books devoted entirely to the interpretation of scripture (as in the rabbinic writings), but the passages that do (some of them lengthy) are consistent with Porton's definition. The basic structure of Jewish midrash, (1) the citation of or allusion to the authoritative scripture and (2) comment upon it, and the typical subforms employed, are found in Paul's interpretation as well.

Like the rabbis, Paul may use chain quotes (Rom. 3:10–11; 11:8–10; 15:9–12) or quote scripture in the order of law, prophets, and writings (Rom. 11:8–10; 15:9–12). Sometimes these passages are linked on the basis of key words or phrases, a typical ploy (see Rom. 9:25f.; 15:9–12; 1 Cor. 15:54–55). In the Pauline literature one finds common introductory formulas ("as it is written," Rom. 1:17; "scripture says," Rom. 4:3; "as God said," 2 Cor. 6:16; "as Moses says," Rom. 10:19) and interpretation based upon grammatical details (see Paul's handling of the word "offspring" in Gal. 3:16). Some of the more common interpretive "rules" listed by the rabbis, such as "light to heavy" (if a principle is true in an insignificant example, how much more will it be true in an important case; see 1 Cor. 9:9; Rom. 5:15–21) and analogy (where one passage is compared to or used to confirm the meaning of another; see the use of Gen. 15:6 and Ps. 32:1f. in Rom. 4:1–8; cf. Deut. 27:26 and 21:23 in Gal. 3:10, 13) are frequently found in Paul.

Although many of the above could be pursued as significant forms in their own right, we would like to define four subforms of midrash in Paul that are important relative to the understanding of his use of the Hebrew scriptures. These four forms are (1) running commentary, (2) pesher interpretation, (3) typological interpretation, and (4) allegorical interpretation.

Running Commentary

Often Paul will develop a theme by referring to several scripture passages and commenting upon them. Structurally, this running commentary consists simply of the alternation of scripture and comment. Galatians 3 is a good example. Galatians 3:6 refers to Gen. 15:6; Gal. 3:7 interprets the passage relative to those who have faith. Galatians 3:8 speaks of the justification of Gentiles, a concept that is affirmed through the use of Gen. 12:3 (v. 8) and commented upon in v. 9. The next paragraph has a new topic (vs. 10–14), but the same alternation of scripture and comment is present. In v. 10, Deut. 27:26 is quoted to point out the curse of the law. Verse 11 contrasts this curse with a comment and quotation (Hab. 2:4) about faith righteousness. Verse 12 quotes Lev. 18:5 to show the difference between faith and "doing" the law. Verse 13 rounds out the argument by quoting Deut. 21:23 to show that Jesus Christ took the curse upon himself and therefore saves humans from the curse. Notice how this form continues in vs. 15–18, albeit on a slightly different topic. See Rom. 9–11 for additional examples of the running commentary. The running commentary is common in rabbinic midrash, although in Paul the comments are more succinct, and he is more concerned with interpreting scripture to support the issue he is addressing than with exegeting a large block of scripture.

Pesher Interpretation

Pesher interpretation refers to the kind of exegesis that took place in the Qumran community. It gets its name from the Hebrew word *pishro*, which means "interpretation." In the Qumran scrolls that comment upon scripture, a three-part form is often evident: (1) quotation of scripture, (2) use of the phrase "its interpretation" (*pishro*) to introduce the interpretation, and (3) the interpretation itself (see especially Qumran Habakkuk Commentary 12:2ff.). Even more significant than this use of *pishro* is the way interpretation is affected by the community's sectarian and eschatological orientation. The Essenes at Qumran were alienated from the religious establishment at Jerusalem. They believed that their leader, the Teacher of Righteousness, was the legitimate religious authority in Israel. The trauma they were experiencing was a sign of the nearness of the end; God would soon usher in the new age and give their community its rightful authority. Scripture is seen as a prophetic mystery that could only be rightly understood in relationship to their eschatological crisis. The Essenes at Qumran believed that they and they alone had the key to understanding scripture. What was written in the past, properly interpreted, is seen as being fulfilled in their own present. As one might expect, this hermeneutical stance allows the Qumran writers to exercise considerable freedom in the interpretation of scripture. Often interpretation begins in the quotation itself: the version or textual reading most advantageous to the interpretation is chosen; letters in words are rearranged; synonyms are substituted for the original word, and so forth. Interpretation is based more upon what is perceived as divine revelation for the immediate situation than upon what we would call rational exegetical methods (see Porton, 75–77; Juel, 49–56).

Paul's concern for the Christian community and his understanding of the eschatological situation in Jesus Christ (see 2 Cor. 6:2) at times produces interpretation very much like the Qumran pesher. Based upon the new revelation he has in Jesus Christ (see 2 Cor. 3:12–18), Paul appears to choose freely among available texts (e.g., the Septuagint, the Masoretic Text, and translations in the Targum; see examples given by Ellis, 144–147, 150–152) and to alter words where it seems appropriate. E. Earle Ellis cites 1 Cor. 15:54–55 as a particularly graphic example. The form of Isa. 25:8 found in 1 Cor. 15:54 appears to be a hybrid based on both the Septuagint and Masoretic Text, except for the phrase "in victory" found at the end. Those words are found in neither version and are a Pauline addition. Hosea 13: 14, used in 1 Cor. 15:55, is similarly altered; unlike either the LXX or MT, Paul writes "O death, where is your *victory.*" Both Isa. 25:8 and Hos. 13:14 are altered by Paul so that they can refer to the victory over death that comes through Jesus Christ (see v. 57). Like the Qumran writers, Paul may interpret a passage even as he cites it (Ellis, 144–145).

Romans 10:6–13 is another helpful example. Notice how, in vs. 6–8, Paul follows each scriptural reference with the words "that is." Like the word *pishro* in the Qumran writings, the phrase "that is" introduces Paul's comment. Even more interesting are the comments themselves. Paul interprets Deut. 30: 11–14 in a way that is quite inconsistent with its original context. In that context, Moses speaks these words to affirm that humans can keep the law. Paul, however, applies the words to Jesus Christ and uses them to contradict Moses' statement about righteousness through the law found in v. 5 (see Lev. 18:5). Paul uses Moses' words against Moses! Alterations are made in the text as well. Instead of asking "Who will go over the sea?" as the MT and LXX read, Paul asks, "Who will descend into the abyss," applying the words to Christ and his descent into Hades after death (v. 7). Romans 10:11 follows the LXX form of Isa. 28:16, except that the word *pas* is added (with the negative, meaning "no one"), thus affirming the statements about the universality of the gospel Paul makes in vs. 12–13. There can be little doubt that Paul is influenced in his interpretation of scripture by the intensity of his eschatological situation (for Paul, the new creation that comes in Jesus Christ). In his use of "that is" before comment, in his selection and alteration of the scriptural text, and in his free interpretation of the text, Paul exhibits an exegetical form very much like what is found in the Qumran writings.

Typological Interpretation

Typology is an interpretive form in which a correspondence is shown between an earlier and later event or person. In Paul and in the framework of N.T. theology, typological interpretation refers to the way in which elements of the Hebrew scriptures are shown to correspond to elements in the Christian faith and thus further illumine God's salvific plan. The typological relationship between Adam and Christ is one of the best examples in Paul. In Rom. 5:12–21, for instance, Adam and Christ are compared and contrasted. Both bring a new reality to the world; but whereas Adam brings sin and condemnation, Jesus Christ brings justification and new life (vs. 16, 18; see also 1 Cor. 15:20–28). Notice how this form differs from the running commentary (above). In his typological interpretation, Paul usually does not quote scripture but rather makes a general reference to a scriptural event or figure. As one might expect, an explicit interpretation of a scripture passage is also usually absent. Paul's primary purpose in alluding to the scriptural element is to show a correspondence between it and an aspect of the Christian faith, to show how some principle enunciated in the Hebrew scriptures illumines God's salvation through Jesus Christ. Interpretation of the Hebrew scriptures does take place, but in a way that is determined by its relationship to the N.T. concept. The word pair that perhaps best describes the structure of typology is type/antitype rather than scripture/interpretation. For further examples of typological interpretation in Paul, see 2 Cor. 3 (the two covenants), 1 Cor. 10:1–5 (the supernatural rock and Christ) and perhaps Gal. 4:21–31 (the two covenants; see Ellis, 126–135 for an excellent discussion of typology in Paul).

Allegorical Interpretation

Allegorical interpretation is not as common in Paul as it is in rabbinic midrash and in Philo. A scriptural interpretation is allegorical when it goes beyond the literal meaning and emphasizes deeper truths or symbolic meaning. Galatians 4:21–31 is probably the best example in Paul, even though the passage resembles typology as well (see Ellis, 53). Paul carefully alludes to the story of Hagar and Sarah in vs. 21–23 (see Gen. 16:15; 21:2) and then states that his interpretation will be an allegory (v. 24). The interpretation Paul offers certainly goes beyond the literal or obvious: Hagar and her son are made to represent Mt. Sinai and the slavery of the law; Sarah and her son Isaac represent the new Jerusalem and freedom from the law (vs. 24–31). Once again the basic structure is obvious. A reference to scripture is followed by an interpretation, although in allegory the interpretation depends less upon the text itself than upon the author's grasp of its symbolic meaning. See also 1 Cor. 9:9 as a possible allegorical interpretation (Longenecker, 126).

The Value for Interpretation

How does knowledge of the four subforms in Paul's midrash help us understand his thought and his use of the Hebrew scriptures? Although it might seem obvious, it must be stated that the forms remind us again of the importance and authority of the scriptures for Paul. Perhaps the running commentary is the best example. Paul builds key arguments through the citation and interpretation of scripture. Galatians 3 is a sophisticated discussion of faith and law (one might argue that it is the theological core of the letter) where Paul feels compelled to quote and interpret the O.T. at every turn. Romans 9–11 is a delicate and emotional discussion of God's will for the Jews built, appropriately, almost entirely on his interpretation of select O.T. passages. In their own way, the pesher, typological, and allegorical forms also affirm the importance of the Hebrew scriptures for Paul; even in the interpretive freedom he has in Jesus Christ, the Hebrew scriptures continue to be his touchstone. Above all else, these forms tell interpreters that they must take seriously the analysis of scripture as it occurs in Paul.

Just as important, the forms remind the interpreter that Paul's use of the Hebrew scriptures may not be like ours. A knowledge of the pesher, typological, and allegorical forms allows the interpreter both to understand what Paul is attempting and to appreciate how his use of the Hebrew scriptures is legitimate within his hermeneutical context. It is very difficult to comprehend Paul's interpretation of Deut. in Rom. 10:5–9 without a knowledge of the pesher method; it is perhaps even more difficult to sympathize with it. Unless one understands the use of allegory in first-century midrash, Paul's interpretation in Gal. 4:21–31 appears to be a fabrication based on a disregard for literary context. Most modern interpreters approach the biblical text with an exegetical method that exhibits a very basic form: (1) the most authentic version of the text is obtained, and (2) it is interpreted in light of its social, historical, and literary context. But Paul may deviate from both points! He may seek out the text that best suits his interpretation (as in pesher interpretation) and interpret it in a christological way far removed from its original use. The interpreter must not simply assume that Paul's exegetical method resembles the ones we use.

It is always important for the N.T. interpreter to determine which version of the Hebrew scriptures is being quoted in Paul (or which textual variant) and, of course, to grasp the passage's original context. This endeavor is emphasized in an interesting way because of Paul's use of the pesher method, which often has a form of (1) *altered* text and (2) interpretation. Ellis notes that twenty scriptural citations in Paul appear to be altered or selected from available versions for interpretive reasons (144f.). The interpreter must ask why the text was altered or structured as it was and how Paul's version of the text relates to its original context. As noted, Paul's allusion to Isa. 25:8 in 1 Cor. 15:54 does not follow any of the versions exactly, and he significantly alters the text by adding "in victory" at the end. Nevertheless, Paul's use of the verse is very much informed by its context in Isaiah, where the prophet speaks of God's eschatological victory. Paul's first step in interpretation is what could be called a christological alteration of the text, giving the verse an interpretation that, in Paul's mind, is quite consistent with Isaiah's intentions.

This awareness of the original settings of scriptural passages is also vital relative to an understanding of the interpretations Paul offers. Paul's interpretive approach is more like that found at Qumran than the type used in mainstream Judaism. The interpretation is not simply an exercise in exegesis but has a powerful eschatological and existential focus. God's revelation in Jesus Christ and the eschatological setting in which the apostle finds himself become the hermeneutical keys to Paul's use of the O.T. It is important for the interpreter to ask how the scriptural passage has given rise to the interpretation Paul offers. In Rom. 10:6–8, for instance, how or to what extent does its original context influence Paul's use of Deut. 30:11–14? What is it about this passage that informs Paul's christological interpretation? Is Paul's interpretive freedom governed at all by a literal or historical understanding of the text?

Finally, mention should be made of the uniqueness of the typology form. Even though typological interpretation interprets the Hebrew scriptures, it does so in the context of a dialectic between type and antitype. The O.T. type points forward to and interprets the Christian antitype even as the antitype illumines the O.T. type. In Paul's Adam/Christ typology, for instance, Adam helps us understand Christ, but Christ also gives us a fuller picture of the significance of Adam (Rom. 4). The same could also be said of the "two covenants" typology in 2 Cor. 3. The interpreter must know that interpretation is not so much stated as it is presented in the comparing and contrasting of type and antitype.

Selected Bibliography

Ellis, E. Earle. 1957. *Paul's Use of the Old Testament*. Grand Rapids: Wm. B. Eerdmans. This older work is still the best introduction to Paul's interpretive methods.

Juel, Donald. 1988. *Messianic Exegesis: Christological Interpretation of the Old Testament in Early Christianity*. Philadelphia: Fortress Press. See especially Juel's second chapter for a helpful introduction to first-century Jewish interpretation.

Lindars, Barnabas. 1961. *New Testament Apologetic*. London: SCM Press. This helpful work shows how the early church used the Hebrew scriptures to formulate its theology.

Longenecker, Richard N. 1975. *Biblical Exegesis in the Apostolic Period*. Grand Rapids: Wm. B. Eerdmans. This work covers a wide range of topics, including Jesus' use of the Hebrew scriptures, early Christian and Pauline interpretation, interpretation in the Gospels, and so forth.

Porton, Gary G. 1981. "Defining Midrash." In *The Study of Ancient Judaism*. Vol. 1. Edited by Jacob Neusner, 55–92. New York: KTAV. This is a succinct and readable definition of midrash.

CHIASM

Definition of the Form

A chiasm (from the Greek *chiazō*, which means to make a mark like the Greek X) is a literary form that has as its most obvious feature a reverse parallelism. Two or more terms, phrases, or ideas are stated and then repeated in reverse order. Paul uses a simple chiasm in Rom. 10:19 where he quotes Deut. 32:21:

A. I will make you jealous
   B. of those who are not a nation;
   B'. with a foolish nation
A'. I will make you angry.

A common and important variation of this simple form occurs when the chiasm has an odd number of parts. In that case, a single element may stand at the center of the chiasm separating the parallel elements. An O.T. example is found in Amos 5:4b–6a:

A. Seek me and live;
   B. but do not seek Bethel,
      C. and do not enter into Gilgal
         D. or cross over to Beersheba;
      C′. for Gilgal shall surely go into exile,
   B′. and Bethel shall come to nothing.
A′. Seek the LORD and live.

Notice how line D stands at the center and is not repeated; it marks the transition to parallel elements that follow (the underlining points out the more obvious parallels). The O.T. examples used above are appropriate because chiasms are especially common in Jewish literature, although they can be found in various writings in the Hellenistic era (Welch; see also *Chiasm* in the Gospels and Acts section of this volume).

The chiasms found in the Pauline tradition are diverse in terms of style. Paul may vary the simple chiastic form by using chiasms to form the individual parts of larger chiasms (as in 1 Cor. 11:8–12) or by producing a larger structure that is composed partly of chiasms and partly of couplets (1 Cor. 6:12–14; Lund, 145). Length can also vary greatly. They range from the simplest four-part expressions ([A] "Neither was man created [B] for the sake of woman, [B′] but woman [A′] for the sake of man"; 1 Cor. 11:9) to chiasms that are several chapters long. Nils Lund, for instance, sees 1 Cor. 12–14 as a chiasm (164ff.):

A. Introduction: The gifts and those who have them: the Spirit, 11:34b–12:3.
   B. The diversity and unity of the spiritual gifts: the principle, 12:4–30.
      C. The gifts and the graces, 12:31–14:1a.
   B′. The diversity and unity of the spiritual gifts: the application, 14:1b–36.
A′. Conclusion: The leaders and the gifts: the Lord, 14:37–40.

The Value for Interpretation

A familiarity with chiasms is essential in the exegesis of Paul and the larger Pauline tradition. Although one might relate the chiastic form to interpretation in many ways, especially considering the variety of chiasms, the following are basic exegetical insights concerning the use of chiasms.

It is important to note that chiasms help the exegete delineate units of thought. Paul writes freely and at times without apparent structure. Identifying a chiasm may tell the interpreter where a teaching or argument begins and where it ends. It may tell the student of scripture exactly what unit should be the topic for exegesis. The chiasm in 1 Cor. 12–14 (above) is a good example: while ch. 13 is often used as an independent unit in the church, the chiastic structure of the larger passage shows the folly of this approach. Chapter 13 and its statements about love must be understood within the larger context of the nature and use of spiritual gifts in the Christian community.

Because chiasms consist of reverse parallelism, it is vital exegetically to find and compare the parallel elements. If the writer intends a relationship between two parts of a chiasm, the interpreter must define that relationship and show how it helps determine the meaning of the passage. The chiasm found in 1 Cor. 13:8–13 could be used as an example (see Lund, 176):

A. Love never ends.
  B. But as for prophecies, they will come to an end;
     as for tongues, they will cease;
     as for knowledge, it will come to an end.
    C. For we know only in part,
       and we prophesy only in part;
       but when the complete comes,
       the partial will come to an end.
      D. When I was a child,
         I spoke like a child,
         I thought like a child,
         I reasoned like a child;
         when I became an adult, I put an end to childish ways.
    C'. For now we see in a mirror, dimly,
        but then we will see face to face.
        Now I know only in part;
        then I will know fully, even as I have been fully known.
  B'. And now faith, hope, and love abide, these three;
A'. and the greatest of these is love.

C and C' are obviously parallel elements and should be compared. As is often the case, the thoughts conveyed in these parallel verses are very similar, yet they are not synonymous. Like C, C' contrasts incomplete present knowledge with the perfect knowledge of the future, but it also introduces the image of the mirror and the idea of God fully understanding the writer. Interpreted together, the parallel elements offer a richer description than either of the individual parts could. B and B′ are also to be related, but they function in terms of contrast. The phrase "these three" (B′) serves to emphasize the three gifts in relationship to the three given in B, but these three remain, whereas the former will pass away. The parallelism in the chiasm effectively contrasts the preferred gifts in Corinth (B) with what Paul knows are the higher gifts (B′). Whether the parallel elements function in terms of comparison or contrast (or have some other relationship), knowledge of the chiastic form allows the exegete to grasp more effectively the meaning the author intends to convey (see *Poetry and Hymn* for further discussion of parallelism).

It is even possible that the presence of a chiasm may help determine issues of grammar and structure in the letters. Lund gives Rom. 11:33–35 as an interesting example (222f.). Is v. 33 to be translated "O the depth of the riches both of the wisdom and knowledge of God!" (as in the KJV, NASB) or "O the depth of the riches and wisdom and knowledge of God!" (NRSV)? Both are possible on the basis of the Greek, but they yield quite different results. In the former translation, we are given two distinct characteristics of God, whereas the latter offers three. This dilemma can be solved if the verses are allowed to function as part of a chiasm:

A.   O the depth of the <u>riches</u>
   B.   and <u>wisdom</u>
      C.   and <u>knowledge</u> of God!
         D.   How unsearchable are his judgments
         D′.   and how inscrutable his ways!
      C′.   "For who has known the <u>mind</u> of the Lord?
   B′.   Or who has been his <u>counselor</u>?"
A′.   "Or who has given a <u>gift</u> to him, . . ."

Lund believes that v. 33 contains three distinct statements about God because they have parallel elements when put into chiastic form (C′, B′, A′). These parallel elements interpret one another in a significant way: Can anyone know the mind of God (C′); that is, can anyone grasp God's knowledge (C)? Can anyone serve as his counselor (B′) considering his wisdom (B)? And who can give to God (A′) considering his riches (A)? Here an awareness of Paul's use of chiasm gives the exegete an important tool for translation (see also Man, 152–153).

Finally, a knowledge of chiasms in the Pauline tradition may help the interpreter see the intended focus of a passage. It is obvious that chiasms have a center point, whether this point is composed of one element or two (see the couplet above, Rom. 11:33–35). This center point often functions in one of two ways; it may stand as the interpretive focal point of the passage, or it may mark an important transition in the movement or thought of the chiasm. The lengthy chiasm found in 1 Cor. 12–14 illustrates well the idea of an interpretive focal point (see above). Chapter 13 and its understanding of the gift of love is the key to understanding the larger section. Paul's statements about the church as the body of Christ (ch. 12) inevitably lead to ch. 13, and his statements about gifts in ch. 14 presuppose it.

Romans 11:33–35 (given above) actually illustrates both focal point and transition. The first three elements (A, B, C) speak of specific characteristics of God (depth of riches, wisdom, knowledge). The center point (D/D′) goes beyond these individual characteristics to state the theme of the entire chiasm, the unsearchableness or inscrutability of God. But D/D′ also marks an important transition in the chiasm in that the elements that follow (C′, B′, A′) do not simply repeat A, B, and C, but speak of these characteristics of God in terms of human ability to grasp or impart them. Romans 11:33–35 is a fine example of the necessity of identifying and taking seriously the center point of a chiasm.

Perhaps a warning of sorts is also in order. While the interpretive points offered above can be very helpful, it is also common to find chiasms that do not readily lend themselves to such an analytical approach. Chiasms have great rhetorical appeal and can be used primarily for aural effect or for purposes of memory (Welch). Parallel sounds might be more important than parallel ideas in any given chiasm. Chiasm is a close relative of Hebrew poetry and must be treated as such. Interpreters must also beware of finding chiasms "everywhere," that is, of seeing a chiasm where none was intended. Nevertheless, because the chiasm is an often-used form in the Pauline tradition, the exegete must be able to identify it and tussle with its implications for interpretation.

Additional Examples

Of the many possibilities, see Rom. 2:6–11; Eph. 5:8–11; Phil. 2:5–11; Col. 1:14–22a. See Lund for a more extensive list.

Selected Bibliography

Lund, Nils Wilhelm. 1942. *Chiasmus in the New Testament: A Study in Form Geschichte*. Chapel Hill: University of North Carolina Press. This older work is still the most helpful volume on chiasm in English.

Man, Ronald E. 1984. "The Value of Chiasm for New Testament Interpretation." *Bibliotheca Sacra* 141, 146–157. Man's article is very helpful in that he explicitly relates the chiastic form to exegetical issues.

Martin, Ralph P. 1983. *Carmen Christi: Philippians 2:5–11 in Recent Interpretation and in the Setting of Early Christian Worship*. Grand Rapids: Wm. B. Eerdmans. Martin offers a useful chiastic interpretation of Phil. 2:5–11.

Welch, John W. 1981. *Chiasmus in Antiquity*. Hildesheim: Gerstenberg Verlag. An excellent resource for the study of chiasms in the Hellenistic world, this book also has a chapter dealing specifically with chiasms in the N.T.

APOCALYPTIC LANGUAGE AND FORMS

Definition of the Forms

Jewish apocalyptic eschatology is a religious orientation that believes that the present world order is evil and that God will soon send a messiah to destroy this evil age and set up a new and lasting kingdom. In the meantime, the faithful are expected to persevere in the trauma and suffering of the end-times. When the messiah comes, the wicked will be judged and the faithful vindicated. This religious orientation can issue forth in a number of different literary forms and genres, the most important of which is the "apocalypse," the genre of the book of Revelation. Succinctly put, an apocalypse is a narrative describing a divine revelation about a future transcendent order, mediated through a supernatural being to a human recipient, and given for the purpose of exhorting or consoling an oppressed community (see Collins 1979, 9; Hanson, 27; *Apocalypse*). While the writings in the Pauline literature are not apocalypses, they do reflect apocalyptic thought and expression. This section illustrates Paul's use of apocalyptic imagery and language, and especially focuses on two forms that have an apocalyptic function in Paul: "prophecies about the end-times" and "pronouncements of holy law."

Paul's apocalyptic language and imagery are based on Jewish apocalyptic eschatology, although they have been modified in light of what he sees as the decisive eschatological event, the coming of Jesus Christ. Much of the apocalyptic language used by Paul relates to the imminent consummation of the new age through the return of Christ and the implications of this event for the Christian life. In 1 Thess. 1:10, Paul talks about how members of the church have given up their old ways to serve God and "to wait for his Son from heaven, whom he raised from the dead—Jesus, who rescues us from the wrath that is coming." Romans 13:11 speaks of the nearness of the end: "Besides this, you know what time it is, how it is now the moment for you to wake from sleep. For salvation is nearer to us now than when we became believers." Compare also 1 Cor. 7:29–31: "I mean, brothers and sisters, the appointed time has grown short; from now on, let even those who have wives be as though they had none. . . . For the present form of this world is passing away."

In Rom. 8:18–23, Paul uses typical apocalyptic themes and images—present sufferings, birth pangs, and cosmic transformation—as he talks about his hope for the new age:

> I consider that the sufferings of this present time are not worth comparing with the glory about to be revealed to us. For the creation waits with eager longing for the revealing of the children of God; for the creation was subjected to futility, not of its own will but by the will of the one who subjected it, in hope that the creation itself will be set free from its bondage to decay and will obtain the freedom of the glory of the children of God. We know that the whole creation has been groaning in labor pains until now . . . (cf. Eph. 1:10; Col. 1:20).

Sometimes Paul uses very brief apocalyptic allusions: *maranatha* ("our Lord, come," 1 Cor. 16:22); "new creation" (2 Cor. 5:17); "we will be saved through him from the wrath of God" (Rom. 5:9). In one unusual passage (2 Cor. 12:2–7a), Paul uses language reminiscent of the vision and otherworldly journey scenes in apocalypses. Referring to himself in the third person, Paul says:

> I know a person in Christ who fourteen years ago was caught up to the third heaven—whether in the body or out of the body I do not know; God knows. And I know that such a person—whether in the body or out of the body I do not know; God knows—was caught up into Paradise and heard things that are not to be told, that no mortal is permitted to repeat. . . . But if I wish to boast, I will not be a fool. . . . But I refrain from it, . . . even considering the exceptional character of the revelations.

Many other examples could be given. Awareness and proper interpretation of such language is vital in the exegesis of Paul and the larger Pauline tradition.

Prophecies About the End-times

David Aune notes a number of passages in Paul that can be called prophecies; they indicate the divine origin or prophetic nature of the statement and give the content of the revelation (1983, 248–261). A good example is 2 Cor. 12:9, found shortly after the "vision talk" related above:

> But he [the Lord] said to me,
> "My grace is sufficient for you,
> for power is made perfect in weakness."

Paul clearly states that the words are from God. The revelation itself has a two-part structure (God's response and its theological rationale) that is similar in form to both Greek and Jewish oracular utterances (Aune 1983, 249, 250). As additional examples, see Rom. 11:25–26; 1 Cor. 14:37–38; Gal. 5:21b; 1 Thess. 3:4; 4:2–6. Two of the examples given by Aune, 1 Cor. 15:51–52 and 1 Thess. 4:15–18, are interesting because the revelations are similar in terms of content and form to end-time predictions commonly found in apocalyptic writings.

Both 1 Cor. 15:51–52 and 1 Thess. 4:15–18 begin by indicating the divine origin of the prophecy, in 1 Thess. by a reference to "the word of the Lord" (v. 15) and in 1 Cor. through the use of the word "mystery," a technical term indicating divinely concealed and revealed information (Aune 1983, 251; see Rom. 11:25). End-time statements in apocalyptic literature often have four components: (1) predictions about sufferings and trauma before the end; (2) a description of the coming of the messiah, often with standard images (angels, clouds, trumpets, etc.); (3) statements about salvation and/or judgment for the people; (4) exhortations or paraenesis. Mark 13 (and parallels) is the best example in the N.T.: Jesus discusses the trauma preceding the consummation of the new age (13:3–22), describes the arrival of the messiah (13:24–27; note the typical images), briefly states the implications for humans (the Son of Man will gather his elect, 13:27), and gives exhortations (see 13:35–37 and vs. 5, 9, 14, etc.; *Apocalyptic Language and Forms* in the Gospels and Acts section of this volume; for further examples of statements about the end-times, see the apocalypses Revelation, 1 Enoch, 4 Ezra, as well as *Assumption of Moses* 10 and *Jubilees* 23). Of course, the two prophecies in Paul are much shorter and less involved than Jesus' statement in Mark, but the structural components are very similar. In both we find (1) details and images about the arrival of the messiah (1 Thess. 4:16, the Lord descends from heaven, archangel's call, trumpet; 1 Cor. 15:52, the immediateness of the event, the trumpet), (2) reference to personal salvation for the faithful, which includes resurrection of the dead and transformation of the living (1 Thess. 4:16, 17; 1 Cor. 15:52), and (3) exhortations or paraenesis (1 Cor. 15:58; 1 Thess. 4:18–5:11). The paraenetical section in 1 Thess. 5:1–11 (see *Paraenesis/Topoi*) is very similar in form and content to Mark 13:28–37 (cf. 2 Thess. 2:1–15). Noteworthy is the fact that neither 1 Cor. 15 nor 1 Thess. 4 includes references to events that precede the end. In fact, Paul de-emphasizes such information in 1 Thess. 5:1–3; after using typical images to stress the suddenness and unexpectedness of Christ's return, he quickly turns to paraenesis (vs. 4–11).

Second Thessalonians 1:5–2:15 has often been compared to the above passages, but it is actually quite different in terms of form and content. There is no reference to divine revelation, nor is there a sharply defined statement about the end that might be construed as an oracular utterance. What we see is a discussion about the end relative to the suffering of the community (1:5). Consistent with this context, there is a strong emphasis upon the judgment of the wicked as a just recompense (1:6–9). Whereas 1 Thess. 5:1–11 emphasizes the suddenness and unexpectedness of the coming of the new age, 2 Thess. 2:1–15 speaks of an elaborate process that occurs before the end. As one might expect, it is especially these differences concerning apocalyptic themes that have caused many people to doubt the Pauline authorship of 2 Thessalonians.

Pronouncements of Holy Law

In the early 1950s, Ernst Käsemann wrote an article in which he defined the structure and function of a certain two-part form found in the N.T. First Corinthians 3:17 is a good example:

> If anyone destroys God's temple,
> God will destroy that person.

According to Käsemann, such pronouncements usually had well-defined features: a conditional logic that reflects an understanding of retributive justice (if someone does something, God will punish or reward accordingly), a chiastic structure, the use of the same verb in both parts of the pronouncement, and a second part that emphasizes God's judgmental action in the last day, often through the use of the passive verb (66–68). Käsemann went on to say that these pronouncements had their origin in Christian prophecy and usually functioned as warnings during the Lord's Supper (69, 70).

Recent scholarship has challenged Käsemann in several ways. The form does not consistently exhibit all of the features Käsemann lists. Aune more accurately and simply defines the pronouncement as a two-part statement, "the first part dealing with the activity of man in the present and the second dealing with the eschatological response of God" (1983, 240). Nor can the setting of the form be limited to Christian prophetic activity. It is employed in various ways and probably has its origin in the wisdom tradition (see Aune 1983, 238).

Nevertheless, Käsemann's original definition remains helpful because it points out that the second part of the pronouncement usually refers to God's eschatological activity as judge (cf. Mark 8:38; Luke 12:8–9). In Paul, this becomes an important part of his apocalyptic framework. Paul almost always uses the form to stress right belief and behavior in light of the imminent judgment of God. Note the basic form and its apocalyptic implications in the following examples: "Let anyone be accursed who has no love for the Lord. Our Lord, come!" (1 Cor. 16:22); "Anyone who does not recognize this is not to be recognized" (1 Cor. 14:38); "If anyone proclaims to you a gospel contrary to what you received, let that one be accursed" (Gal. 1:9); "The one who sows sparingly will also reap sparingly, and the one who shows bountifully will also reap bountifully" (2 Cor. 9:6); "All who have sinned apart from the law will also perish apart from the law, and all who have sinned under the law will be judged by the law" (Rom. 2:12). Of course, a person might also classify this pronouncement as a paraenetical form, but in Paul it is one that is inseparably linked to an eschatological motivation.

The Value for Interpretation

There are several important ways in which knowledge of Paul's use of apocalyptic language is helpful in interpretation. Simply identifying certain language or images as apocalyptic can be a significant step in the exegetical process. Knowing, for instance, that a reference to future salvation from wrath (Rom. 5:9) carries apocalyptic connotations can be very helpful when trying to understand how Paul employs the phrase. Discovering that the numerous end-times images found in Paul (e.g., birth-pangs, the trumpet's call, the resurrection) are common in Jewish apocalyptic literature enables the interpreter to see Paul as he should be seen, as part of a larger apocalyptic tradition. What context, one might ask, is the language given in Paul, and how does that setting compare to the one it might be given in Jewish apocalyptic writings? Exactly how does Paul use apocalyptic language to develop a theme or discussion? Does the apocalyptic language have an internal connection with the subject being discussed (as in the relationship between suffering and the end-times in Rom. 8:18–25), or is it simply used as an afterthought or "prooftext" (see 1 Cor. 6:9f.; Gal. 5:21; Gager, 325–337)? The pervasive influence of apocalyptic eschatology upon Paul's thought makes a knowledge of apocalyptic language a central interpretive concern. The careful exegete is one who comes to Paul with a good understanding of the wide range of Jewish and Christian apocalyptic literature (e.g., Rev.; 4 Ezra; 1 Enoch; Daniel 7–12; *Assumption of Moses*; Mark 13, etc.).

Certainly Paul's apocalyptic language and thought are not always consistent with Jewish apocalyptic eschatology. Language that is used in apocalyptic writings to stress the tension between the present and future and to emphasize the increasing trauma of the end-times is often downplayed in Paul. As J. Christiaan Beker states (1980, 145):

> The reduction of apocalyptic terminology and the absence of apocalyptic speculation signifies that the Christ-event has strongly modified the dualistic structure of normal apocalyptic thought. Although death is "the last enemy" (I Cor. 15:26), Paul strongly emphasizes both the openness of the present to the future glory of God and the incursion of the present into the future.

The interpreter is called upon not only to identify Paul's apocalyptic language and thought but also to wrestle with its uniqueness relative to what Paul asserts is the decisive eschatological event, the coming of Jesus Christ.

An awareness of the form called "prophecy about the end-times" is helpful especially in that it allows the interpreter to compare the content and form of the prophecy, the description of the coming of the messiah, with other apocalyptic scenarios and thus see more clearly the emphases found in Paul. Why, for instance, does Paul not speak of the traumatic events leading up to the coming of the new age, and why does he not emphasize the resurrection and judgment of the wicked in 1 Cor. 15 and 1 Thess. 4 (cf. Mark 13:3–23; *Assumption of Moses* 10:7; 2 Thess. 1:7ff.)? To what extent does the absence of this material reflect his apocalyptic thought; to what extent does it reflect Paul's desire simply to speak directly to the pastoral issue at hand in both 1 Cor. 15 and 1 Thess. 4, the nature of the resurrection for believers? Of course, both the judgment of the wicked and the trauma of the last days (discussed relative to the time of the end in 2:1–15) are included in the discourse found in 2 Thessalonians. These topics would be relevant indeed to the context of suffering given in 1:5. Interpreters of Paul must be attuned to the use of the form both as it indicates Paul's theological thought and as it points to the pastoral situation being addressed.

Although a hortatory purpose is not unusual in Jewish apocalyptic literature, paraenesis is especially important in Christian apocalyptic expressions. Nowhere is this more obvious than in Paul, where paraenesis is intimately related to the forms discussed and also functions in relationship to general apocalyptic language (1 Cor. 7:25–31; Rom. 13:11–14). Although the pronouncement form more explicitly states the inevitable relationship between an action and judgment, both Paul's prophecies about the end-times and his pronouncements of holy law point to his use of eschatological motivation. The interpreter must tussle with this relationship between paraenesis and Christian apocalyptic eschatology. To what extent is Paul's paraenesis a product of his apocalyptic thought? Would Paul's ethical exhortations be changed significantly if they were somehow removed from an awareness of Christ's imminent return? How might the meaning of 1 Cor. 15:58 be altered, for instance, if it were located after a passage describing what Christ had already done for us, rather than after one describing his second coming? This remains an important issue in N.T. scholarship, one that relates directly to many basic questions concerning the nature of Pauline theology (Beker 1980, 135–181). The interpreter of Paul is never far removed from the question of the influence of apocalyptic language and forms.

Selected Bibliography

Aune, David E. 1983. *Prophecy in Early Christianity and the Ancient Mediterranean World*, 237–240. Grand Rapids: Wm. B. Eerdmans. Aune gives a vast amount of material dealing with prophetic and oracular forms. See especially his discussion of Käsemann's pronouncement of holy law.

———. 1987. *The New Testament in Its Literary Environment*, 226–253. Philadelphia: Westminster Press. This very helpful section deals with the various types of apocalyptic literature, with special emphasis upon the book of Revelation.

Beker, J. Christiaan. 1980. *Paul the Apostle: The Triumph of God in Life and Thought*, 135–181. Philadelphia: Fortress Press. Beker's section on the apocalyptic nature of Paul's thought provides a useful introduction.

———. 1982. *Paul's Apocalyptic Gospel: The Coming Triumph of God*, 29–54. Philadelphia: Fortress Press. This book provides a readable introduction; see especially his chapter "The Apocalyptic Character of Paul's Gospel."

Collins, Adela Yarbro. 1986. "Introduction: Early Christian Apocalypticism." *Semeia* 36, 1–12.

Collins, John J. 1979. "Introduction: Towards the Morphology of a Genre." *Semeia* 14, 1–20.
  The above two articles provide useful analyses of the apocalyptic genre. The larger issues (*Semeia* 14, 36) also contain helpful studies of specific apocalypses.

Gager, John G. 1970. "Functional Diversity in Paul's Use of End-time Language." *Journal of Biblical Literature* 89, 325–337. Gager illustrates the various ways Paul can employ apocalyptic language.

Hanson, Paul D. 1976. "Apocalypse" and "Apocalypticism." *Interpreter's Dictionary of the Bible*, Suppl. vol., 27–34. Nashville: Abingdon Press. Hanson's succinct definitions of such terms as apocalypse, apocalyptic eschatology, and apocalypticism, and his clear analyses are excellent introductory material.

Käsemann, Ernst. 1969. *New Testament Questions of Today*. Translated by W. J. Montague, 66–107. Philadelphia: Fortress Press. See especially "Sentences of Holy Law in the New Testament" and "The Beginnings of Christian Theology."

PARAENESIS/TOPOI

Definition of the Form

Paraenesis is ethical exhortation, instruction concerning how or how not to live (from the Greek *parainesis:* "advice," "exhortation"). It is characterized by verbs in the imperative mood, the mood of command. In the Pauline tradition, indeed throughout the N.T., paraenesis tends to be traditional. It often reflects typical Christian practice and commonly borrows ethical insight from the larger Hellenistic world. Paraenesis can either occur throughout the letters (see 1 Cor. 5, 7, 8, 10; 1 Tim. 2, 3, 5) or in large concluding sections (Rom. 12–14; 1 Thess. 4:1–5:22; Eph. 4:1–6:20). Of the many possible forms that might be examined under the paraenetical heading (e.g., "proverbs," Gal. 5:9; 1 Cor. 5:6; Rom. 12:21; 1 Cor. 15:33; "admonitions" or short imperative statements strung together loosely, Rom. 12:9–21; 1 Thess. 5:12–22), this discussion will focus on topoi, one of the three more important and sharply defined forms. (The other two—vice and virtue lists and household codes—will be dealt with in separate sections in this volume.)

Topoi (plural of the Greek topos: *"place," "theme")*

Topoi are extended paraenetical statements on particular themes or topics. In Paul, see Rom. 13:1–7 on duty to the state; Rom. 14:1–23 on eating certain foods; 1 Thess. 5:1–12 on the Christian life relative to the eschaton; 1 Cor. 8:1–13 on relations with fellow Christians. This topical approach to paraenesis is common in Hellenistic literature, where issues such as the state, civic responsibility, and sexual conduct are often discussed (see Malherbe, 144–161, for many examples). Topoi are easily distinguished from admonitions, which are simply individual paraenetical statements strung loosely together (see Rom. 12:9ff., 1 Thess. 5:12–22). As one might expect in arguments or treatises, topoi often exhibit a rhetorical structure.

Perhaps the most helpful analysis of the topos is the one given by Terence Mullins (542f.), who argues that Paul's ethical discussions employ a structure like that found in the ethical arguments of Hellenistic rhetoric: (1) *injunction* (statement of the desired ethical action), (2) *reason* (the rationale for such action), and (3) *discussion* (persuading by showing the consequences of the behavior). Sometimes two other elements are also present— *analogous situation* and *refutation.*

There is no doubt that the above provides a useful rhetorical structure for interpreting Paul's topical discussions. Romans 13:1–7 is a good example (Mullins, 543):

> *Injunction:* Let every person be subject to the governing authorities (v. 1a).
> *Reason:* For there is no authority except from God . . . (v. 1b).
> *Refutation:* Therefore whoever resists . . . (v. 2).
> *Discussion:* For rulers are not a terror to good conduct . . . (vs. 3–7).

Note the form of the final argument in Rom. 14 (Mullins, 546):

> *Injunction:* So do not let your good be spoken of as evil (v. 16).
> *Reason:* For the kingdom of God is not food and drink . . . (v. 17).
> *Discussion:* The one who thus serves Christ . . . (vs. 18–23).

Note also the structure in 1 Cor. 10:25–30 (Mullins, 546):

> *Injunction:* Eat whatever is sold in the meat market . . . (v. 25).
> *Reason:* For "the earth and its fullness are the Lord's" (v. 26).
> *Discussion:* If an unbeliever invites you to a meal . . . (vs. 27–30).

The Value for Interpretation

If not only the structure but also the subject matter of Paul's topoi are similar to those found in Hellenistic literature, then a key interpretive issue will be the relevance of his ethical exhortations for the communities being addressed. In Rom. 13:1–7, for instance, is Paul giving the people advice that is written specifically for them and their situation, or is this passage simply a standard argument Paul has often employed, one that reflects typical Christian or even typical Hellenistic thought? In this case, the question is made even more difficult than it normally might be because Paul had neither founded nor visited the Roman church, and it is difficult to know how much he knew about it. It has been argued that there is nothing in Rom. 13:1–7 to preclude its being used in various religious and civic settings.

The exegete can approach this problematic issue in various ways. One should ask how 13:1–7 relates to its literary context and whether the statements in vs. 1–7 reflect Pauline teaching elsewhere. It is also important to ask if there are elements in the passage that link it specifically with the Roman context. Some have said, for instance, that the two types of taxes mentioned in v. 7 are precisely the types collected in Rome. It should be emphasized that the rhetorical form proposed by Mullins certainly does not rule out concern for a specific audience or situation. Both the "reason" and "discussion" sections, for example, point toward ethical statements that are not mere pronouncements but attempt to respond to questions or objections. The form itself exhibits at least some social awareness.

Finally, the topos form given above offers the interpreter another means of analyzing Paul's train of thought. Larger topos sections can be divided into smaller logical units (e.g., Rom. 14:13–15 as distinct from vs. 16–23; Rom. 13:1–7 as distinct from vs. 8–10 and vs. 11–14). Interpreters will be able to note when Paul deviates from this standard form. Having some formal basis on which to analyze the topoi gives the interpreter a tremendous advantage over someone who can see in a topos only a haphazard discussion on certain ethical issues. Certainly this rhetorical definition of the form offered by Mullins is open to further definition. Rhetorical criticism will increasingly sharpen our understanding of such forms as it draws parallels between the N.T. and Greco-Roman rhetoric (see *Forms of Argumentation* in the Pauline Tradition and Gospels and Acts sections of this volume).

Additional Examples

See 1 Cor. 5, 6, 7; 10:14–33; 11:1–26; Gal. 6:1–10; 1 Thess. 4:1–12.

Selected Bibliography

Brunt, John C. 1985. "More on the *Topos* as a New Testament Form." *Journal of Biblical Literature* 104, 495–500. Brunt sharpens the definition of the term "topos" and further defines Mullins's understanding of the form.

Malherbe, Abraham J. 1986. *Moral Exhortation: A Greco-Roman Sourcebook.* Philadelphia: Westminster Press. This book is an invaluable resource for Hellenistic parallels to N.T. ethical exhortation and topoi.

Mullins, Terence Y. 1980. "Topos as a New Testament Form." *Journal of Biblical Literature* 99, 541–547. Mullins gives a very helpful analysis of the structure of the topos from a rhetorical perspective.

VICE AND VIRTUE LISTS

Definition of the Form

Lists of virtues and vices are very common in the Pauline tradition (and elsewhere in the N.T.) and serve a basic paraenetical function; they offer examples of acceptable and unacceptable ethical behavior. The form itself usually consists of a listing of independent items, although considerable variation is possible. A typical vice list is found in Rom. 1:29–31:

> They were filled with every kind of wickedness, evil, covetousness, malice. Full of envy, murder, strife, deceit, craftiness, they are gossips, slanderers, God-haters, insolent, haughty, boastful, inventors of evil, rebellious toward parents, foolish, faithless, heartless, ruthless.

Colossians 3:12 is a good example of a virtue list: "Clothe yourselves with compassion, kindness, humility, meekness, and patience."

Sometimes vice and virtue lists are closely linked, as in Gal. 5:19–23 (cf. Eph. 4:31–32; Titus 1:7–10):

> Now the works of the flesh are obvious: fornication, impurity, licentiousness, idolatry, sorcery, enmities, strife, jealousy, anger, quarrels, dissensions, factions, envy, drunkenness, carousing, and things like these. . . . By contrast, the fruit of the Spirit is love, joy, peace, patience, kindness, generosity, faithfulness, gentleness, and self-control.

It is true that there are a few short vice lists in the O.T. (see Jer. 7:9; Prov. 6:17–19; Hos. 4:2), but they do not appear to be a well-developed literary form. Virtue lists are absent. Most scholars agree that the N.T. form (and in many cases the content, the specific vices and virtues enumerated) has been borrowed from Hellenistic literature and rhetoric, where it is very common (Berger, 149f.). Hellenistic Judaism readily adopted the form and used it to condemn the sinfulness of Gentiles, especially their idolatry and immortality (see Wisdom of Solomon 14:22–31; cf. Rom. 1:29–31). Burton Easton gives a graphic example of the traditional nature of the virtue list when he quotes Onosander (*Strategoi*, first century) and compares his list to the description of a bishop found in 1 Tim. 3:2–7:

> I say that the general should be chosen as sober minded, self-controlled, temperate, frugal, hardy, intelligent, no lover of money, not too young or old, if he be the father of children, able to speak well, of good repute. (Easton, 10, 11)

It appears that generals and bishops need similar moral qualifications! In reality, both Onosander and the writer of 1 Timothy are tapping stereotyped Hellenistic views concerning the virtues of a responsible person, and both are using the standard list form. Obviously, this traditional nature of the lists will be an important issue for the interpreter.

The Value for Interpretation

The power of vice and virtue lists lies in repetition. Content is emphasized through the cadence established. Variations in the standard form of repetition often affect how the list is heard and what meaning is conveyed. Although there may be little difference in meaning between lists that have conjunctions (1 Cor. 5:9–10; 6:9–10) and those that do not (Gal. 5:19–21), considerable impact is felt when the writer "slows down" and expands upon certain items (2 Tim. 3:2–5; 1 Tim. 3:2–7). Often the power of repetition is enhanced through consonance or euphony (note the repetition of initial sounds in the Greek in 2 Tim. 3:2–4 and Rom. 1:29–32; McEleney, 214).

Even though it might seem that each item in a list would have equal value, sometimes arrangements of the words or other associations give interesting emphases. The nine virtues in Gal. 5:22–23 beg to be arranged into three groups with three items each, based upon rhetorical balance and content (love, joy, peace; patience, kindness, generosity; faithfulness, gentleness, and self-control; Furnish, 87). Many scholars feel that the vice list in 1 Tim. 1:9, 10 is arranged roughly according to the two tables of the decalogue (Easton, 207). Victor Furnish argues that the virtue lists in Paul cluster around the themes of love, purity, and truthfulness (86). The vice lists in Paul appear to emphasize certain key sins—adultery/fornication, idolatry, murder, and drunkenness—similar to their Hellenistic Jewish counterparts. When vice and virtue lists occur together, comparison is called for, although not all the items listed have "opposites" (see Gal. 5:19–23; Eph. 4:31–32). It is these nuances of rhythm and arrangement that interpreters must be aware of as they analyze this form.

It is also important for the interpreter to ask how these lists relate to their literary and social contexts. Is the N.T. writer simply borrowing common Hellenistic virtues or vices, items that have no relationship to the specific situation being addressed, or is he listing virtues or vices that are immediately relevant to the community in mind? Certainly the content of many of the lists found in the N.T. is very similar to that found in Hellenistic literature. Perhaps this indicates an apologetic function (as in the case of the household codes), or it may simply indicate the pervasive influence of the Hellenistic environment. Of course, the traditional nature of the lists need not preclude relevance, because Christians can share virtues and vices with other religious groups!

Many of the N.T. lists do appear to have been shaped relative to the situation at hand. In Gal. 5:19–23, for instance, several of the listed vices (enmity, strife, jealousy, anger, selfishness, dissension, party spirit, envy) and virtues (love, joy, peace, patience, etc.) speak directly to the problems the church is experiencing (Easton, 5). The vice list in 2 Cor. 12:20–21 seems to be tailor-made for Corinth and its errors. Impurity, sexual immorality, and licentiousness (v. 21) relate to the problems of immorality (1 Cor. 5, 6), and the vices in v. 20 relate directly to the problem of dissensions and divisions that pervades the correspondence (Furnish, 84). Even the list in 1 Tim. 3:2–7, though it begins by sounding like a typical Hellenistic virtue list, is concluded with several descriptive statements that tie it directly to the situation ("How can he take care of God's church?", v. 5; "He must not be a recent convert," v. 6). Paul and the later writers in the Pauline tradition felt free both to borrow typical vices and virtues and to shape their lists based upon the situation addressed and the uniqueness of the Christian faith.

The question of literary context can perhaps be asked in another way: exactly how do the lists function within their respective passages? Are they representative of typical, universal behavior, as is more often the case with the vice lists, or are they the basis for narrowly Christian paraenesis? Are the lists the basis for threats or exhortations? How are they used to further the argument? How do both the form and content of the lists serve the author's purpose in ethical instruction?

Additional Examples

Vice lists: Rom. 13:13; 2 Cor. 6:14; Eph. 5:3–4; Col. 3:5–8; 1 Tim. 6:4–5 (see also Mark 7:21; 1 Peter 4:3; Rev. 9:20–21).

Virtue lists: Eph. 6:14–17; Phil. 4:8; 1 Tim. 3:2 (see also Matt. 5:3–11; Heb. 7:26; James 3:17).

Selected Bibliography

Berger, Klaus. 1984. *Formgeschichte des Neuen Testaments,* 148–150. Heidelberg: Quelle and Meyer. Unfortunately, this work is untranslated, but is an excellent resource for background information on this and other N.T. forms.

Easton, Burton Scott. 1932. "New Testament Ethical Lists." *Journal of Biblical Literature* 51, 1–12. This is an excellent older article, especially with reference to the Hellenistic background of the form.

Furnish, Victor Paul. 1968. *Theology and Ethics in Paul,* 84–89. Nashville: Abingdon. This helpful section shows Paul's influence in the structuring of the lists.

McEleney, Neil J. 1974. "The Vice Lists of the Pastoral Epistles." *Catholic Biblical Quarterly* 36, 203–219. Although significant in many ways, this article is very helpful in pointing out arrangements and emphases within the lists in the Pastorals.

THE HOUSEHOLD CODE

Definition of the Form

Another form located under the umbrella of paraenesis is the household code (in German, the *Haustafel*). The form usually addresses three key pairs in the household—master and slave, husband and wife, father and children—and describes how these relationships properly function. Wives, children, and slaves are considered subordinate members and owe their obedience to the household head. Adult males, whether as husbands, fathers, or masters, were thought to possess the natural right of authority in these relationships, although they were not to abuse this authority. Recent research has shown that the form has its origin in the Hellenistic belief that a strong and properly regulated family leads to a strong society (Balch 1981, 21–62).

An excellent N.T. example of the form is found in Col. 3:18–4:1:

> Wives, be subject to your husbands, as is fitting in the Lord. Husbands, love your wives and never treat them harshly.
>
> Children, obey your parents in everything, for this is your acceptable duty in the Lord. Fathers, do not provoke your children, or they may lose heart.
>
> Slaves, obey your earthly masters in everything, not only while being watched and in order to please them, but wholeheartedly, fearing the Lord. Whatever your task, put yourselves into it, as done for the Lord and not for your masters, since you know that from the Lord you will receive the inheritance as your reward; you serve the Lord Christ. For the wrongdoer will be paid back for whatever wrong has been done, and there is no partiality. Masters, treat your slaves justly and fairly, for you know that you also have a Master in heaven.

It is noteworthy that this form does not appear in the letters undisputably authored by Paul. Rather, it occurs in those writings of the later tradition whose Pauline authorship is debated (Col. 3:18–4:1; Eph. 5:21–6:9) or even unlikely (1 Tim. 2:8–15; 5:1–2; 6:1–2; Titus 2:1–10; 3:1–7). In addition, a form of the household code surfaces in 1 Peter 2:18–3:7, a later writing directed to churches in Asia Minor faced with suffering.

The Value for Interpretation

Interpretation of the household codes found in the N.T. demands (1) an awareness of the sociopolitical situation of the form and (2) an understanding of how the typical form can be embellished or "Christianized." As is the case in the literature of other minority religions in the Roman world, N.T. household codes often have an apologetic function (Balch 1981, 63–116). They exhort behavior that is acceptable in Roman society and hence show that Christianity is not dangerous to the norms of the state. The use of the household code in the N.T. points to communities that are aware of their own political environment and, in some

cases, indicates the threat of persecution. These factors explain
in part the presence of this form in the later N.T. books. In
contrast to the asceticism and strong apocalypticism of earlier
communities, these Christian groups stress their ongoing witness
in the world. As they settle down for a long stay, they are forced
to deal with the political structures around them, sometimes as
a matter of survival. The exegete must be willing to ask how this
apologetic function has shaped the material and how it should
impact his or her interpretation and application. What aspects of
the community's situation have prompted them to use this Hellenistic form? To what extent does the use of the form represent
a desire to become socially acceptable? To what extent does its
use represent merely an attempt to avoid conflict with society
while, nevertheless, remaining true to the essential teachings of
Christianity?

In several cases, there are embellishments or alterations of the
form that suggest that these Christian communities did not readily submit to the ideological status quo. In the household code
found in Colossians, for instance, both the ruling males and the
subordinate groups are given Christian rationales for their actions. Wives are to be subject, "as is fitting in the Lord" (v. 18).
Children are expected to obey because it is their duty in the Lord
(v. 20). The code claims that whatever slaves do they do in
service to the Lord, not humans, in the knowledge that they will
receive their reward from the Lord (vs. 22–25). Household
heads are told to love their wives, to avoid provoking children,
and to treat their slaves fairly because they too have a master in
heaven (3:19; 4:1). Although this code may sound crudely patriarchal to us, in light of its setting in a Hellenistic world in which
the household head had absolute power over his subordinates,
this Christianizing of the form surely represents a liberating
tendency.

Ephesians 5:21–6:9 offers an even clearer example. The entire code reflects the radical command that people are to be
subject *to one another* in reverence for Christ (v. 21). The long
exhortation to husbands to love their wives (vs. 25–33) finds its
reason in the emulation of Christ's love for the church as well as
their instinctive care for their own bodies. Verse 30 associates
the word "body" (*sōma*) with being members of Christ's church.
The responsibilities of the husband/wife relationship, summed
up in v. 33, are rooted in a christological and ecclesialogical
model. Genesis 2:24 is included as a scriptural warrant for the
relationship, even though it does not directly support the subor-

dination of the wife to the husband. Fathers are not only not to provoke their children, but are also to bring them up in the discipline and instruction of the Lord (v. 4). Masters are to treat their slaves in a way that reflects the fact that they share an impartial master in heaven (v. 9). Although the basic features of the form are still intact (wives, be subject; children, obey; slaves, obey), the writer has so emphasized the mutuality of household relationships that he is actually challenging Hellenistic views of subordination (for a helpful interpretation of 1 Peter 2:11–3:12 and its liberating statements, see Balch, 1984).

Of course, not all the household codes found in the N.T. Christianize the form and thus challenge the status quo. Those in the Pastorals (1 Tim. 2:8–15; 5:1–2; 6:2; Titus 2:1–10; 3:1–7) appear to accept uncritically the Hellenistic worldview. The church is rigidly defined on the basis of sex and age differences in order to protect the established order (see Verner; Fiorenza, 288–294). The interpreter must evaluate the hierarchical assumptions of these household codes in light of the unity and equality enunciated by Paul in Gal. 3:28 and by Jesus in the Gospels. Because we do not urge the reinstitution of slavery just because the household code assumes the master/slave relationship, so we must critically assess the code's interpretation both of the husband/wife relationship and that of the parent/child. At times it may be necessary to disagree with some parts of scripture based upon our understanding of the whole.

It should also be noted that emphases within the household codes may indicate where the author's primary concern lies. The code in Ephesians deals at length with the husband/wife relationship (5:22–33), whereas the one in Colossians dwells upon the relationship between master and slave (3:22–4:1). The place of women, whether as wives or widows, appears to be a primary concern in 1 Tim. (2:9ff.; 5:3ff.). In 1 Timothy, in fact, the household code is broadened out to include statements about positions and behavior in the church (see 3:1–13; 5:1, 2, 9ff., 17ff.) and becomes what could be called a community code. The code in 1 Peter addresses slaves but not masters (2:18–22) and omits the standard father/child relationship. It begins with a general admonition to be subject to ruling institutions, emperors, and governors (vs. 13, 14); perhaps the church was composed of those from the lower end of the socioeconomic scale who faced the threat of official persecution. All of the above are clues interpreters must wrestle with as they try to understand the use of this Hellenistic form.

Selected Bibliography

Balch, David L. 1981. *Let Wives Be Submissive: The Domestic Code in I Peter*. SBL Monograph Series Vol. 26. Missoula, Mont.: Scholars Press.

————. 1984. "Early Christian Criticism of Patriarchal Authority: I Peter 2:11–3:12." *Union Seminary Quarterly Review* 39, 161–173.
    Balch's discussion of the historical setting and apologetic use of household codes is very helpful, as is his insightful analysis of 1 Pet. 2:11–3:12.

Fiorenza, Elisabeth Schüssler. 1984. *In Memory of Her*. New York: Crossroad, 251–284. This book is a helpful and much needed interpretation of the household codes from the feminist perspective.

Lohse, Edward. 1971. *Colossians and Philemon*. Translated by Robert J. Karris and William R. Poehlmann. *Hermeneia*. Philadelphia: Fortress Press.

Sampley, J. Paul. 1971. *"And the Two Shall Become One Flesh": A Study of Traditions in Ephesians 5:21–33*. Cambridge: Cambridge University Press.
    Lohse's and Sampley's works contain useful studies of the household codes in Colossians and Ephesians.

Verner, David C. 1983. *The Household of God: The Social World of the Pastoral Epistles*. SBL Dissertation Series No. 71. Chico, Calif.: Scholars Press. Verner offers an insightful study about the Pastorals' use of the household codes as a means of supporting the established order in the church.

LITURGICAL FRAGMENTS: BLESSINGS AND DOXOLOGIES

Definition of the Forms

It is no surprise that liturgical language and forms are found scattered throughout the letters in the Pauline tradition. Paul himself most certainly led worship in the churches he founded and would have been influenced in his correspondence by these traditional elements of worship. Equally important is the fact that the letters were expected to be read aloud in the churches (1 Thess. 5:27; Col. 4:16), perhaps as part of a worship experience. In light of this setting, it would be only natural for the letter writer to include common liturgical elements.

These elements are diverse, and not all can be classified as literary forms. *Acclamations*, for instance, are simply short expressions of praise reflecting the joy of worship or prayer. In the Pauline literature, examples include "Amen" (1 Cor. 14:16, and the many occurrences in blessings and doxologies, see below); *"Maranatha"* ("Our Lord, come!" 1 Cor. 16:22), and *"Abba"* ("Father," Rom. 8:15; Gal. 4:6). Another liturgical element, the *grace benediction*, usually comes at the end of the letters (Rom. 16:20; 2 Cor. 13:14; Gal. 6:18; Phil. 4:23; 1 Thess. 5:28; 2 Thess. 3:18) and does have a standard form: (1) the pronouncement of grace, (2) the source of the grace (usually Jesus Christ, but in 2 Cor. 13:14 the entire Trinity is mentioned), and (3) the recipient of the grace. Romans 16:20 is typical: "The grace of our Lord Jesus Christ be with you." In the Pastorals, the second element is often missing (1 Tim. 6:21; 2 Tim. 4:22; Titus 3:15). Grace benedictions are probably Christianized versions of the Hebrew peace greeting ("peace be with you"), but their exact use in worship is unclear. They might have functioned in prayer or as liturgical greetings (cf. 1 Cor. 16:20 and the kiss greeting), or they might have been used to conclude worship, consistent with their placement at the end of the letters. Compare these grace benedictions with the grace salutations used by Paul (Rom. 1:7; 1 Cor. 1:3; 2 Cor. 1:2; see *The Pauline Letter*). The salutations appear to be Christianized versions of the typical greeting in a letter (instead of *chairein*, "greetings," Paul declares *charis*, "grace," to the recipients).

Worship instructions, although they are not literary forms, do offer helpful information about the nature of early Christian worship. In 1 Cor. 11, Paul instructs about dress (vs. 2–16) and the celebration of the Lord's Supper (vs. 17–34). In 1 Cor. 14:26f., he mentions common elements of worship at Corinth: hymns, lessons, revelations, and tongues. The author of the Pastorals discusses the nature of corporate prayer in 1 Tim. 2:1–9. It has even been suggested that the letters contain partial *orders of worship*. First Corinthians 16:20–24, with its sequence of kiss greeting (v. 20), exclusion of unbelievers (v. 22), *maranatha* (v. 22), and grace benediction (v. 23), may have preceded the Lord's Supper (Cullmann, 24), whereas Eph. 4:11–16 and 1 Tim. 3:1–10 may reflect ordination liturgies. *Hymns* and *creeds*, other important elements of worship, are dealt with in separate sections of this volume (see *Poetry/Hymn* and *Creeds*). In this section, two short but significant forms are the focus—*blessings* and *doxologies*.

Blessings and Doxologies

Prayer is a very important theme in the Pauline tradition. Paul often mentions his prayers in the thanksgiving sections (Rom. 1:9; Phil. 1:4; 1 Thess. 1:2; in the deutero-Pauline letters, see Col. 1:3; 2 Thess. 1:3), and thanksgiving itself is a typical part of Jewish/Christian prayer. Both blessings and doxologies are forms used to express praise to God, and as such can be seen as prayers in their own right, although they can be found in various contexts in the letters. Blessings are common in the O.T. (see Ps. 41:13; 66:20; 1 Chron. 16:36) and typically conclude synagogue prayer. The basic form in Paul is like that in Jewish literature: (1) reference to God, (2) description of God as one "who is blessed forever," and (3) the concluding "Amen" (Rom. 1:25; 9:5; 2 Cor. 11:31). Paul does, however, feel free to alter this traditional form. Note the description of God as the Father of Jesus Christ, along with other attributes, in 2 Cor. 1:3ff. In Eph. 1:3ff., the writer embellishes the blessing into an extended hymn about the history of salvation (cf. 1 Tim. 6:15–16).

Doxologies are similar in terms of form. They (1) begin with a reference to God in the dative case (often using relative or personal pronouns to refer to God; see Rom. 11:36; Gal. 1:5; 1 Tim. 6:16), (2) ascribe to God eternal glory (*doxa*), and (3) conclude with an "Amen." Romans 11:36 is typical: "To him be glory forever. Amen." As with the blessings, there is a tendency to expand upon the basic form. In Eph. 3:21 we read: "to him be glory in the church and in Christ Jesus to all generations, forever and ever. Amen" (cf. 1 Tim. 1:17). The most embellished doxology is found in Rom. 16:25–27. Although it may have been added by a later editor (Elliott, 124–130), it most certainly reflects the faith and practice of the worshiping community.

> Now to God who is able to strengthen you according to my gospel and the proclamation of Jesus Christ, according to the revelation of the mystery that was kept secret for long ages but is now disclosed, and through the prophetic writings is made known to all the Gentiles, according to the command of the eternal God, to bring about the obedience of faith—to the only wise God, through Jesus Christ, to whom be glory forever! Amen.

Even though the doxology is not as common as the blessing in Jewish literature, ascriptions of glory to God are found in the O.T. (see Pss. 29:2, 3; 66:2; 96:8), and the complete form is used at times to conclude prayers (Pr. Man. 15) or texts (4 Macc. 18:24). In the Pauline tradition as well, the benediction is often used to conclude a section of thought (Rom. 11:36; Phil. 4:20; 2 Tim. 4:18).

The Value for Interpretation

Because blessings and doxologies have a fairly standard form in both Jewish literature and in the Pauline tradition, one aspect of interpretation has to do with alterations of the forms. The embellishments in the blessing in 2 Cor. 1:3 and the doxology in Eph. 3:21, for instance, attest to the power of Christology in the life of the early church. As one might expect, it is difficult for these writers (reflecting the attitudes of the Christian communities they serve) to ascribe blessings and glory to God without also mentioning God's greatest revelation, Jesus Christ. We perhaps underestimate the boldness that was necessary to alter these traditional Jewish forms.

The interpreter must also be aware of how these short liturgical elements function within the Pauline text. It is true that blessings and doxologies are prayer language, but in Paul they usually do not occur as part of a larger prayer. The interpreter must be attuned to the train of thought being developed and how these elements accentuate or develop that thought. In Rom. 1:25, for example, Paul appears to use the blessing as a means of emphasizing the righteousness of God in contrast to the wicked people he has been describing (vs. 21–25). In Rom. 9:5, the blessing is an emotional outburst that accentuates his helplessness before God's authority relative to the plight of his fellow Jews. If it is true that the doxologies (like their Jewish counterparts) often have a concluding function in Paul, that fact must not be lost to the interpreter. One must not fail to notice, for example, that the rhetorical crescendo leading up to the doxology in Rom. 11:36 is the conclusion to an important section (Rom. 9–11), and that ch. 12 begins a different discussion.

Not only would blessings and doxologies have been recognized by the communities hearing the letters read, but the concluding "Amens," used elsewhere in worship, would have been a familiar element. The interpreter should ask how the use of these common liturgical elements would have affected the hear-

ing of the letters. Did Paul place them at certain points in his
letters knowing that the people would join in the "Amens," thus
affirming what he was saying? To what extent did Paul employ
this language to link himself with the churches he was addressing, and how should this liturgical relationship affect our interpretation? These are not easy questions, but they must not be
avoided considering the common liturgical function of these
forms.

Selected Bibliography

Berger, Klaus. 1984. *Formgeschichte des Neuen Testaments*, 236–238.
    Heidelberg: Quelle and Meyer. For the German reader, this is an
    excellent resource concerning the doxology and a host of other forms.

Champion, L. G. 1934. *Benedictions and Doxologies in the Epistles of
    Paul.* Oxford: Kemp Hall Press. This older work is still the best
    resource for these forms in Paul.

Cullman, Oscar. 1953. *Early Christian Worship.* London: SCM Press.
    This classic is well worth reading. Cullmann's special emphasis in
    this book is the Gospel of John.

Elliott, J. K. 1981. "The Language and Style of the Concluding Doxol-
    ogy to the Epistle to the Romans." *Zeitschrift für die neutestament-
    liche Wissenschaft* 72, 124–130. According to Elliott, Rom. 16:25–27
    is not from Paul's hand but is an interesting representative of doxolo-
    gies used in the early church.

POETRY AND HYMN

Definition of the Forms

Poetry

Although poetry has evolved over the years, it is quite possible
to give a general definition of the form that applies to both
first-century and modern expressions. Two elements are central.
First, poetry often employs what is called figurative language.
Instead of simply stating directly the thought she or he wishes to
convey, the poet uses word pictures, images, symbols, metaphors, and so forth, to encourage the reader to wrestle creatively
with the issue at hand. In 1 Cor. 13:1, for instance, Paul (or

perhaps a pre-Pauline writer) does not say, "Without love, speaking in tongues is meaningless." Rather he states, "If I speak in the tongues of mortals and of angels, but do not have love, I am a noisy gong or a clanging cymbal." The image of angelic speech forces the reader to imagine the beauty and positive qualities of this language, yet it also heightens the irony when one realizes that such a speaker, without love, is only a noisy gong or clanging cymbal. The latter metaphors stimulate the reader to compare speaking in tongues (without love) with the meaningless sound produced by instruments in pagan worship; the nuances of interpretation are endless and the impact is powerful. Figurative language involves the reader by stimulating the imagination.

Second, poetry usually exhibits some type of sustained rhythm. Of course, rhythm can be expressed in various ways, through patterns of repetition in syllable stresses (meter), through the repetition of vowel or consonant sounds, through the arrangement of clauses or thoughts, and so forth. If rhythm occurs in some larger pattern, it can become the basis for dividing a poem into verses. Again, 1 Cor. 13 serves as a helpful example. Each of the first three lines in the chapter has the same structure: (1) an "if clause" that describes some very desirable gift, (2) the phrase "but do not have love," and (3) a clause that states the effects of the gift apart from love (i.e., is a noisy gong, a clanging cymbal, v. 1; is nothing, v. 2; gains nothing, v. 3). Although we may more commonly think of poetic rhythm in terms of meter, such as iambic pentameter, the rhythm in vs. 1–3 is easily discernible and effective; it even helps the reader to distinguish vs. 1–3 from vs. 4–7 and vs. 8–13, both of which have their own distinct rhythms.

First Corinthians 13:1–3 illustrates the most common rhythmic structure or verse form found in the Pauline tradition, a structure called *parallelism*. It consists of the repetition of lines that are parallel to one another in terms of sentence structure and meaning. The use of parallelism in the New Testament most certainly has its origin in Hebrew poetry. Isaiah 54:1, quoted by Paul in Gal. 4:27, is a fine example:

> "Rejoice, you childless one,
>   you who bear no children,
>   burst into song and shout,
>   you who endure no birthpangs."

The reader feels the rhythmic impact of these lines, not primarily through the repetition of sounds or stresses, but through parallel syntax and meaning (see Paul's use of Ps. 19:4, Deut. 32:21, and Isa. 65:1 in Rom. 10:18–20 for more examples). Obviously, many types of parallelism are possible, but three are often mentioned: synonymous, antithetic, and synthetic. Synonymous parallelism refers to lines that convey roughly the same meaning, as in Rom. 11:33:

> O the depth of the riches and wisdom and knowledge of God!
> How unsearchable are his judgments
>   and how inscrutable his ways!

Antithetic parallelism uses lines that stand in contrast to one another, as in Rom. 6:23:

> For the wages of sin is death,
> but the free gift of God is eternal life in Christ Jesus our Lord.

Synthetic parallelism has a second line that completes or expands the meaning of the first, as in 1 Cor. 13:12:

> For now we see in a mirror, dimly, but then we will see face to
>   face.
> Now I know only in part; then I will know fully, even as I have
>   been fully known.

Parallelism lies at the heart of poetic expression in the New Testament.

Of course, the Pauline tradition comes to us in the form of prose letters, not poetry. Although these letters do contain what appear to be complete poems (as we shall see), most often we find bits of poetic language hidden among the prose (as are Rom. 11:33; 6:23, above). Such language usually occurs in the midst of a rhetorical crescendo where both the rhythm and figurative power of the writing distinguish it from the surrounding prose. Note the poetic qualities in 2 Cor. 4:8–10:

> We are afflicted in every way, but not crushed;
> Perplexed, but not driven to despair;
> Persecuted, but not forsaken;
> Struck down, but not destroyed;
>
> Always carrying in the body the death of Jesus,
> So that the life of Jesus may also be made visible in our bodies.

The first four lines might be said to function in terms of synonymous parallelism, using similar sentence structure and meaning to nuance the message and heighten its impact. The last two lines use synthetic parallelism; there the second line clearly expands upon the meaning of the first. And note the powerful images—contrasting images of despair and hope in the first stanza, and images of life, death, and body in the second. Obviously, it is important for the reader to recognize such poetic outbursts when they occur, even if they represent only a small portion of a larger prose context, and interpret them accordingly (of the many possible examples, see 1 Cor. 12:4–6; Phil. 3:8; Rom. 8:37–39).

Hymns

Some of the poetry found in the Pauline letters, indeed most of the larger, more complete units, were borrowed by Paul (or in the case of deutero-Pauline letters, a later writer) from the liturgies of the early church. Many scholars think that these rhythmic, image-filled pieces were used as hymns during worship. Ralph Martin (19) further classifies hymns according to their function and content: (a) sacramental (Eph. 5:14; Titus 3:4–7; perhaps Rom. 6:1–11 and Eph. 2:19–22); (b) meditative (Eph. 1:3–14; Rom. 8:31–39; 1 Cor. 13); (c) confessional (1 Tim. 6:11–16; 2 Tim. 2:11–13); (d) christological (Col. 1:15–20; 1 Tim. 3:16; Phil. 2:6–11). Hymns in the last category (christological) most certainly function as creeds or theological confessions as well. See the section *Creeds* for further examples, especially of those that are somewhat less poetic (less reliance upon figurative language) and that focus more precisely on the essential content of the faith. In terms of form, the above hymns are largely poetry, but there are other formal characteristics to note. The hymns are often introduced by introductory formulas that set them apart from the surrounding prose and give some indication that they have been borrowed from the tradition ("The saying is sure," 2 Tim. 2:11; "Therefore it says," Eph. 5:14). The poetry of the hymn is often begun with a relative pronoun ("Who, though he was in the form of God," Phil. 2:6; "Who is the image of the invisible God," Col. 1:15, author's translation reflecting the Greek). Theological concepts abound, especially in the christological hymns.

Probably the most well known of the hymns is the christological hymn found in Phil. 2:6–11. Although it is widely agreed that vs. 6–11 are poetry, there has been considerable debate about how they should be divided into verses. Two factors lie at the heart of the discussion—the nature of the rhythm in the piece and the question of Pauline additions to the original hymn. Ernst Lohmeyer, for instance, divided the hymn into six three-line verses, each line having three stresses (see *Kyrios Jesus: Eine Untersuchung zu Phil. 2,5–11*). Thus he understood the rhythm to be based on meter, which is typical in Greco-Roman poetry of the first century. Part of one line does not fit into this metrical pattern ("even death on a cross," v. 8), so Lohmeyer considered it a Pauline addition not found in the original poem.

Quite a different verse form is offered by Martin (38). Following other scholars, he considers three phrases ("even death on a cross," v. 8; "in heaven and on earth and under the earth," v. 10; "to the glory of God the Father," v. 11) to be Pauline additions. All three come at the end of a line and are in a typically Pauline style. The deletion of these phrases allows versification on the basis of parallelism:

Who, though he was in the form of God,
Did not regard equality with God as something to be exploited;

But emptied himself,
Taking the form of a slave;

Being born in human likeness,
And being found in human form;

He humbled himself,
And became obedient to the point of death;

Therefore God also highly exalted him,
And gave him the name that is above every name;

So that at the name of Jesus every knee should bend,
And every tongue should confess that Jesus Christ is Lord.

Surely this is some of the most sophisticated poetry in the New Testament. It appears to be a complete unit, moving as it does from exaltation to humiliation and back to exaltation. The nuances of meaning communicated in the parallel lines are powerful, as are the images and metaphors employed. It is not hard to imagine this poem being sung or chanted in the early church. Paul may well have borrowed it not only because of its beauty and insight, but also because it was widely known and revered.

The Value for Interpretation

Perhaps the most essential thing to be said is that poetry, through its rhythm and figurative language, signals to the reader that she or he is entering a literary world far different from that of prose or dogma. Here the purpose is not tight definition but stimulation, getting the reader to wrestle with the images and moods generated by the poetic experience. Rhythm offers a cadence that heightens the power of language. The numerous metaphors and symbols employed indicate that meaning is open-ended, dependent to a certain extent upon the creativity of the interpreter. As poetry, Phil. 2:6–11 should not be seen as propositional theology. To say that Jesus "was in the form of God" (v. 6) is to suggest infinite interpretations; like all good poetry it also communicates the limitations of human language.

The verse form of poetry often provides important clues for interpretation as well. Lohmeyer's arrangement of Phil. 2:6–11 into three-line verses actually separates into different verses some lines that Martin considers parallel (i.e., "being born in human likeness," "being found in human form," vs. 7b, 8a), leading to the possibility of quite different interpretations. Both Lohmeyer and Martin determine the Pauline additions to this traditional hymn at least in part based upon their understanding of the verse form and what does not fit that form.

Because parallelism is such an important structure in New Testament poetry, as in Hebrew poetry, special attention should be paid to it. Terms such as synonymous parallelism and antithetic parallelism, while they are somewhat helpful, are perhaps also deceptive in that the relationship between the parallel lines is always much more complex than simply "the same" or "the opposite." James Kugel, in a study of Hebrew poetry, speaks of the "afterwardness" of the second line in the couplet (13). The second line often completes the meaning of the first; it adds a richness to the interpretation. Simply to say that the lines "he humbled himself" and "he became obedient to the point of death" (Phil. 2:8) are synonymous may indicate a failure to grasp the nuances of meaning presented by the second line. Robert Alter also emphasizes the dynamic relationship between the lines: "The characteristic movement of meaning is one of heightening or intensification, of focusing, specification, concretization, even what could be called dramatization" (19). Interpreters must not overlook the richness and complexity of New Testament parallelism.

We might also note the significance of the introductory formulas typically part of the New Testament hymns. At the very least they indicate a pre-Pauline setting, probably one in worship, as we have noted. The interpreter is called upon to think about that setting and how it compares to the setting it is given in the Pauline tradition. The original setting might shed some light upon Paul's use of the hymn, even if it shows only that Paul is using it in a nonliturgical way.

Selected Bibliography

Alter, Robert. 1985. *The Art of Biblical Poetry.* New York: Basic Books. A delight to read, Alter's book offers a sophisticated definition of Hebrew poetry with many biblical examples.

Berger, Klaus. 1984. "Hellenistische Gattungen im Neuen Testament." In *Aufstieg und Niedergang der römischen Welt,* 1149–1169. II.25,2. Berlin & New York: Walter de Gruyter. In this section Berger describes the nature of hymns in the larger Hellenistic world and points out similarities to N.T. hymns.

Charlesworth, J. H. 1982. "A Prolegomenon to a New Study of the Jewish Background of the Hymns and Prayers in the New Testament." *Journal of Jewish Studies* 33, 265–285. The methodological principles Charlesworth offers are helpful, but see especially his succinct overview of N.T. scholarly works on the subject.

Kugel, James L. 1981. *The Idea of Biblical Poetry: Parallelism and Its History.* New Haven: Yale University Press. Like Alter, Kugel provides a helpful analysis of parallelism, although he comes to quite different conclusions about the nature of Hebrew poetry.

Martin, Ralph P. 1983. *Carmen Christi: Philippians 2:5–11 in Recent Interpretation and in the Setting of Early Christian Worship.* Grand Rapids: Wm. B. Eerdmans. Martin provides the definitive work on the form and content of Phil. 2:5–11.

Sanders, Jack T. 1971. *The New Testament Christological Hymns: Their Historical Religious Background.* Cambridge: Cambridge University Press. This book is a fine overview of the christological hymns in the New Testament.

CREEDS

Definition of the Form

Creeds, or confessions of faith, were used in worship in the early church and most probably reflect the use of *Shema* (a confession that "God is one," cf. Mark 12:29) in synagogue worship. Of course, these creeds functioned in other settings in the church as well—catechism (instruction), polemic, and preaching. The creeds found in the Pauline tradition are largely traditional; that is, they have been borrowed from the worshiping community. These confessions exhibit somewhat diverse formal characteristics. Some of the hymns, for instance, function as faith statements (see *Poetry and Hymn*). Here we are primarily concerned with those confessions that focus more precisely on the essential content of the faith and that are usually less poetic than the hymns; that is, they show less reliance upon figurative language.

Vernon Neufeld suggests that confessions of faith found in Paul's writings can often be identified by the following characteristics (42–68): (1) the presence of *homologeō* ("confess") or some similar introductory word indicating a context of confession; (2) the presence of *hoti* ("that" or "because") or some other grammatical device indicating either quoted material or indirect discourse; (3) in the creed or confession itself, the use of relative clauses, participles, or parallelism to give a rhythmic or "creedal" character; (4) the presence in the confession of a theme that often has a dual or antithetical nature. Scholars argue that this dual character may reflect the twofold nature of what they think was one of the earliest creeds, "Jesus is Lord." In this creed, both the earthly life of Jesus and his divine authority ("Lord") are being confessed. This two-part confession may have led to other dual statements about Jesus: He is one who died and rose (Rom. 8:34; 1 Cor. 15:3–5); he was crucified in weakness but lives in power (2 Cor. 13:4); in him previously hidden things are being revealed (Col. 1:26–27; 2 Tim. 1:9–10).

Romans 10:9 is a fine example of an early creed exhibiting most of the elements listed above:

> Because if you confess with your lips that Jesus is Lord and believe in your heart that God raised him from the dead, you will be saved.

The initial *hoti* (here translated as "because") is perhaps best used recitatively, that is, as an indication that quoted or traditional material is to follow. Notice the presence of a form of *homologeō* ("confess") and, of course, the primitive creed "Jesus is Lord." Notice also the obvious parallelism between the first and second clauses (confess/believe; with your lips/in your heart), giving the lines a formal character. It is quite possible that Paul is borrowing an early Christian creed or fragment of one.

Among many possible examples, Rom. 1:3–4 and 1 Cor. 15:3–5 illustrate well the dual or two-part theme of many of the confessions.

> . . . concerning his Son, who was descended from David according to the flesh and was declared to be Son of God with power according to the spirit of holiness by resurrection from the dead, Jesus Christ our Lord. (Rom. 1:3–4)

> For I handed on to you as of first importance what I in turn had received: that Christ died for our sins in accordance with the scriptures, and that he was buried, and that he was raised on the third day in accordance with the scriptures, and that he appeared . . . (1 Cor. 15:3–5)

Although Rom. 1:3 lacks a formula indicating quoted or traditional material, such is especially obvious in 1 Cor. 15:3. There Paul uses the verbs "handed on" *(paradidōmi)* and "received" *(paralambanō)*, technical words used to indicate that traditional material will follow. The same verbs are used in 1 Cor. 11:23 to introduce Jesus' words about the Lord's Supper. Both Rom. 1:3–4 and 1 Cor. 15:3–5 have a rhythmic character: the passage in Romans repeats relative clauses (in the Greek, "who was descended" and "who was declared"), whereas I Corinthians establishes a cadence through the repetition of *hoti* ("that"). Both passages exhibit structural parallelism as well. But notice especially the two-part Christology in the creeds. Reflecting the human and divine emphases found in the creed "Jesus is Lord," Rom. 1:3–4 speaks of Jesus as "descended from David according to the flesh" and "declared to be Son of God . . . by resurrection from the dead." First Corinthians 15:3–5 relates both that Christ died and was buried and that he was raised and seen (cf. the dual themes in 2 Cor. 13:4; 1 Tim. 3:16; Col. 1:26–27). These borrowed fragments give us helpful insight concerning the form and content of the confessions used in the early church.

The unity of God is another focus of the confessions in the Pauline tradition (as in the Jewish *Shema*), and at times this oneness of God is paralleled with a statement about the one lordship of Jesus Christ. Note the beautiful parallelism in 1 Cor. 8:6:

> Yet for us there is one God, the Father, from whom are all things and for whom we exist, and one Lord, Jesus Christ, through whom are all things and through whom we exist.

A similar confession is found in 1 Tim. 2:5:

> For there is one God; there is also one mediator between God and humankind, Christ Jesus, himself human, who gave himself a ransom for all.

In both of the above, the perhaps more typical two-part christological focus is replaced by another confessional dualism, the one God and one Lord (or mediator).

The Value for Interpretation

The parallelism found in many of the creeds invites the interpreter to compare or think about the relationship between the parallel parts. In Rom. 10:9, for instance, one is compelled to think about the use of the parallel verbs "confess" and "believe." Why does a person *confess* that Jesus is Lord and *believe* that God raised him? Are these verbs interchangeable? Why are they given in the order that they are, considering that a person usually believes before she or he confesses? One might ask similar questions about the parallel participles in Rom. 1:3–4, "descended" and "declared," or in any of the situations where parallel lines occur. In what sense do the parallel parts help interpret one another, whether through contrast or amplification (see *Poetry and Hymn*)?

The importance of this structural parallelism is enhanced by the presence of what could be called christological or theological parallelism. As seen above, often two aspects of Christ are compared or contrasted, or there is a two-part statement about Christ and God. In many cases, the theological parallelism is not just a poetic nicety but reflects the deepest christological concerns of the early church. The interpreter who takes seriously the dualistic nature of the confessions will be confronted with essential questions regarding the presence of the human and divine in Christ, and regarding the relationship of Christ and God.

Because these confessions were borrowed from the tradition, from the liturgies of the early church, the interpreter must also ask how they were used and understood by the biblical writers. The creed in Rom. 1:3–4 is interesting because it does not appear to be consistent with other statements of Pauline theology. The Davidic descent of Christ and adoptionism (the teaching that Jesus is appointed Son of God at a certain time) are not found elsewhere in Paul. Why would Paul employ this confession? Coming as it does at the beginning of a letter written to a church he had not founded, it may have been used to demonstrate his orthodoxy to the Christians at Rome (Neufeld, 51; Käsemann, 12, 13). Perhaps the community there used a similar confession.

A similar kind of tension between a creed and Paul occurs in Rom. 10:9. Although the order in the confession is "confess" and "believe" (consistent with the references to lips and heart in Deut. 30:11–14, alluded to in v. 8), Paul prefers to deal with the concepts in the opposite order (see v. 10). It is possible, as many have suggested, that the creed found in Rom. 10:9 was used at baptism, where public declaration or confession would have been important, and where both the words "confess" and "believe" would have referred to the content of the confession learned by the initiate (that "Jesus is Lord" and that "God raised him from the dead"; see Käsemann, 291). Paul, however, does not so much want to deal with the content of the creed found in v. 9 as he wants to emphasize that faith and confession lead to salvation for all people (vs. 11–13).

Obviously, there are various ways in which the N.T. writers can employ the creeds and influence how they are understood. Each new context inevitably leads to new interpretation. A knowledge of the form and content of early Christian creeds not only allows the interpreter to recognize these traditional pieces in the Pauline literature, but also gives the exegete a basis for understanding the writer's use of the material.

Additional Examples

Apart from the lengthy creedal hymns not dealt with in this section (Phil. 2:6–11; Col. 1:15–20; 2 Tim. 2:8–13; see the Selected Bibliography in *Poetry and Hymn*), scholars have detected creedal fragments in Rom. 4:24–25; 1 Cor. 12:3; Gal. 3:20; Eph. 5:2; 1 Tim. 3:16.

Selected Bibliography

Käsemann, Ernst. 1980. *Commentary on Romans*. Edited and translated by Geoffrey W. Bromiley. Grand Rapids: Wm. B. Eerdmans. Always the basic resource for study in Romans, Käsemann's book provides fascinating insight about the creeds in Rom. 1:3–4 and 10:9.

Kelly, J. N. D. 1949. *Early Christian Creeds*. London: Longmans, Green & Co. This older work is still worth consulting, especially the first chapter dealing with N. T. creeds.

Martin, Ralph P. 1978. *New Testament Foundations: A Guide for Christian Students*. Vol. 2, pp. 268–275. Grand Rapids: Wm. B. Eerdmans. Martin's section "Pre-Pauline Statements of Faith" is one of the best introductions to the Pauline use of confessions.

Neufeld, Vernon H. 1963. *The Earliest Christian Confessions*. Grand Rapids: Wm. B. Eerdmans. This work is the best treatment of the form and content of N.T. creeds.

THE GOSPELS
AND ACTS

GOSPEL

Definition of the Genre

"Gospel" is a translation of the Greek term *euangelion*, which in Paul refers to the oral proclamation centered on the saving significance of Jesus' crucifixion and resurrection. But because in Mark (1:1) this same term is used to designate the entire narrative about the career of Jesus, Gospel has become the generic designation for all narratives about Jesus Christ. Hence, to inquire about the genre of the Gospels is to discuss the traits that define these complex literary works, including structure, formal units, techniques of style, motifs, and subject matter. As a preliminary definition of the genre of the Gospels, the following is offered: A Gospel is a narrative, fashioned out of selected traditions, that focuses on the activity and speech of Jesus as a way to reveal his character and develops a dramatic plot that culminates in the stories of his passion and resurrection. This multifaceted narrative about Jesus relates to the larger framework of biblical history, because the life of Jesus not only emerges from that history but also transforms and transcends it.

As part of the current scholarly debate concerning the genre of the Gospels, two views predominate. The one approach, largely accepted since the turn of the century, argues that the written Gospels constitute a unique literary genre resulting from the earliest preaching of the church. By producing the first written Gospel, the author of Mark brought this oral process to creative fruition. The other approach explains the Gospel genre in terms of its similarities with existing literary types in the Greco-Roman world, especially biography. This second approach revives an earlier view of the Gospels as biographical, yet does so with a more sophisticated appreciation of the features and functions of ancient biography: (1) ancient biography incorporates sayings and anecdotes attributed to the person; these sayings and anecdotes are used to reveal the person's character; (2) the biographer focuses more on the ideal and typical than that which is individual; (3) the character of the person is presented as fixed rather than changing; and (4) the biography often has an apologetic function (see Berger, 1236–1243).

Some scholars are now suggesting that the canonical Gospels combine traits and features both of biblical history and Greco-Roman biography. Because of this, the Gospels represent a "mixed genre." Viewing the Gospels as a mixed genre avoids the less fruitful enterprise of explaining them exclusively in terms of one Jewish or Hellenistic literary type. Given their religious history and cultural environment, it makes sense that the evangelists would both appeal to the Hebrew scriptures for authority and guidance and draw on Hellenistic literary and rhetorical practices known to their audience in constructing the Gospel narratives. Indeed, this mixing of literary genres accords with one purpose of the Gospels; that is, to present Jesus as a unique figure and the community established in his name as a "new" alternative in both the Jewish and Hellenistic world. Stanley Saunders notes:

> Adoption of an existing genre could represent a form of parody. The mixing of existing genres into a "new" pattern might be a way of investing the old genres with new meaning, or such an action might also express a rejection of the values associated with the existing genres. (83)

Although David Aune concludes that "an analysis of the constituent literary features of the Gospels situates them comfortably within the parameters of ancient biographical conventions in form and function" (1987, 46), he nonetheless recognizes that in the first century C.E. the literary boundaries between biography and history were quite fluid: "History and biography moved closer together with the increasing emphasis on character in historiography. Biography and history become more and more difficult to distinguish" (1987, 30). Formerly, according to literary canons, history focused on the significant deeds *(praxeis)* of great figures as part of a larger political, social, and military framework, whereas biography concentrated on the character of an individual and how his deeds *(praxeis)* revealed that character *(ethos)*, with little or no interest in the wider historical picture (Talbert 1977, 16–17; Cox, 12; Aune 1987, 29–31). Yet it is significant that by the time of the New Testament, interests in history and biography could merge.

In summary, then, it must be said that the Gospels offer us richly textured and multifaceted literary works that exhibit biographical interest in the figure of Jesus but do so within the context of biblical history. In particular, the synoptic Gospels develop a narrative pattern that creatively adapts literary and rhetorical forms and motifs used in Jewish and Hellenistic literary traditions. All the Gospels obviously focus on the identity and significance of Jesus, presenting him as a paradigmatic figure whose actions and words represent his character and possess

immense import for his followers. In this regard, they accord
with the general purpose of much biography in the ancient
world. Moreover, Charles Talbert (1977, 108) concludes that the
Gospels are designed to dispel false images of Jesus, a function
again similar to the apologetic function of Hellenistic biography.
It is clear that the Gospel writers present the story of Jesus as the
figure who embodies the history and destiny of the Jewish people, and whose death and resurrection make possible a newly
reconstituted and universal people of God.

The Value for Interpretation

Knowledge of ancient literary genres and rhetoric is helpful to
interpreters of the Gospels if they remember that concern about
genre is not so much to classify precisely a literary document but
rather to clarify and understand better its structure and literary
features. What follows is an attempt to offer a few suggestions
about each Gospel in light of the discussions about the Gospel
genre.

Mark, probably the first Gospel, offers a chronologically ordered narrative of Jesus' public ministry, which culminates in his
arrest, trial, crucifixion, and resurrection. At first glance, the
Markan narrative appears to have an episodic character because
of its use of traditional units, yet after a more careful reading it
actually presents a coherent plot that displays dramatic movement. In fact, some scholars even suggest that the Markan
narrative possesses the basic ingredients of Greek tragedy: introduction or exposition, rising action or complication, climax or
crisis, falling action, catastrophe, and denouement (Aune 1987,
48–49; Robbins 1980, 389). Throughout the narrative, Jesus acts
and speaks with divine authority. His words and deeds reveal his
character as the messianic Son of God, yet his disciples and
others in the story do not recognize him as such but rather
respond with fear and puzzlement. Misunderstood and completely rejected, in the end Jesus is crucified by the Romans. Yet
Mark 16:1–8 announces his resurrection and a new beginning.

Both Jewish and Greco-Roman literary traditions have apparently contributed to the Markan Gospel. On the one hand, the
apocalyptic theme that permeates the entire narrative suggests
dependency on Jewish prophetic apocalyptic literature, which
anticipates a divinely wrought transformation of present history
into a new age. Mark's use of individual anecdotes and sayings
associated with a popular figure, on the other hand, is reminis-

cent of certain biographical literature in the Hellenistic world (see Robbins 1980, 392–393). The Markan "popular literary style" corresponds to this more popular type of biography.

Unlike most early Greco-Roman biography, Mark places great emphasis on Jesus' suffering and death. This is not without analogy, however, because by the first century c.e. there surfaced biographical interest in the hero's death. This was premised on the ancient Greek notion that "a person's life could be evaluated only when completed by death" (Aune 1988, 122–123). Aune lists Mark 14:32–42, 53–65 par., 15:2–5 par., John 18:29–38, and 19:8–15 as texts that witness to Jesus' "calmness and courage in the face of death," a motif corresponding to a Hellenistic conception of a hero figure. As an aid in understanding the shaping of the passion narrative, however, this observation needs to merge the roles played by models of the righteous sufferer, the Jewish martyr, the dying teacher, and the humiliated king in biblical, Jewish, and Greco-Roman literature (Robbins 1984, 180–194; see also *Stories About Jesus*).

Matthew also seems to draw on both Jewish and Hellenistic traditions. For example, some scholars argue that Matthew's fivefold form, with its alternation of narrative and discourse, suggests the pattern of the Deuteronomistic historiography. Yet it is also maintained that Matthew displays characteristics belonging to Greco-Roman biography. Like a biography, Matthew begins with the birth of Jesus and ends with his passion and resurrection. Both focus on the identity and person of Jesus. Moreover, Matthew lays stress on the teaching of Jesus, because the evangelist's alternation of narrative and discourse incorporates a great deal more of it. For this reason, Matthew might best be termed a didactic biography. And even more than Mark, Matthew emphasizes the integrity of Jesus' words and actions, which together illumine his identity and character. The juxtaposition of Jesus' words of authority in chs. 5–7 and his acts of mercy in chs. 8–9 offers an example of this. This accent on the integrity of word and deed corresponds to the concerns of Hellenistic biography as well.

In a somewhat different vein, George Kennedy (101–107) describes Matthew's alteration and expansion of the Markan framework in rhetorical terms. Whereas Mark presents what Kennedy calls a "radical Christian rhetoric," which involves absolute claims with little argumentation, Matthew has his characters engage in forms of logical argument. According to Kennedy, Matthew arranges materials in a fashion that resembles argumentation (e.g., Matt. 1:1–17 as the proem, 5–7 as the proposition, etc.; see *Forms of Argumentation*). Matthew's repeated use of scriptural quotations serves this pattern of argumentation.

Turning to Luke-Acts, the judgment of Kennedy offers a starting point: "Luke in the Gospel comes close to being a classical biographer, just as in Acts he comes close to being a classical historian" (108). Other scholars, arguing that the two volumes must be taken as a unity, have classified Luke-Acts as either biography (Robbins 1979) or history (Aune 1987), whereas Richard Pervo has developed a more tenuous thesis that contends that Acts by itself exhibits characteristics of the historical novel. Most scholars conclude correctly that Acts shows traits of both Hebraic and Hellenistic historiography (Beardslee, 42–52).

In any case, it seems clear that certain features move the volumes closer to more sophisticated literary forms in the Hellenistic world. First, Luke writes in more cultivated Greek, altering the paratactic style of Mark (i.e., the pattern of connecting clauses by using the conjunction *kai*—"and/but"). Second, a formal preface begins each volume (Luke 1:1–4; Acts 1:1–5), intimating knowledge of literary conventions in writing history (Aune 1987, 89–90, 120–121) and/or didactic biography (Robbins 1979, 95–108). Third, the evangelist incorporates, especially in Acts, various constituent forms that appear frequently in ancient history and biography: dramatic episodes, symposia, speeches, letters, digressions, travel sections, and summaries. Fourth, Luke exhibits other techniques employed in ancient literature such as recapitulation and resumption (used to connect the two volumes; see Aune 1987, 117), parallelism (the death of Jesus and the death of Stephen, Jesus' sermon in Luke 4:16ff. and Paul's sermon in Acts 13:15ff., and Jesus in Jerusalem and Paul in Rome), and interlacement (focusing on one character, then another, and then back to the previous character: see Acts 8:4–13 [Philip], 8:14–25 [Peter], and 8:26–40 [Philip]; 9:1–30 [Paul], 9:32–11:18 [Peter] and 13:1–14:28 [Paul]; see Pervo, 134).

As does Mark, the Johannine Gospel focuses on the public career of Jesus, but this author uses the myth of the "descending-ascending redeemer" to depict Jesus' preexistence and eternal relationship with God. In many respects, John is more literary than the other Gospels. It is less episodic, and it develops its story line with more explicit interplay between parts of the narrative. With literary artistry, the Johannine author fashions narrative scenes with fascinating exchanges between Jesus and his interlocutors (John 6), or forms dialogues and monologues that assume front and center stage in the overall drama (John 9 and John 14–17). Furthermore, the author's clever use of dramatic irony (John 18:33–38) and deliberately ambiguous symbols (e.g., water or bread) represents a highly developed literary style. Kennedy (108–113) describes the Johannine Gospel as possessing the quality of "elevation and sublimity," which was identified in the ancient world with great writing. Conceptual power, profound emotional quality, use of figures or metaphors, choice of diction, and arrangement of words characterized this type of writing (John 1:1–18 and John 3:1–21). Clearly, the fourth Gospel displays a character of writing quite different from the Synoptics. Nonetheless, in both cases a common narrative pattern appears, one that finds its culmination in Jesus' passion and resurrection.

Largely because of their content, the Gospels and Acts have no exact literary analogues in the Jewish or Greco-Roman world. This fact, however, does not mean that there is no benefit in studying the Gospels alongside of ancient literature. If, for example, the Gospels exhibit traits shared by Hellenistic biographies, we would expect a stress on actions and sayings as revealing Jesus' character, which would then become a pattern for his disciples to copy. This approach to character differs, it should be noted, from the concern for psychological development and historical facticity so central to modern biography. Although it is the case that both ancient biography and history were concerned with "things that happened," they were more concerned with underlining the importance of a person, demonstrating the person's representative character and heroic qualities. They might describe the significance of a movement, anchoring it in the past to guarantee its antiquity and its legitimacy.

To convey this larger significance of Jesus and the Christian movement required complex and flexible literary compositions like those represented in the Gospels and Acts. What is obvious is that each evangelist used creativity in presenting Jesus as both source and paradigm for the church. Luke does this quite explicitly by writing two volumes, one featuring Jesus and one the early church. Each evangelist, it seems clear, was indebted to the biblical history but also drew on rhetorical and literary conventions practiced in the Greco-Roman world. Their literary outcomes offer coherent wholes that avoid reducing the Christian tradition about Jesus simply to a collection of sayings or miracle stories, which could mislead or even distort its meaning.

Selected Bibliography

Aune, David E. 1987. *The New Testament in Its Literary Environment*, 17–157. Philadelphia: Westminster Press. Aune presents a concise and insightful treatment of the genre issues for the Gospels and Acts.

————. 1988. "Greco-Roman Biography." In *Greco-Roman Literature and the New Testament: Selected Forms and Genres*, edited by David E. Aune, 107–126. Atlanta: Scholars Press. Aune describes the types and features of Greco-Roman biography, demonstrating that biography is a genre that incorporates various shorter forms.

Beardslee, William A. 1970. *Literary Criticism of the New Testament*, 14–29, 42–52. Philadelphia: Fortress Press. These brief chapters discuss "The Form of the Gospel" and "History as a Form"; the latter includes a segment on the book of Acts as history.

Berger, Klaus. 1984. "Hellenistische Gattungen im Neuen Testament." In *Aufstieg und Niedergang der römischen Welt*, 1231–1245. II.25,2. Berlin & New York: Walter de Gruyter. This entry includes a chronological list of Greek and Latin biographies, as well as a description of the features for comparison with the Gospels.

Cox, Patricia. 1983. *Biography in Late Antiquity: A Quest for the Holy Man*, esp. 3–65. Berkeley, Calif.: University of California Press. Cox provides a discussion of ancient biographies of philosophers.

Kennedy, George A. 1984. *New Testament Interpretation Through Rhetorical Criticism*, 97–113. Chapel Hill: University of North Carolina Press. Chapter 5 provides a brief yet useful analysis of the rhetoric of the Gospels.

Pervo, Richard I. 1987. *Profit with Delight*. Philadelphia: Fortress Press. The author argues that Acts resembles the literary genre of a Hellenistic novel.

Robbins, Vernon K. 1979. "Prefaces in Greco-Roman Biography and Luke-Acts." *Perspectives in Religious Studies* 6, 94–108. This investigation of the Lukan prefaces is done in connection with similar conventions in ancient biographical literature.

————. 1980. "Mark as Genre." *SBL Seminar Papers* 19, 371–399. Chico, Calif.: Scholars Press. The author offers a review of the discussion about the genre of the Gospels before suggesting that Mark is best described as "eschatological memorabilia."

―――. 1984. *Jesus the Teacher: A Socio-Rhetorical Interpretation of Mark*. Philadelphia: Fortress Press. Robbins interprets Mark as an eschatological teacher-disciple biography.

Saunders, Stanley P. 1990. *"No One Dared Ask Him Anything More": Contextual Readings of the Controversy Stories in Matthew*. Unpublished dissertation. Princeton Theological Seminary. Saunders includes a helpful discussion about the genre of Matthew.

Shuler, Philip L. 1982. *A Genre for the Gospels: The Biographical Character of Matthew*. Philadelphia: Fortress Press. Shuler's thesis is that Matthew represents a "laudatory biography."

Talbert, Charles H. 1977. *What Is a Gospel?* Philadelphia: Fortress Press. Talbert reintroduces the argument that the Gospels fit within the biographical genre of the Hellenistic world.

―――. 1988. "Once Again: Gospel Genre." *Semeia* 43, 53–73. This article provides a helpful summary of Talbert's position.

APHORISM

Definition of the Form

Aphorism is a term used for the briefest form of Jesus' sayings. Aphorisms, parables, dialogues, and stories containing sayings of Jesus are the major types of sayings-material in the synoptic Gospels (Crossan 1986, xv–xvi). Normally, when describing this briefest form, scholars draw a distinction between aphorism and proverb. John Dominic Crossan (1983, 18–25), for example, accepts the following as the major distinction: a proverb represents "collective wisdom or ancestral authority," whereas an aphorism represents "personal insight or individual authority." In response to Crossan's study on aphorism, Vernon Robbins (33ff.) suggests that the distinction between proverb and aphorism needs to be more precisely described. A proverb, according to Robbins, is always unattributed, general, useful for daily living, and either concrete or abstract in content. Proverbs 15:1 offers an example: "A soft answer turns away wrath, but a harsh word stirs up anger." Although this proverb might have begun as an aphorism (some person, to whom it was initially attributed, could have said something like this), it now functions as popular wisdom that is unattributed, general in that it does not relate to a specific occasion, concrete (not abstract) in that it deals with the effects of gentle and harsh words in a relationship, and clearly applicable to everyday living.

In contrast to a proverb, the aphorism is attributed speech or, more precisely, "a saying attributed to a specific person and perceived within the horizons of that person's wisdom and action" (Robbins, 37). Because an aphorism is a brief saying ascribed to a specific person and thus tied to a specific situation related to that person, it is appropriate to use this term to describe all sayings of Jesus. This means, for example, that even a saying that formerly functioned as a proverb and was subsequently used by Jesus becomes, thereafter, an aphorism that, although its content remains constant, now functions differently because it is bound to his specific vision and situation. Jesus' saying in Mark 6:4 is likely an example of an aphorism that first circulated as a proverb:

> Prophets are not without honor, except in their hometown,
> and among their own kin, and in their own house.

In addition to the characteristics of attribution and specificity, which are the major distinguishing marks, Robbins stresses that both aphorism and proverb can be concrete or abstract. Further, although a proverb always offers guidance for daily living, an aphorism may or may not. Consider Mark 10:43–44 as an example of an aphoristic saying of Jesus. It is both concrete (suggesting a reversal of the way people act in society) and specifically directed to those who are his disciples (recommending how they should think and act)—and thus not applicable to life in general:

> Whoever wishes to become great among you must be your servant,
> and whoever wishes to be first among you must be slave of all.

There are additional features of Jesus' aphorisms worth noting. First, an aphoristic saying can appear in one of three grammatical forms: statement, question, or imperative. The statement form occurs most frequently. For example, in Matt. 10:24–25 Jesus warns his disciples of coming persecution by employing two declarative statements:

> A disciple is not above the teacher,
> nor a slave above the master;
> it is enough for a disciple to be like the teacher,
> and the slave like the master.

Though less numerous, there are ample instances of Jesus' posing a question. Use of the question, more so than a statement, directly engages hearers in pondering the intent of the saying. For example, Jesus' questions in Mark 8:36–37 invite hearers to reflect on the very meaning of life:

> For what will it profit them to gain the whole world and forfeit their life?
> Indeed, what can they give in return for their life?

Finally, some sayings of Jesus are in the imperative mood, implying entreaty, exhortation, or command. Luke 13:24 provides an example of an exhortation followed by a rationale for doing so:

> Strive to enter through the narrow door;
> for many, I tell you, will try to enter and will not be able.

Hence, the grammatical form of the aphorism reveals how the text relates Jesus as speaker to the hearers. A statement invites hearers to accept as true what Jesus asserts, a question seeks to engage hearers directly in pondering his saying, and an imperative challenges them to envision and act in line with the rhetorical force of his words.

Another feature of many of Jesus' aphoristic sayings is their parallelism, a chief characteristic of Hebrew poetry. This means that two or more lines express their thoughts in forms parallel to one another. For example, if an aphorism consists of two balanced segments (semantic units that can stand on their own), how do these two segments interact? Are they formally parallel, with the second one repeating in somewhat different words the meaning of the first? If so, this is what has been termed "synonymous parallelism." Matthew 10:27 is an example of synonymous parallelism in which Jesus' words in the second line repeat and thus reinforce the first line:

> What I say to you in the dark, tell in the light;
> and what in the ear you hear, proclaim upon the housetops.
> (author's translation)

This parallel form orally establishes a cadence for the hearers; they can feel the rhythmic movement of the lines. The words affect them both mentally and bodily. The second line verbally reinforces the first one, providing the hearers yet another opportunity to understand. Indeed, the second line actually furthers the message of the saying because "hearing in the ear" is more secretive than "saying" and "proclaiming upon the housetop" is more public than "telling in the light." In both instances, the second part of the saying has developed the contrasting images by use of hyperbole. What the disciples have heard and learned from Jesus in private, even in the secrecy of whispering, is to be shared in public, openly and boldly, as part of their mission.

Antithetical parallelism is another variation, a form in which the second line is the opposite of the first. Matthew 7:17 provides a clear example of this type:

> In the same way, every good tree bears good fruit,
> but the bad tree bears evil fruit. (author's translation)

Another type of parallelism in which there is tension between the two lines is chiasm (see *Chiasm*). In this case, the second line reverses the order of the key words in the first line (A B/B′ A′). Mark 8:35 provides an example:

> For those who want to save their life will lose it,
> and those who lose their life for my sake,
> and for the sake of the gospel, will save it.

This chiasm creates semantic tension between "saving life" and "losing life," with the goal of disturbing hearers and thereby challenging them to reconsider the conventional notions of how to "save" one's life. It invites them instead to risk "losing life," which paradoxically results in saving it. In this instance, as Crossan points out, "the positives frame the negatives" (1983, 90). Furthermore, close examination of Mark 8:35 reveals that the phrase "for my sake and for the sake of the gospel," which breaks the overall pattern, probably indicates the hand of a redactor. Likely the author of Mark or someone before him wanted to make clear the crucial reason for risking life—for Jesus' sake, or what the church summarized with the term "the gospel."

Sometimes parallelism involves more than two lines. In Matt. 7:7–8, three synonymously parallel lines occur. In this example, two future passive verbs, signaling the promised fulfillment from God, and one future active verb follow the initial three imperatives (ask, search, knock) that intensify the action. Then the second triad in v. 8 reiterates the content in indicative statements that reassure the hearers:

> Ask, and it will be given you;
> search, and you will find;

knock, and the door will be opened for you.
For everyone who asks receives,
and everyone who searches finds,
and for everyone who knocks, the door will be opened.

Three semantic units are also involved in Jesus' words in
Matt. 8:20/Luke 9:58:

Foxes have holes,
and birds of the air have nests;
but the Son of Man has nowhere to lay his head.

In this aphoristic saying, the first two semantic units represent
synonymous parallelism, but the third segment stands as their
strong antithesis. The interplay of these three lines created a
rhetorical punch for first-century hearers. In Palestine, people
probably did not readily observe the dens of foxes or bird nests.
If, as the saying claims, even foxes and birds have "homes," then
how extremely unsettled and risky was Jesus' existence as an
itinerant preacher. The context implies the same risk for those
who follow Jesus. The use of the "Son of Man" title further
accentuates the irony of this aphorism, for Jesus is depicted as
one with divine authority over all the world, yet finds himself
homeless in the world.

Finally, Jesus' sayings use a wide range of images such as
analogies drawn from nature (Matt. 7:17; 8:20) and human
experience (Matt. 7:7–10; Luke 6:29–30), sometimes developing these by use of paradox (Mark 8:35) and hyperbole (Matt.
10:27). Particularly striking is the use of hyperbole in a number
of Jesus' aphoristic sayings. Exaggeration jolts the hearers into a
new perception. For example, the hyperbolic sayings in Matt.
5:29–30 compel an audience to sense the utter seriousness of
lusting after a woman:

If your right eye causes you to sin,
tear it out and throw it away;
it is better for you to lose one of your members
than for your whole body to be thrown into hell.
And if your right hand causes you to sin,
cut it off and throw it away;
it is better for you to lose one of your members
than for your whole body to go into hell.

The parallelism of these sayings generates some of the rhetorical power, but the driving force comes from the hyperbole. This

particular exaggeration can shock hearers if it is not quickly assumed that Jesus intends his words to be taken figuratively. Indeed, a listener can conceive of actually tearing out an eye or cutting off a hand. The willingness to entertain a literal fulfillment brings home the meaning—allowing lustful thoughts to grow in one's heart is more serious than maiming one's body.

The Value for Interpretation

Close attention to the content and form of the aphoristic sayings of Jesus begins to illustrate the rich variety of aphorisms in the Gospels. Clearly, interpreters advance their understanding of a specific saying by analyzing its formal features: grammatical form, parallelism, and any metaphorical images or devices used. But this is only the beginning of what the interpreter can do.

If by definition aphorisms are attributed to a person—normally in the Gospels to Jesus—then they must be interpreted as part of that person's context. Aphorisms are not like proverbs that are unattached and thus applicable to innumerable situations. It is crucial for the interpreter to observe the actual way a particular aphorism ascribed to Jesus functions. Robbins (38–41) illustrates this need for precise interpretation when he compares the proverb "A stitch in time saves nine" with the aphoristic compound (coupling of two similar sayings) attributed to Jesus in Mark 2:21–22. In contrast to the proverb, which focuses on timely action with its favorable results, Jesus' two aphorisms combine to develop a process of argumentation. Their rhetoric invites hearers to deliberate future action that is the opposite of that suggested by the two aphorisms: "No one sews a piece of unshrunk cloth on an old cloak" and "no one puts new wine into old wineskins." The hearers will want to avoid the improper action implied.

Moreover, according to Robbins, these aphorisms function as rhetorical syllogisms (called enthymemes) that together involve both inductive and deductive reasoning. Beginning with the two examples (mixing old and new with regard to clothing or wineskins) suggests an inductive pattern, yet a deductive syllogism is also implied. Robbins (41) states it in the following way:

General Premise: No one damages or destroys a thing useful for life.
Hypothetical Concrete Premise: If someone puts an unshrunk patch on a new garment or new wine into old wineskins, he

or she tears the garment, or bursts the wineskins and loses
the wine.

Conclusion: Therefore, no one sews an unshrunk patch on a
new garment or puts new wine into older wineskins.

Thus, although the "stitch in time saves nine" proverb seeks
to "move a person from inaction (not stitching) to action (stitching), the 'Patches and Wineskins' compound is designed to cen-
sure or defend a particular form of action" (Robbins, 40). In
Mark 2:18–22, Jesus' sayings assume that something new has
happened and that "not fasting" (rather than "fasting") is the
new action that is appropriate and faithful in the actual circumstances. Mark 2:21–22 represents "then, an argumentative compound arising out of a situation of conflict and designed for
argumentation in a setting of conflict" (Robbins, 40–41).

Robbins' explanation of Mark 2:21–22 demonstrates how important it is for interpreters to discover how aphorisms, when
they are grouped together, function as part of a rhetorical argument (Crossan uses "compound" where two aphorisms are com-
bined, and "clusters" where more than two are joined). Hence
the interpretive task involves far more than analyzing the formal
features of the separate aphorisms; it must also investigate how
these aphorisms contribute to the larger argument implied in the
speech of Jesus.

Finally, it is also important for the interpreter, as part of this
analysis, to determine if a particular aphorism is general or
specific, concrete or abstract, concerned with daily living or not.
For example, the aphoristic compound in Mark 2:21–22 is general, concrete, and concerned with daily living. These two aphorisms are general in that they are not directed to a particular
party or group but are addressed to everyone. They are concrete
in that they describe the imprudent action of patching old cloth
with new and putting new wine into old wineskins, and they are
concerned with daily living in that their argument suggests a
course of action that is the opposite of what is readily recognized
as a foolish endeavor in everyday life. As another example,
Robbins (41–42) cites Matt. 23:13 as an aphorism that is specific
(tied to the scribes and Pharisees), abstract (keeping others from
the "kingdom"), and not concerned with daily living (only useful
if one is a certain type of person). Recognizing these distinctions
can deepen the interpreter's understanding of both the form and
function of Jesus' aphorisms.

Additional Examples

The aphorisms attributed to Jesus and others in the Gospels and Acts are numerous. Refer to Crossan's compilation of aphorisms in *Sayings Parallels* for a more complete listing.

Selected Bibliography

Beardslee, William A. 1970. *Literary Criticism of the New Testament,* 30–41. Philadelphia: Fortress Press. This chapter deals with proverb and beatitude.

————. 1979. "Uses of the Proverb in the Synoptic Gospels." *Interpretation* 24, 61–73. The author argues that the proverbial forms attributed to Jesus function more like paradox and hyperbole.

Bultmann, Rudolf. 1963. *The History of the Synoptic Tradition.* Translated by John Marsh, 69–166. New York: Harper & Row. This earlier study of Jesus' sayings considers them according to subgroups: sayings or logia in a narrower sense, wisdom-sayings, prophetic or apocalyptic sayings, and laws and community regulations.

Crossan, John Dominic. 1983. *In Fragments: The Aphorisms of Jesus.* San Francisco: Harper & Row. This significant book has prompted scholarly advancement in understanding the aphorisms in the New Testament.

————. 1986. *Sayings Parallels: A Workbook for the Jesus Tradition.* Philadelphia: Fortress Press. This is a helpful workbook for studying the sayings-tradition.

Robbins, Vernon K. 1985. "Picking Up the Fragments." *Foundations and Facets Forum* 1, 31–64. The author seeks to enrich Crossan's analysis of the aphorisms by introducing a rhetorical analysis.

Tannehill, Robert C. 1975. *The Sword of His Mouth.* Philadelphia: Fortress Press. Tannehill focuses on the rhetoric of Jesus' sayings by offering insightful studies of various texts.

PARABLE

Definition of the Term

The parables of Jesus are widely known both in the church and in our culture. The word "parable" itself is derived from the Greek term *parabolē* that appears frequently in the Gospels; in the Septuagint it is the normal translation for the word *mashal*. The Hebrew root *mshl* apparently means "to be like" and as a noun primarily designates a proverblike saying (1 Sam. 10:12), but it can also be used to name other forms of figurative speech such as riddle (Judg. 14:10–18), allegory (Ezek. 17:2–24), or even taunt song (Micah 2:4; see Scott, 8–19, and Jeremias, 20). Whereas Jesus' parables definitely stand within this wisdom tradition of the *mashalim*, they represent short stories uncharacteristic of the Hebrew scriptures, with the possible exception of Nathan's story to David in 2 Sam. 12:1ff. Their closest parallels appear in the post–70 C.E. rabbinic tradition, where parabolic-type stories explore the meaning of Torah. Or, as a Jewish scholar assesses the relationship, "The compositions attributed to Jesus are our earliest datable evidence in Late Antiquity for the tradition of the *mashal* that attains its full maturity in Rabbinic literature" (Stern, 43). Klaus Berger (1110–1124), however, also cites numerous similarities and differences between the New Testament parables—especially those narrated in Luke—and Hellenistic materials.

The Greek word *parabolē*, which literally means "to cast alongside," implies a comparison or juxtaposition. In the case of Jesus' parables, it involves an everyday phenomenon or situation being likened to the kingdom of God. Scholars have proposed more elaborate definitions of "parable," and the following is the oft-quoted one by C. H. Dodd:

> At its simplest the parable is a metaphor or simile drawn from nature or common life, arresting the hearer by its vividness or strangeness, and leaving the mind in sufficient doubt about its precise application to tease it into active thought.(5)

Dodd's definition draws attention to various characteristics of Jesus' parables: their metaphorical character, their vivid realism, and their surprising and often ambiguous features that engage the listener and prompt active participation in the story. In a recent volume on parables, Bernard Brandon Scott offers an even briefer definition that squarely identifies parable as a particular type of *mashal*, one that "employs a short narrative fiction to reference a transcendent symbol" (8). This definition—with its stress on brevity, narrative fiction, and the "kingdom of God" as a symbol pointing to transcendent reality—provides an update on the scholarly understanding of parable since the time of Dodd.

Since the monumental work of Adolf Jülicher, scholars have

characteristically enumerated several subtypes of parable. Among these, the figure of speech probably stands at the genesis of parabolic language. For example, Jesus uses the figure of "a city built on a hill cannot be hid" (Matt. 5:14b) as a follow-up to the promise to the disciples, "You are the light of the world." This suggests a comparison between the light of an elevated city and that issuing from the disciples' good works. Or, in Matt. 15:14, to characterize the Pharisees Jesus speaks of a blind person guiding another blind person, causing both to fall into a ditch. Such figures of speech, or similes, imply a simple comparison and involve at most one sentence.

When the figure of speech is elaborated into a brief picture-narrative that entails more than one verb, scholars term it a "similitude." The following examples will illustrate:

> To what should I compare the kingdom of God?
> It is like yeast that a woman took
> and mixed in with three measures of flour
> until all of it was leavened. (Luke 13:20–21)

> But to what will I compare this generation?
> It is like children sitting in the marketplaces
> and calling to one another,
> "We played the flute for you, and you did not dance;
> we wailed, and you did not mourn". (Matt. 11:16–17)

These similitudes depict typical, recurring situations or processes that are universally known, and the comparisons have their rhetorical effect when the kingdom of God or people's reaction to it respectively is pondered in light of a familiar scene—rising bread or playing children.

In distinction to the similitude—though the difference should not be overemphasized—is what has been called the parable proper. This is a longer narrative that builds a comparison to the reign of God by describing a particular situation in a rhetorically striking manner. So, for example, Matt. 20:1–15 compares the kingdom of heaven to the hiring and paying of day laborers for work in a vineyard. The parabolic effect of this story results from the surprising way in which this particular scene is narrated: only the first hour workers agree to an exact amount of money (v. 2); the perfect tense in the question of v. 6 suggests that the workers hired last have been waiting in the marketplace the whole day; for rhetorical effect the five groups of workers are paid in reverse order of their hiring (v. 8); at the end of the parable only the last and first hour workers remain because the conflict is between them (vs. 9–10); the householder's final questions imply affirmative answers and are addressed to the first hour workers whose sour grapes over his generosity is the problem (v. 15). Although Jesus' parables largely draw on traditional motifs within Judaism, their power issues from the imaginative manner in which they are told. For this reason, a parable is aptly described as a fictional narrative.

Scholars have frequently listed yet another subtype—the example story. This type of story exhibits the characteristics of the parable with one major difference; it does not refer by analogy to another reality. Instead, it offers a pattern of correct behavior to emulate or wrong behavior to avoid. According to this definition, the story of the Good Samaritan in Luke 10:29–37 would be an example story. Recently, however, Scott (28–30) has questioned if example story should be understood as a separate type told by Jesus himself. All four stories normally classified in this way appear only in Luke (10:29–37, 12:16–21, 16:19–31, and 18:9–14) and likely have been reshaped in the direction of example by the evangelist himself.

Recent research on parables has shed light on certain characteristics of Jesus' parables already mentioned. First, the parables are amazingly *brief*. By far the longest parable is that of the father and two sons in Luke 15:11–32, which is told in fewer than four hundred words in Greek or approximately one typed double-spaced page in today's print world. This remarkable economy of words reflects oral usage and is indicative of all Jesus' teaching. The parables do not waste words; each detail has some reason for being mentioned in the narrative. For example, only the characters necessary to the plot appear, and much about them and their motives is typically left unsaid. John Dominic Crossan, one scholar who claims brevity as a vital element of Jesus' parables, even suggests "it may well be the very brevity of the narrative that first impels us to look elsewhere for its fuller meaning" (1980, 4–5). Brevity is a feature of narrative that communicates by means of deliberate vagueness and lack of explanation.

Second, the parables are *narrative*. Put most simply, as Jesus' speech, they present happenings in a sequence. Even the briefest similitude must narrate actions in a temporal sequence. For example, in Matt. 13:44, "the kingdom of heaven" is likened to a "treasure hidden in a field," and then the one-verse narrative depicts in sequence a man's actions: finding, covering up, going, selling all, and buying that field.

As a related observation, others have remarked about the "realism" or "everydayness" of Jesus' parables. For the most part, the parables are brief narratives that juxtapose vivid, concrete, and everyday scenes familiar to the hearers, with the reality implied in the phrase "the kingdom of God." Although these stories offer little direct talk about God, they invite the hearers to discern divine movement and purpose in the ordinary happenings of life. Glimpses of the kingdom of God are evoked by talking about a shepherd going after a lost sheep, a woman searching and finding a valuable coin, a rich man building more and bigger barns, day laborers being hired to work in a vineyard, and so on. Amos Wilder comments upon the significance of this everydayness:

> Jesus, without saying so, by his very way of presenting man [*sic*], shows that for him man's destiny is at stake in his ordinary creaturely existence, domestic, economic and social. This is the way God made him. The world is real. Time is real. Man is a toiler and an "acter" and a chooser. (82; see also Dodd, 10)

The narrativity of the parables has been a focus of much parable scholarship during the last two or three decades. Employing various aesthetic and rhetorical approaches, scholars have sought to analyze both the plots and characterization of the parables. Already in the early part of the century, Rudolf Bultmann (188–192) drew attention to features of narrative style that Jesus' parables have in common with other folk literature: they are concise, there is stage duality (only two characters or two groups interact at the same time), they focus on one matter at a time in single perspective, they employ direct speech, there is repetition that often involves a pattern of three, the important part of the story is at the end, they are open-ended often without a clear conclusion, and they build on the anticipated judgment made by the hearers.

The parables can also be seen as *metaphors*. Jesus' parables initiate the hearer into a metaphorical process that is not only provocative but iconoclastic. Characteristically, a parable begins by offering the hearer a picture world that appears largely familiar and typical. That familiar world, however, is shattered by means of a hyperbole or some strange feature. In this way, the parable evokes a new vision of reality for the hearers, inviting them to imagine the world differently and consequently to live differently (for example, in Matt. 18:23–35 the incredibly huge debt canceled in scene 1 causes the hearers to view the demand to pay up in scene 2 as unreasonable and unmerciful). In a sense, the parable has the character of an argument; it invites the hearers to choose its alternative view of reality (according to God) rather than their own. Robert Funk underlines this decision prompted by the parable when he writes, "[The listener] must choose to unfold with the story, be illuminated by the metaphor, or reject the call and abide with the conventional. . . . [The parables] are language events in which the hearer has to choose between worlds" (162).

Another point needs to be made. Paul Ricoeur has discussed metaphorical (or parabolic) language in relation to the polysemy of words—that is, the multiple meanings of words arising from their ambiguity. According to Ricoeur, certain language strategies seek to lessen or eliminate the ambiguity of words. Metaphorical language, however, does quite the opposite by intentionally enhancing it. Thus, as metaphorical language, Jesus' parables are narratives that seek to encourage listeners to widen and deepen their notion of the kingdom of God, a symbol that points to divine reality and cannot be reduced to an abstract concept. Jesus' parables invite hearers to increase their sense of reality, an invitation often accomplished by shattering their inadequate and even idolatrous notions.

There is a longstanding Christian tradition of interpreting the polysemy of the parables allegorically, that is, by assuming that every important feature of the parable represents a reality outside the story. The problem with this practice is that the allegorical interpretation destroys the polysemic function of the parable. To paraphrase Ricoeur, the parable as metaphor speaks of a mysterious reality so rich and so new that the parable is not reducible to clear language. That reality can only be grasped, though always partially, through the parable itself (quoted in Crossan 1973, 13). For Jesus, "the kingdom of God" stands as his primary symbol for this new and mysterious transcendent reality, and for him parabolic language became the only way to invite hearers to participate in this divine/human actuality.

Mark 4:14–20 provides an allegorical explanation of the parable of the sower in Mark 4:3–8, an interpretation likely introduced by a Christian community when the meaning of Jesus' parable had become obscure. Undoubtedly, some characters or features in Jesus' stories possessed rich symbolic—namely, allegorical—meaning for first-century Jewish hearers (e.g., "king" in Matt. 18:23ff. or Matt. 22:1ff.; "father" in Luke 15:1ff. connotes "God"; "wedding banquet" in Matt. 22:1ff. alludes to the messianic feast). Nevertheless, as a whole, Jesus' stories are not allegories because, unlike allegories, their intention is not to describe in cryptic terms a world the hearers already know, but to draw the outlines of a world they have scarcely begun to imagine. Point by point, Mark 4:14–20 translates elements of the story into another reality outside the story itself (e.g., the seed represents the Word of God; the various soils, the types of hearers; the birds, Satan; the thorns, the cares of the world, and so on). But this kind of interpretation replaces the parable with another kind of story, a story that does not have the rich, mysterious quality of the parables themselves. The goal of parable interpretation can be, and should be, to illumine the nature of a parable as a polysemic story.

The Value for Interpretation

Parable as metaphor has endless possibility for further development. The implications for metaphorical interpretation of the parables of Jesus in the Gospels are many, as well. First, interpreters make a mistake in their preaching and teaching if they attempt to explain the meaning of a parable in abstract terms. The parables cannot be reduced to concepts or teachings, whether they be moralistic or religious, that render the parable itself expendable. In Ricoeur's words, it is repeatedly necessary to think *"through* the Metaphor and never *beyond"* (242). The parabolic metaphor must be reexperienced in new contexts to sense in fresh ways its potential to "redescribe reality." This is why every time the parable of "the father and two sons" is retold, it creates new meaning for hearers.

Second, it is important to realize that Jesus' parables are frequently open-ended and polyvalent. Contrary to the conclusion of earlier scholars, these metaphorical stories do not have just one legitimate point but sponsor multiple interpretations. Whether intended or not, the final segment of Dodd's definition seems to describe this open-ended or polysemic quality of the parables: ". . . and leaving the mind in sufficient doubt about its precise application to tease it into active thought." A parable creates meaning by inviting the hearer to participate in that creation. For example, even a brief parable like Matt. 13:44 can sponsor various meanings: the challenge to value the kingdom of

God as the man valued the treasure, or the challenge to sell all for the sake of the kingdom, or the invitation into the "joy" that motivates one to sell all to secure the field. All three of these emphases are integral to the parable, but each one can be heard and appropriated with differing nuance by various hearers. In preaching Matt. 13:44, it is critical to design a strategy that does not override the story's intentional ambiguity. By means of this parable, Jesus does not clearly explain a point to us. Instead, he describes a man's urgent action when he finds a treasure in a field, leaving the interpretation of the action to individuals who have been encouraged to participate in it. Faithfulness to the parabolic form implies that the preacher will not soften the story's provocative nature; it is intended to engage hearers by "teasing their minds into action."

Above all, interpreters need to be clear that Jesus' parables are not simply pleasant and polite stories that cause no offense. Rather, they function as iconoclastic stories that shake up the world as we know it. And, if we are really hearing the parable, we might sense deep resistance in ourselves to its profound challenge to the fortified areas of our lives.

Additional Examples

Scott organizes the parables of Jesus according to the social realities in the peasant culture of first-century Palestine: (1) "Family, Village, City, and Beyond"—see Matt. 21:28–31a; Luke 15:11–32; 12:16–20; 16:19–31; 14:16–24; 18:2–5; 10:30–35. (2) "Masters and Servants"—see Matt. 24:45–51; 25:14–30; Mark 12:1–12; Luke 16:1–8a; Matt. 18:23–34; 20:1–15. (3) "Home and Farm"—see Luke 15:8–10; Matt. 13:33; Luke 13:6–9; Mark 4:1–9; 4:26–29; 4:30–32; Matt. 18:12–14.

Selected Bibliography

Berger, Klaus. 1984. "Hellenistische Gattungen im Neuen Testament." In *Aufstieg und Niedergang der römischen Welt*, 1110–1124. II.25,2. Berlin & New York: Walter de Gruyter. Berger places Jesus' parables within their wider Hellenistic environment.

Bultmann, Rudolf. 1963. *The History of the Synoptic Tradition*. Translated by John Marsh, 166–205. Oxford: Basil Blackwell. This work is a standard source for the saying-tradition of Jesus.

Crossan, John Dominic. 1973. *In Parables*. New York: Harper & Row. This study investigates the parabolic language of the historical Jesus.

———. 1980. *Cliffs of Fall*. New York: Seabury Press. The focus is on paradox and polyvalence in the parables of Jesus.

Dodd, C. H. 1961. *The Parables of the Kingdom*. Rev. ed. First published in 1936. New York: Charles Scribner's Sons. Following Jülicher's *Die Gleichnisreden Jesu*, 2 vols. (Tübingen: J. C. B. Mohr, 1910), which ended the allegorical tyranny over Jesus' parables, Dodd was the first to pursue a historical interpretation.

Funk, Robert W. 1966. *Language, Hermeneutic, and Word of God*, 123–222. New York: Harper & Row. Funk's work advanced the metaphorical understanding of parable.

Jeremias, Joachim. 1963. *The Parables of Jesus*. Rev. ed. Translated from 6th German ed. (1st German ed. in 1947). New York: Charles Scribner's Sons. One of the most widely read books on parables, this work searches for the meaning of the parables as told by the historical Jesus.

Perrin, Norman. 1976. *Jesus and the Language of the Kingdom*, 89–205. Philadelphia: Fortress Press. This book contains a helpful survey of modern research on parables and argues for viewing "the kingdom of God" as a symbol rather than a concept.

Ricoeur, Paul. 1978. "Creativity in Language" and "Listening to the Parables of Jesus." In *The Philosophy of Paul Ricoeur*, edited by C. E. Reagan and D. Stewart, 120–133, 239–245. Boston: Beacon Press. The first article demonstrates how various strategies of language build on the ambiguity of words; the second one discusses how the parables speak to the listener's imagination.

Scott, Bernard Brandon. 1989. *Hear Then the Parable*. Minneapolis: Fortress Press. After an insightful introduction, Scott analyzes each parable as to its function in its present context, the effect of its structure on meaning, and its parabolic effect in its reference to the symbol of the kingdom.

Stern, David. 1989. "Jesus' Parables from the Perspective of Rabbinic Literature: The Example of the Wicked Husbandmen." In *Parable and Story in Judaism and Christianity*, edited by C. Thoma and M. Wyschogrod, 42–80. New York: Paulist Press. This article offers a careful comparison of Jesus' parables with those appearing in the rabbinic materials.

Via, Dan O. 1967. *The Parables*. Philadelphia: Fortress Press. Via offers an aesthetic and existential understanding of the parables.

Wilder, Amos N. 1964. *The Language of the Gospel*, 79–96. New York: Harper & Row. This chapter initiated the discussion of parable as a literary metaphor.

PRONOUNCEMENT STORY

Definition of the Form

Another literary form frequently occurring in the Gospels is the pronouncement story. Simply defined, it is a brief story about Jesus that culminates in a short, striking saying (and possibly an action) and reveals something of his character and facility in repartee when challenged by others. Both the specific situation described and the response it prompts, normally by Jesus, are indispensable to this type of story. Mark 2:15–17 provides an example:

> And while he was reclining at meal in his [Levi's] house,
> also many tax collectors and sinners were reclining
>   with Jesus and his disciples;
> for there were many also following him.
> And when the scribes of the Pharisees saw
>   that he was eating with sinners and tax collectors,
> they began to say to his disciples,
>   "Why does he eat with the tax collectors and sinners?"
> And when he heard, Jesus said to them,
>   "The ones who are strong do not have a need of a physician,
>   but the ones who are sick;
>   I did not come to call righteous people but sinners." (author's translation)

Stories fitting this definition occur in all strands of the tradition in the Gospels and Acts. Most of them portray Jesus as the main character, but a few focus on John the Baptist (Luke 3:10–11, 12–13, 14). Most are relatively brief, varying in length from two or three verses to approximately twelve. Although the narrative of a number of the stories is elaborated (Mark 2:23–28; 3:23–30; 10:2–9; 14:3–9), Luke 11:27–28 is an example of an exceedingly brief one that includes only Jesus' saying as a direct response to another's saying.

Until recently, scholarly work on the pronouncement stories achieved little advancement beyond the earlier studies of Dibelius and Bultmann. Martin Dibelius designated this type of story a "paradigm" *(paradeigma)*, a standard rhetorical term for a brief example used in a speech to support an argument. He assumed that nonliterary persons in the early church produced them to use in sermons designed to proclaim the good news about Jesus. Rudolf Bultmann, on the other hand, called these stories "apophthegms" *(apophthegma)*, defined as "sayings of Jesus set in a brief context" (Bultmann, 11); he tended to focus on the culminating saying at the expense of the other features in the story.

To label this type of story a "pronouncement story," as most current scholars have until recently, is to use a term first employed by Vincent Taylor (30) and one that, with Bultmann, lays stress on the saying-component. Accepting "pronouncement story" as the overarching category, scholars have tended to use either "conflict story" or "controversy story" to designate a subtype that depicts Jesus involved in a confrontation with a person or a group cast in an adversarial role. Recently, Robert Tannehill (1981a, 1–13, and 1981b, 101–119) has proposed a far more comprehensive typology of subtypes in an attempt for greater terminological clarity. Vernon Robbins (1988b, 5) summarizes these six subforms of the pronouncement story as follows:

1. *Correction stories,* where the story ends with the main character correcting one or more individuals (e.g., Mark 1:35–38; 9:33–37).
2. *Commendation stories,* where the story ends with the main character commending one or more individuals (e.g., Matt. 13:51–52; Luke 10:17–20).
3. *Objection stories,* where an objection calls forth the response from the main character (e.g., Mark 2:15–17; Matt. 3:13–15).
4. *Quest stories,* where a secondary person's success or failure in a quest of something important to human well-being has prominence alongside the main character's response (e.g., Mark 10:17–22; 12:28–34).
5. *Inquiry stories,* where the story ends with a response by the main character to an inquiry (e.g., Mark 7:17–23; Luke 3:10–14).
6. *Description stories,* where the story ends with a description

of the situation by the main character (e.g., Luke 14:15–24).

In addition, Tannehill points out that some are hybrid stories that contain at least two of the types.

Although this classification clearly moves beyond the generality of most former descriptions of pronouncement stories, some scholars have noted a logical inconsistency in this expanded typology. Types 1 and 2 classify the stories from the vantage point of the response of the main character, whereas types 3, 4, and 5 classify the stories from the vantage point of the secondary person who approaches the main character, Jesus. So questions remain: Has Tannehill actually described types of stories deliberately fashioned in the ancient world, or does his typology represent a theoretical abstraction (Berger, 1107–1110)?

As a further development of the current scholarship on pronouncement stories, some scholars have studied the features and function of the *chreia,* a brief narrative form used in Greco-Roman rhetoric, to shed additional light on the Gospel stories. "Chreia," derived from the Greek word meaning "useful," is defined by Ronald Hock as "a saying or action that is expressed concisely, attributed to a character, and regarded as useful for living" (26). This definition highlights the following: (1) action as well as speech as a climax for the chreia; (2) the characteristic of attribution, so that these are not unattached or anonymous stories; and (3) the intended relevance of the story. Moreover, Burton Mack and Vernon Robbins (1–67) have shown that the basic form of the chreia was frequently altered or elaborated in a number of ways by ancient rhetoricians to become part of a pattern of argumentation.

The Value for Interpretation

Recent scholarship suggests that there are two interrelated tasks involved in interpreting a pronouncement story in the Gospels: (1) an analysis of the interplay in the brief narrative between the particular situation described and Jesus' response to it; and (2) an overall assessment of the rhetorical strategy and effect of the entire story, not just of the final pronouncement of Jesus. To accomplish this second task, knowledge of the rhetorical patterns of the Hellenistic chreia is helpful, if not essential.

Three examples will illustrate this interpretive process, beginning with a very brief pronouncement story in Luke 11:27–28.

As noted above, it offers a story that consists almost entirely of the interplay of two sayings—a woman's blessing of Jesus' mother and his challenging rejoinder:

> While he [Jesus] was saying this,
> a woman in the crowd raised her voice and said to him,
>> "Blessed is the womb that bore you
>> and the breasts that nursed you!"
> But he said,
>> "Blessed rather are those who hear the word of God
>> and obey it!"

This story lacks an elaboration of the situation that prompts the exchange between the woman and Jesus. Rather, it depends on the Lukan context that signals, in Jesus' exorcisms, the arrival of the reign of God (11:14–26) and invites people to discern the significance of Jesus' presence (11:29–32). In 11:27–28, a woman in the crowd extols Jesus by testifying to the blessedness of his mother. Jesus' reply counters the suspicion that he might be susceptible to the woman's flattery (Mack and Robbins, 188–189). Clearly, the rhetorical effect of this story results from Jesus' quick, concise, and clever response to the woman's indirect accolade of him. Using the same form, he responds by restating her beatitude, but his restatement serves as a challenge and correction to her blessing. She expresses the traditional belief that the maternal relationship to a famous son constitutes a special connection and benefits much, but Jesus' response redirects attention to a relationship to God and himself available to everyone—hearing the Word of God and keeping it.

Second, Mark 12:13–17 provides an example of a pronouncement story that is far more elaborated than Luke 11:27–28 and resembles a "mixed chreia" with its emphasis on both Jesus' action (vs. 15b–16) and memorable reply (v. 17).

> Then they sent to him some Pharisees and some Herodians to trap him in what he said. And they came and said to him, "Teacher, we know that you are sincere, and show deference to no one; for you do not regard people with partiality, but teach the way of God in accordance with truth. Is it lawful to pay taxes to the emperor, or not? Should we pay them, or should we not?" (vs. 13–15a)

> But knowing their hypocrisy, he said to them, "Why are you putting me to the test? Bring me a denarius and let me see it. (v. 15b)

> And they brought one. (v. 16a)

Then he said to them, "Whose head is this, and whose title?" (v. 16b)

They answered, "The emperor's". (v. 16c)

Jesus said to them, "Give to the emperor the things that are the emperor's, and to God the things that are God's." (v. 17ab)

And they were utterly amazed at him. (v. 17c)

Not only is the situation in this story more fully described, but it is also essential for understanding the pronouncement. The presence of the coin prepares us for Jesus' final words.

In this case, the story begins by telling us the motive of the Pharisees and Herodians; they intend to entrap Jesus with an impossible question. They start by complimenting him as a teacher who is not swayed by the prominence of others but is, rather, impartially concerned with the truth. Their flattery sets up the question about the lawfulness (under Torah) of paying taxes to the Roman emperor, a question designed to force Jesus to take a compromising political position. Jesus' initial response reveals his awareness of their deceptive intent. Next, the request that his antagonists bring him a denarius initiates a dynamic that turns the tables on them. Their willing obedience causes them to handle a Roman coin, an activity forbidden to pious Jews and something Jesus has evidently not done.

The last exchange in the story prepares us for Jesus' stunning pronouncement. He asks his antagonists, "Whose head is this and whose title?" In order to answer, they must utter the name of the emperor. The story ends by Jesus declaring, "Give to the emperor the things that are the emperor's, and to God the things that are God's." This puzzling saying has generated various explanations, but not all interpreters understand the rhetorical function of such a saying in a story like this. In this contest with the Jerusalem leaders, Jesus' final saying is designed to win the day. Their impossible question, contrived to expose Jesus' subversive political attitude, prompts from him a clever and deliberately ambiguous pronouncement, which extricates him from the entrapment. On the one hand, Jesus' saying seems to acknowledge an obligation to the emperor, but, on the other, if the stress lies with the second half of the parallel lines, then the obligation to give back to God the things that are God's relativizes all else. This would demand their wholehearted devotion to God.

Interpreters only begin to sense the rhetorical power of the story when they analyze the interplay between the situation of entrapment and Jesus' apt response, which not only allows him to escape but also to demonstrate mastery over his opponents. Jesus meets their shrewd question with an action (calling for the coin) that puts them on the defensive and also with a saying that overturns their presuppositions and thwarts their hostile intentions. Put simply, Jesus outwits them, and the only appropriate reaction on their part—and ours—is utter amazement (v. 17c).

A final example is Burton Mack's interpretation of Mark 14:3–9, the anointing of Jesus. Mack analyzes the story's pattern in light of the major components of a chreia as rhetorically developed (see *Forms of Argumentation*): setting, question, response (Mack and Robbins, 92–100).

Narratio—setting for chreia, only slightly amplified (v. 3):
> While he was at Bethany in the house of Simon the leper, as he sat at table, a woman came with an alabaster jar of very costly ointment of nard, and she broke open the jar and poured the ointment on his head.

Quaestio—the challenge or question that is amplified by emphasizing the objectors' hostile reaction and specifying their objection (vs. 4–5):
> But some were there who said to one another in anger, "Why was the ointment wasted in this way? For this ointment could have been sold for more than three hundred denarii, and the money given to the poor." And they scolded her.

Argumentatio—a response that is extensive, engaging the objectors (vs. 6–9):
> v. 6a—a response that redirects the question:
> But Jesus said, "Let her alone; why do you trouble her?"
> v. 6b—a rationale that serves as a thesis:
> "She has performed a good service for me."
> v. 7a,c—a contrary that acts as a contrast:
> v. 7b—an analogy that is implied:
> "For you always have the poor with you,
> and you can show kindness to them whenever you wish;
> but you will not always have me."
> v. 8—an example:
> "She has done what she could; she has anointed my body beforehand for its burial."
> v. 9—a judgment:
> "Truly I tell you, wherever the good news is proclaimed

in the whole world, what she has done will be told
in remembrance of her."

This analysis seeks to understand the rhetorical argumentation at work in the story. For example, Mack calls attention to
the skillful crafting of the objection in vs. 4–5. The situation
could be most embarrassing for Jesus, but the stated objection—
that the woman's use of the expensive perfume was wasteful
and its sale could have provided money for the poor—shifts the
argument to another level. Their mention of the poor, to quote
Mack,

> puts the objectors strongly on the side of piety and conventional
> ethics. And it begins to explain their indignation. With this sug-
> gestion they have proposed another course of action as better (a
> deliberative thesis), and it sets the stage nicely for Jesus' response
> as a rebuttal over a deliberative issue. (95)

The rhetorical pattern of Jesus' response unfolds quite creatively as a definite argument. His first words in v. 6a define his
opposition to the objectors ("Let her alone") and question the
true intentions behind their objection ("why do you trouble
her?"). His next words in v. 6b serve as a thesis that Jesus will
defend: the woman's action is "good" and not "wasteful"
(*kalon*—a word rhetorically important in the epideictic type of
speech). Jesus' words in v. 7 offer both a contrast between the
poor as *always* present and Jesus as *not always* present, a point
derived from a midrash on Deut. 15:11 ("The poor will always
be with you in the land"), and an analogy of "doing good
works." The analogy is set up between Jesus and the poor,
objectors and the woman, alms and good deeds. Finally, the
argument reaches its climax in the two declarations in vs. 8–9.
With a bit of sarcasm, Jesus intimates that the objectors could do
good (for the poor) whenever they want, but in contrast to their
neglect to do good stands the woman's good deed of anointing
him, an example that points to his death (v. 8). Not only has
Jesus' argument justified the woman's action, but it has disclosed
its christological significance. Then follows v. 9 as a final authoritative *amēn* declaration, linking the woman's good act with the
ongoing proclamation of the gospel.

Thus, according to Mack, Mark 14:3–9 represents not "a simple chreia" with a "pointed saying" but a chreia with an elaborated argument as Jesus' serious and convincing response to his
objectors. Their challenge has been met. "The woman's action

turns out to have been a good deed; and Jesus turns out to be the Christ in anticipation of his death" (100).

The Gospels offer a rich array of brief narratives that can be properly classified as pronouncement stories. It is crucial to analyze not only the specific setting that prompts Jesus' response but the particular character of that response as well. Interpretive insights emerge as exegetes become sensitive to the rhetorical logic of these brief, provocative stories.

Additional Examples

Pronouncement stories in Mark: 2:16–17; 2:18–22; 2:23–28; 3:31–35; 6:1–6; 7:1–13; 8:11–13; 9:33–37; 9:38–41; 10:2–12; 10:13–16; 10:17–22; 10:35–40; 11:27–33; 12:18–27; 12:28–34; 12:35–37a; 12:41–44. Pronouncement stories in Q: Matt. 4:1–11/Luke 4:1–13; Matt. 8:18–22/Luke 9:57–62; Matt. 11:2–6/Luke 7:18–23. Pronouncement stories in Special Matt. and Luke: Matt. 9:36–38; 12:10–12; 17:24–27; Luke 3:10–11, 12–13, 14; 10:17–20; 10:38–42; 13:31–35; 17:20–21; 19:1–10. Pronouncement stories in John: 1:24–27; 2:13–22; 3:25–36; 6:30–34; 7:1–9; 8:1–11; 11:8–10; 12:1–8. Pronouncement stories in Acts: 2:37–39 and 16:30–31.

Selected Bibliography

Berger, Klaus. 1984. "Hellenistische Gattungen im Neuen Testament. In *Aufstieg und Niedergang der römischen Welt*, 1092–1110. II.25,2. Berlin & New York: Walter de Gruyter. Berger offers numerous examples in a discussion of the structure of the chreia.

Bultmann, Rudolf. 1963. *The History of the Synoptic Tradition*. Translated by John Marsh, 11–69. Oxford: Basil Blackwell.

Dibelius, Martin. 1971. *From Tradition to Gospel*, 37–69. 2d ed. Cambridge & London: James Clarke & Co.
   The works of Bultmann and Dibelius represent early form-critical studies.

Hock, Ronald F., and Edward N. O'Neil. 1986. *The Chreia in Ancient Rhetoric*. Vol. 1. Atlanta: Scholars Press. In addition to a helpful introduction, this volume includes sections from ancient rhetorical handbooks that treat the chreia.

Mack, Burton L., and Vernon K. Robbins. 1989. *Patterns of Persuasion in the Gospels*. Sonoma, Calif.: Polebridge Press. This volume illustrates the value of knowledge of the ancient chreia for interpreting pronouncement stories in the Gospels.

Robbins, Vernon K. 1988a. "The Chreia." *Greco-Roman Literature and the New Testament.* SBL Sources for Biblical Study No. 21, edited by David E. Aune, 1–23. Atlanta: Scholars Press. This article offers a summary of recent study on the chreia, with implications for interpreting pronouncement stories in the New Testament.
———. 1988b. "Pronouncement Stories from a Rhetorical Perspective." *Foundations and Facets Forum* 4, 3–32. This article traces the work of the Society of Biblical Literature Pronouncement Story group and comments on how a knowledge of Hellenistic rhetoric contributes to an understanding of pronouncement stories.
———. 1989. *Ancient Quotes and Anecdotes.* Sonoma, Calif.: Polebridge Press. This volume provides a major collection of anecdotal materials from the Hellenistic world.

Tannehill, Robert C. 1981a. "Introduction: The Pronouncement Story and Its Types." *Semeia* 20, 1–13.
———. 1981b. "Varieties of Synoptic Pronouncement Stories." *Semeia* 20, 101–119.
———. 1984. "Types and Function of Apophthegms in the Synoptic Gospels." In *Aufstieg und Niedergang der römischen Welt,* 1792–1829. II.25,2. Berlin & New York: Walter de Gruyter.
The two *Semeia* articles represent Tannehill's early study of the pronouncement stories; the *ANRW* article offers the fuller elaboration of his typology.

Taylor, Vincent. 1933 *The Formation of the Gospel Tradition,* 63–87. London: Macmillan and Co. Taylor discusses pronouncement stories in this chapter.

APOCALYPTIC LANGUAGE AND FORMS

Definition of the Forms

According to most definitions, neither the Gospels nor the book of Acts can be classified as an apocalypse, a literary genre represented by the book of Revelation (see *Apocalypse*). Nonetheless, the Gospels and Acts unquestionably use apocalyptic language wherever they speak about judgment and resurrection or include terms like "the reign of God" and "Son of Man." In the ancient world, apocalyptic speech most often originated when some figure in the religious community became privy to a "revelation" of what God was about to do in the near future and then spoke to that community, calling people to a new vision of the present order in light of God's impending future action. Thus apocalyptic language expresses a religious perspective that views the immediate future as a time when divine saving and judging activity will deliver God's people out of the present evil order into a new order. This transformation, according to the apocalyptic seer, will be cataclysmic and cosmic in scope (see *Apocalyptic Language and Forms* in the Pauline Tradition section of this volume).

Apocalyptic Language

Clearly, the synoptic Gospels present Jesus as using apocalyptic speech; at the same time, they include only a few passages that hint at his "revelatory experiences" that would account for this way of speaking (see Mark 1:9–11; 9:2–8; Luke 10:17–20; Matt. 11:25–27/Luke 10:21–22). Jesus' apocalyptic language surfaces in his sayings and parables. For example, in Mark 1:15, Jesus announces the imminent arrival of "the reign of God," clearly an apocalyptic symbol: "The time is fulfilled, and the kingdom of God has come near; repent, and believe in the good news" (see also Matt. 10:7; 12:28; Luke 11:20). Or, in Mark 14:62, Jesus responds to the high priest's question about his messianic identity by alluding to an apocalyptic scene in Daniel: "I am; and 'you will see the Son of Man seated at the right hand of the Power,' and 'coming with the clouds of heaven.'" The beatitude is yet another type of Jesus' apocalyptic sayings, as the use of future verbs confirms. The two beatitudes in Luke 6:21 offer specific examples: "Blessed are you who are hungry now, for you *will be filled*. Blessed are you who weep now, for you *will laugh.*" Those followers of Jesus who are hungry and in pain in the present age will experience joy and be satisfied by God's action in the new age.

As further illustration of the pervasiveness of apocalyptic motifs in Jesus' speech, all the following parables of Jesus depend on an apocalyptic background for developing their message: Luke 12:13–21; Luke 16:19–31; Matt. 18:23–35; Matt. 20:1–16; Matt. 22:1–10/Luke 14:16–24; Matt. 24:45–51/Luke 12:42–46; Matt. 25:1–13; Matt. 25:14–30/Luke 19:12–27; Matt. 25:31–46. In the material about John the Baptizer, there also appear apocalyptic images: "the wrath to come" (Luke 3:7);

"the ax . . . lying at the root of the trees" (Luke 3:9); the Coming One with "winnowing fork . . . in his hand" (Luke 3:17); and chaff burning "with unquenchable fire" (Luke 3:17).

Formally, many sayings of Jesus exhibit a "two-part structure in which the first part is related to the present and the second to the future" (Aune 1983, 166). This "present/future polarity reflects the Jewish apocalyptic conception of two ages," according to David Aune. The following examples demonstrate this structure:

> For those who want to save their life/will lose it,
> and those who lose their life for my sake . . ./will save it. (Mark 8:35)
> . . . whoever does not receive the kingdom of God as a little child/ will never enter it. (Mark 10:15)
>
> . . . for all who exalt themselves/will be humbled,
> but all who humble themselves/will be exalted. (Luke 18:14b)

The "present/future" polarity in the sayings of Jesus also functions in an ethical way. Jesus' apocalyptic vision of the future becomes the basis for paraenesis, that is, for his exhorting hearers to think and act in specific ways.

Pronouncements of Holy Law

Some of Jesus' sayings that have the two-part structure also exhibit other formal characteristics. In an important article (66–81), Ernst Käsemann analyzed sayings in Paul and the Gospels that he called "sentences of holy law." Aune (1983, 166–167) summarizes the characteristics of the "holy law" form as follows:

1. The pronouncement is structured in the form of a chiasmus;
2. The same verb is found in both parts of the pronouncement;
3. The second part of the pronouncement deals with the eschatological activity of God and has the verb in the future passive (the passive is frequently a circumlocution for divine activity);
4. The central feature of the pronouncement is the principle of retributive justice (*jus talionis*);
5. The first part of the pronouncement is introduced by the

casuistic legal form "if anyone" or "whoever," whereas the second part is in the style of apodictic divine law.

First Corinthians 3:17 and 14:38 are examples of this form in Paul; Mark 8:38 and Luke 12:8–9 provide examples in the Gospels:

> For whoever is ashamed of me and my words
>   in this evil and sinful generation,
> the Son of Man also will be ashamed of him/her,
> whenever he comes in the glory of his father
>   with the holy angels. (Mark 8:38, author's translation)

> And I tell you,
> everyone who acknowledges me before others,
> the Son of Man also will acknowledge before the angels of God;
> but whoever denies me before others
> will be denied before the angels of God. (Luke 12:8–9)

An analysis of Mark 8:38 illustrates the formal characteristics of the "holy law" in the following manner: (1) the words "whoever" (A) and "of me" (B) in the first line and "Son of Man" (B') and "him/her" (A') in the second line form the chiastic pattern; (2) the verb "ashamed" appears in both the first and second part of the saying; (3) the verb "will be ashamed" in the second part is a future passive form in Greek; (4) the principle of retributive justice, where the penalty fits the offense, is manifested in Jesus' (as the Son of Man) being ashamed of the one who was ashamed of him; (5) the "whoever" is one way to introduce the casuistic form to indicate that this saying applies to anyone who fits the situation described.

Eschatological Correlatives

"Eschatological correlative" is another related form that was identified and labeled by Richard Edwards (1960, 9–20). As noted by Edwards: "A correlative construction is one which brings together two items or persons in order to show a reciprocal relationship between them. The standard correlative form would be: As is the case with A, so it is with B" (11). This form occurs five times in Luke and Matthew (Luke 11:30/Matt. 12:40; Luke 17:24/Matt. 24:27; Luke 17:26/Matt. 24:37; Luke 17:28, 30/Matt. 24:38–39; Matt. 13:40–41), but it never appears in Mark or John. Jesus' saying in Luke 11:30 displays the pattern of the eschatological correlative:

> For just as Jonah became a sign to the people of Nineveh,
> so the Son of Man will be to this generation.

In an eschatological correlative, the first clause begins with the comparative word "just as" *(kathōs)* or "even as" *(hōsper)* and contains a verb in past or present tense, whereas the second clause usually begins with the correlative word "so"/"in this way" *(houtōs)* and includes the future tense "will be" *(estai)*. This form, which resembles the sentence of holy law, always mentions the "Son of Man" in its second clause. Because this form appears frequently in the Septuagint version of the Hebrew prophets, some scholars prefer to label it a "prophetic correlative" (Schmidt, 517–522).

End-times Prophecies

Finally, it should be observed that Mark 13:3–37 is an example of an extended discourse in which Jesus predicts the destruction of the Temple and the events surrounding the end-time (see also Matt. 24:1–36 and Luke 21:5–33). The material of this chapter, which was probably arranged by Mark, presents Jesus' apocalyptic scenario: he predicts the tumultuous events leading up to the end, including the appearance of false messiahs (vs. 6, 21–22), conflicts between nations (vs. 7–8a), earthquakes and famines (v. 8b), and the trials and suffering of the faithful (vs. 9–13). Further, he describes the dissolution of the cosmic order (vs. 24–25) and the appearance of the Son of Man to gather the elect from all parts of the world (vs. 26–27).

> But in those days, after that suffering,
> the sun will be darkened,
> and the moon will not give its light,
> and the stars will be falling from heaven,
> and the powers in the heavens will be shaken.
> Then they will see "the Son of Man coming in clouds" with great power and glory. Then he will send out the angels, and gather his elect from the four winds, from the ends of the earth to the ends of heaven. (13:24–27)

This description echoes apocalyptic language in Joel 2:30–31 and Daniel 7:13.

Whether Mark 13 represents a literary genre is a matter of

some debate (see Aune 1983, 186). In its present form in Mark, however, it definitely exercises a paraenetic or exhortative function. A close reading reveals a series of present-tense imperative verbs ("beware" in v. 5; "beware" in v. 9; "do not worry beforehand" in v. 11; "be alert" in v. 23; "learn" in v. 28; "beware, keep alert" in v. 33; "keep awake" in v. 35; and "keep awake" in v. 37) that all address the Markan community. Hence Jesus' prolonged discourse is apparently designed to teach the Markan audience about the final days and, of more importance, to call them to constant vigilance in the midst of dismaying and uncertain times. This discourse section, especially with its stress on the glorious coming of the Son of Man, provides the apocalyptic symbols to make sense of the unnerving and threatening events facing the community. Mark 13:9–13, in particular, suggests that the Christians to whom Mark wrote were experiencing harsh repercussions from the catastrophic events surrounding the Romans' destruction of Jerusalem with its Temple in 70 C.E.

The Value for Interpretation

Knowledge of apocalyptic language and forms helps the interpreter to recognize their evocative character. Apocalyptic language is language stretched to its limits, evoking images and memories from Israel's past and, above all, as a response to their present loss of meaning, creating a picture of reality that transcends the everyday and historical circumstances of the audience to whom it is directed. In Amos Wilder's terms (153–168), it is language that is "precultural" and "prepersonal," that is, language devoid of the normal human and cultural features.

Moreover, apocalyptic language is richly symbolic, sometimes offering strange and hyperbolic images. It is inappropriate to identify apocalyptic symbols with specific historical or transhistorical referents too easily because this reduces the expressive power of the symbols. It is far more appropriate to approach apocalyptic language as ambiguous and polyvalent, as language that can be interpreted at various levels of meaning, because it seeks to envision reality beyond our imagination. For example, the apocalyptic phrase on the lips of Jesus "the reign of God" is best approached as a polyvalent term that cannot be conceptually explained. As a rich and ambiguous symbol, its use can continue to evoke fresh insights into God's activity vis-à-vis the world.

The interpreter should also consider the nature of the first-century contexts addressed by apocalyptic language. Language becomes hyperbolic in the face of situations of cultural and religious loss and in the face of an actual or perceived chaos, when the continuities and patterns counted on by a community seem to be disrupted or are being destroyed. As noted, it is crucial to understand Jesus' apocalyptic discourse in Mark 13 in terms of its Markan context, which was overlaid with anxiety and fear generated by the events surrounding the Roman siege of Jerusalem in 70 C.E.

The more exegetes understand apocalyptic speech in its original context, the more likely they are to detect its misuse in contemporary preaching and teaching. As noted by Paul Hanson: "Genuine apocalypticism arose within a setting of alienation and was never a theological program self-consciously constructed in security and repose" (33). In order to use apocalyptic speech in appropriate ways today, we need awareness both of the characteristics of this daring and unconventional language and of the type of context out of which it emerged.

Selected Bibliography

Aune, David E. 1983. *Prophecy in Early Christianity and the Ancient Mediterranean World*. Grand Rapids: Wm. B. Eerdmans. This study includes descriptions of prophetic forms with an apocalyptic focus.

————. 1987. *The New Testament in Its Literary Environment*, 226–252. Philadelphia: Westminster Press. The final chapter provides a helpful discussion of apocalyptic literature both in Jewish and Greco-Roman circles.

Edwards, Richard A. 1960. "The Eschatological Correlative as a *Gattung* in the New Testament." *Zeitschrift für die neutestamentliche Wissenschaft* 60, 9–20.

————. 1971. *The Sign of Jonah in the Theology of the Evangelists and Q*, 47–58. Naperville, Ill.: Alec R. Allenson.

   Both entries contain the author's discussion of the "eschatological correlative."

Hanson, Paul D. 1976. "Apocalypticism." *Interpreter's Dictionary of the Bible*. Suppl. vol. Nashville: Abingdon Press. This entry includes definitions of terms (apocalypse, apocalyptic eschatology, and apocalypticism) and a historical-sociological sketch of apocalypticism.

Käsemann, Ernst. 1969. "Sentences of Holy Law in the New Testament." *New Testament Questions of Today*. Translated by W. J. Montague, 66–81. London: SCM Press. This chapter is a translation of the author's influential article published in 1954.

Schmidt, Daryl. 1977. "The LXX *Gattung* 'Prophetic Correlative,'" *Journal of Biblical Literature* 96, 517–522. Schmidt concludes that the correlative form of saying was not a creation of the early church, but was adopted from an earlier prophetic form.

Wilder, Amos N. 1982. "Apocalyptic Rhetorics." *Jesus' Parables and the War of Myths*, 153–168. Philadelphia: Fortress Press. This chapter offers an insightful discussion of the rhetorical effect of apocalyptic speech.

FORMS OF ARGUMENTATION

Definition of the Form

In recent years, New Testament scholars have undertaken what is called rhetorical criticism, a study of biblical texts in terms of the patterns of Hellenistic rhetoric, on the assumption that the New Testament was not isolated from its Greco-Roman culture. Even if most of the New Testament writers were not formally trained in rhetoric, a subject taught in the schools of the Roman Empire during the first century C.E., they did speak the Greek language and were likely influenced by the public rhetoric used in the courts and civil space.

The main aim of rhetoric in the ancient world was persuasion. Even though rhetoric functioned primarily in the civil life, knowledge of it is relevant to religious language as well, because reasons are often given why people should believe what is proclaimed or live in a certain manner. Whenever this occurs in the New Testament, there begins, if only rudimentarily, a process of persuasion or argumentation.

To summarize briefly the explanation of Hellenistic rhetoric (see *Forms of Argumentation* in the Pauline Tradition section of this volume), the practice of rhetoric involved five aspects: *invention* (decisions about the subject addressed, the nature of the issue, and the type of argument), *arrangement* (decisions about the ordering of the material), *style* (choices of diction, grammar, and syntax), *memory* (use of mnemonic devices and process of memorizing the speech), and *delivery* (use of voice, gesture, and other techniques).

Writers about rhetoric did not fail to discuss the social nature of speech, because they realized that the character of the speaker (called *ethos*) and the state of mind of the audience (called *pathos*) affected persuasion. Because of this, speakers were taught to present themselves as authoritative and trustworthy and to develop ways of affecting the emotions of the audience as a means of constructing a convincing speech *(logos)*.

For the actual development of the argument itself, speakers had to decide what rhetorical strategy would in fact accomplish their purposes. Three types of speeches were described by the rhetoricians: judicial, deliberative, and epideictic. Judicial speech was designed for the courtroom and sought to convince the hearers about matters of truth and justice regarding past events. Judicial speech typically involves a *proem* or *exordium* (introduction), *narratio* (statement of the facts), *proposition* (enunciation of the major point), *proof* (development of the evidence in support of the proposition), *refutation* (sometimes the opposing argument is rebutted), and *epilogue* (conclusion). Certain speeches in Acts follow this judicial pattern, for example, Acts 22:1–21 and 24:10–21.

Deliberative speech has its home in the political arena and seeks to persuade the audience to act in a certain way in the future. Its structure resembles that of judicial in a somewhat modified form without a narration; it contains a *proem, proposition, proof,* and *epilogue.* George Kennedy (39ff.) argues that the Sermon on the Mount (Matt. 5–7) and the Sermon on the Plain (Luke 6:20ff.), as well as most of the speech of Jesus, constitute deliberative rhetoric.

Burton Mack (41–43) points out that during the second century B.C.E. the deliberative pattern was transformed into a slightly reduced outline for an argument that was normally called "elaboration" or "refinement." This involved (1) introduction, (2) proposition, (3) reason (rationale), (4) opposite (contrary), (5) analogy (comparison), (6) example, (7) citation (authority), and (8) conclusion.

The third type, epideictic speech, was directed to the present in order to praise or condemn some person or thing. Between the introduction and the conclusion, the speaker normally offered a series of topics about the person, thing, or idea under consideration. Kennedy (73ff.) classifies the "farewell discourses" in John

13–17 as epideictic speech. Also, Vernon Robbins analyzes the Beelzebul controversy in Mark 3:22–30 and Luke 11:18–28 on the basis of a sequence of epideictic topics designed to condemn the scribes (in Mark) and the people in the crowd (in Luke) for asserting that Jesus possesses Beelzebul and casts out demons by the prince of demons (Mack and Robbins, 171–177, 185–191).

Rhetorical argument can use various formal units in developing either a pattern of inductive or deductive reasoning. Inductive reasoning tends to employ examples from the past (*paradeigma*) to move toward a generalization, whereas deductive reasoning builds upon rhetorical syllogisms called *enthymemes*. An enthymeme characteristically assumes the form of a statement supported by a reason. For instance, the first beatitude displays this form: "Blessed are the poor in spirit, *for* theirs is the kingdom of heaven" (Matt. 5:3). Behind this beatitude lies the rather remarkable syllogism: Those who inherit the kingdom of God are blessed (major premise); the poor inherit the kingdom of God (minor premise); therefore, the poor are blessed (conclusion). Many of Jesus' sayings (see *Aphorism*) employ a similar kind of logic and could be labeled "enthymemes."

Rhetorical criticism provides a needed correction to form criticism (see *Introduction*), because a concern for rhetoric focuses not only on the short formal units such as pronouncement story (see *Pronouncement Story*) with its development of the *chreia*, but also on longer scriptural segments. Rhetorical critics are primarily concerned to trace the argument that a specific segment of scriptures pursues to persuade the audience. For example, the speeches in Acts employ both deliberative and judicial patterns of argumentation (see *Speech [Acts]*).

To date, most of the efforts of rhetorical critics have been directed to the Pauline letters (see *Forms of Argumentation* in the Pauline Tradition section of this volume); yet some scholars are now tackling rhetorical analysis of segments in the Gospels and Acts (see, for example, Kennedy, Mack and Robbins, and Mack). Below are examples of such analysis.

Employing the pattern of the "elaboration" or "refinement" (introduction, proposition, reason, opposite, analogy, example, citation, and conclusion), Burton Mack (50–52) proposes the following outline for Jesus' sayings in Luke 12:22–31:

Proposition: One should not worry about life (food) or body (clothing) (v. 22).

Reason: Life is more than food, and the body is more than clothing (v. 23).

Analogy: Ravens do not work for food: God provides for them. You are worth more than birds (v. 24).

Example: No one can add a cubit to life by worry (vs. 25–26).

Analogy: Lilies do not work, yet are "clothed" (v. 27).

Paradigm: Solomon was not so arrayed (v. 27).

Analogy: Notice the grass that is burned. If God clothes it, how much more will he clothe you? (v. 28).

Conclusion: You should not seek food (or worry) (v. 29).

Example: All the nations do that (v. 30).

Exhortation: Seek instead the reign of God, and all the rest will be added to you (v. 31).

Whether or not the evangelist Luke, or the historical Jesus before him, was consciously employing a rhetorical argument known in the Roman world, Mack claims that a pattern practiced in Hellenistic rhetoric is evident. The argument begins with a proposition or thesis in v. 22 and then immediately offers the reason in v. 23 (signaled by the "for"). Support for the proposition assumes the form of analogy (from the world of nature), example (from the social world of human interaction), and paradigm (an example of a historical personage). The analogies (vs. 24, 28) are based on reasoning "from the lesser to the greater" (human beings are *more* than ravens or lilies), whereas the final exhortation in v. 31 moves "from the greater to the lesser" (concern for the kingdom takes precedence over all else in life). The passage as a whole develops the following rhetorical syllogism: Life is more than food and clothing (major premise); God will provide for human needs (minor premise); therefore, there is no reason for humans to worry (conclusion). Also, according to Mack, the imperatives in the passage reveal a stress on the authority of Jesus as teacher (ethos) and underline the audience's need to accept his teaching (pathos).

An awareness of the pattern of the "elaboration" brings new light not only to deliberative rhetoric in which Jesus gives advice but to judicial rhetoric where Jesus defends either himself or his disciples. Vernon Robbins (Mack and Robbins, 132–133) outlines Jesus' argument in Matt. 12:1–8 as follows:

Introduction:
    At that time Jesus went through the grainfields on the sabbath; his disciples were hungry, and they began to pluck heads of grain and to eat.

Statement of the Case:
But when the Pharisees saw it, they said to him, "Look, your disciples are doing what is not lawful to do on the sabbath."

Argument from Example in Written Testimony:
He said to them, "Have you not read what David did, when he was hungry, and those who were with him: how he entered the house of God and ate the bread of the Presence, which it was not lawful for him to eat nor for those who were with him, but only for the priests?"

Analogy:
"Or have you not read in the law how on the sabbath the priests in the temple profane the sabbath and are guiltless?"

Comparison (lesser to greater):
"I tell you, something greater than the temple is here."

Citation Containing the Opposite:
"And if you had known what this means, 'I desire mercy, and not sacrifice,' you would not have condemned the guiltless."

Rationale as Conclusion:
"For lord of the sabbath is the Son of Man."

In this instance, the proposition is a judicial accusation. It states a case against the disciples just as a trial begins with an announcement of the accusation. Jesus, defending his disciples, cites a story from scripture that presents David as a person whose action establishes legal precedent for the action of the disciples. With this statement, Jesus uses two arguments at once: citation and example. Jesus continues by drawing an analogy to priests who are not guilty of violating the law when they do their work on the sabbath. This is an especially effective analogy because it is based on the Torah rather than the prophets, where one finds the story of David. After the analogy, Jesus draws a specific comparison between himself and the Temple, a clever move because priests serve in the Temple. This leads to a citation that introduces the opposite of what the Pharisees have claimed: if the Pharisees were guided by mercy rather than concerns of the Temple, they would not consider the disciples to be guilty of violating God's law. The conclusion introduces a rationale that functions as a minor premise for the guiltlessness of the disciples:

Major premise: The one who is lord of the sabbath is judge over sabbath laws.

Minor premise: The Son of Man is lord of the sabbath.

Conclusion: Therefore, the Son of Man has legal authority to declare the disciples not guilty.

Jesus' powerful use of argument in Matt. 12:1–8 emphasizes his authority to interpret God's law (ethos) and attempts to evoke a decision of not guilty from the audience that sits as jury over the case (pathos).

Rhetorical analyses have also been made of longer scriptural portions such as the Sermon on the Mount (Matt. 5–7). George Kennedy (39–72) proposes this broad outline for the Sermon on the Mount:

5:3–16	Proem
5:17–20	Proposition
5:21–7:20	Proof
7:21–27	Epilogue

Although Kennedy thinks that the sermon as a whole is deliberative speech, because Jesus is offering guidance for the way the audience is to live in the immediate future, he claims that the opening beatitudes are epideictic in character. As part of the proem or introduction, they celebrate qualities (poor in spirit, merciful, pure in heart, etc.) important to the hearers. The beatitudes build a bridge between the speaker and the audience, one of the expressed purposes of the proem. The two metaphors of salt and light in 5:13–16 suggest further that as blessed ones the hearers enjoy a mission, that of doing good works as a witness to God.

Matthew 5:17–20 articulates the proposition of the sermon but does not explain its two principles: the law is to be observed in all its details, and the righteousness of Jesus' disciples is to surpass that of the scribes and Pharisees. Kennedy suggests that ethos and pathos play more of a role here than does logos; Jesus makes these two points in an uncompromising manner, with an emphasis on his authority (ethos) and in v. 19 with an implied punishment or reward for the hearers (pathos).

The argumentation in 5:21ff. first takes up the law (5:21–48), illustrating what is involved in the "greater righteousness," and then offers an additional characterization of that "righteousness" (6:1–18). Although the rhetorical examples in 5:21–48 are largely supported by appeals to ethos and pathos, those in

6:1–18 include rhetorical syllogisms and thus develop more of an argument. The third section of supporting proof for the proposition unfolds in 6:19–7:20, but its connection to 5:17–20 is less apparent. Some of the examples take up the theme of "righteousness," whereas others demonstrate the radicality of the kingdom way of life.

Matthew 7:21–27 provides the epilogue for the sermon. These concluding verses accomplish two things normally appropriate to an epilogue: a recapitulation of the main points of the argument (vs. 21–23) and an attempt to stir the hearers to action (vs. 24–27).

The Value for Interpretation

Modern interpreters of the Bible need to understand the character and function of specific forms like chiasm, aphorism, miracle story, and pronouncement story, but their interpretation is further enriched if they have a working knowledge of the rhetorical patterns practiced in the Hellenistic environment in which the Gospels and Acts were written. Even if the Gospel writers did not study rhetoric formally, it seems probable that some awareness of ancient rhetoric influenced how they shaped the tradition about Jesus and that of the early church.

One important contribution of rhetorical critics is their attention to the rhetorical argument developed in larger segments of scripture. As we have seen, a rhetorical analysis can be made of the Sermon on the Mount as well as a smaller rhetorical unit such as Luke 12:22–31 or Matt. 12:1–8. Robbins even suggests the pattern of argumentation evident in the entire Gospel of Mark at the end of his rhetorical interpretation of that Gospel (201–206). Such analyses can alert the interpreter to what role a particular saying—which might represent a rhetorical analogy, example, or syllogism—plays in the entire argument. Also, a rhetorical analysis normally differentiates between the major point of the argument (thesis or proposition), with its reason, and the supporting proof. Thus, for example, it is critical to understand that in Matt. 5:43–48 the thesis is v. 44 (you should love your enemies . . .), with its reason in v. 45a (so that you may be children of your Father in heaven), while vs. 45b–47 offer the supporting argument.

Rhetorical critics also helpfully remind us that the New Testament authors were essentially concerned with structuring their writings as rhetoric designed to function as aural communica-

tion. Most members of Christian communities in the first century C.E., for example, would have heard a Gospel narrative read
aloud to them in a public setting rather than have read it silently
to themselves. Because reading the Gospel meant an oral per-
formance, rhetorical strategies and techniques would have had
their impact on the audience in much the same way as when a
trained speaker attempted to have a persuasive effect on hearers. Rhetorical criticism can help us discern the intended rhetorical strategy and effect of a text.

Additional Examples

Other texts analyzed rhetorically by Mack include Mark 8:34–
9:1; Luke 3:1–18; John 5:30–47; Acts 2:1–42 (Mack); and Mark
13:3–9; Luke 7:36–50; Mark 4:1–34 (Mack and Robbins).
Kennedy offers rhetorical analyses of Luke 6:20–49 and John
13–17, and suggests that Matt. 23, Luke 10, and Luke 1:46–55
provide other examples of epideictic speech. In addition, Robbins applies rhetorical analysis to Matt. 8:18–22; Luke 9:57–60;
Mark 2:23–28; Mark 3:22–30; Matt. 12:22–37; and Luke 11:
18–28 (Mack and Robbins).

Selected Bibliography

Kennedy, George A. 1984. *New Testament Interpretation Through
Rhetorical Criticism*. Chapel Hill: University of North Carolina
Press. After a helpful introduction, Kennedy analyzes portions of the
New Testament that are examples of judicial, deliberative, and
epideictic speech.

Mack, Burton L., and Vernon K. Robbins. 1989. *Patterns of Persuasion
in the Gospels*. Sonoma, Calif.: Polebridge Press. This book uses
Greco-Roman rhetorical procedures for elaborating an argument to
interpret passages in the synoptic Gospels.

Mack, Burton L. 1990. *Rhetoric and the New Testament*. Minneapolis:
Fortress Press. This volume is a concise, valuable introduction to
rhetorical criticism.

Robbins, Vernon K. 1984. *Jesus the Teacher: A Socio-Rhetorical Interpretation of Mark*. Philadelphia: Fortress Press. This book offers a
socio-rhetorical interpretation of the entire Gospel of Mark.

MIRACLE STORY

Definition of the Form

The broadest definition of miracle story includes any narrative that contains a description of a miraculous event, but such a definition suggests nothing about the structural characteristics of the stories themselves. Even when the miracle story is described as having three sections (opening, main, and concluding; see Betz, 72) or as following the sequence of depicting a problem, a miraculous resolution, and its proof (Wire, 108), one has revealed little about the variety of ways these stories unfold in the Gospels and Acts. Antoinette Clark Wire acknowledges this variety, yet points to narrativity as the essential ingredient when she writes:

> The whole miracle story is in the first place an affirmative statement, not a question or command; a narrative of specific events, not a description, analysis or deduction. The narrative tells a marvelous breakthrough in the struggle against oppressive restrictions on human life. (109)

Beyond these rather general characterizations of the miracle story, both Gerd Theissen (85–112) and Wire (88–108) suggest that certain subforms can be isolated.

1. **An Exorcism.** This type of Gospel story depicts Jesus' encounter with a demon-possessed person. Struggle is central. In such a story, the destructive activity of the demon might be depicted, yet in the presence of Jesus the demoniac becomes defensive and conciliatory. Clearly, Jesus as the miracle worker is in the commanding position; he expels the demon with a word. Following the expulsion, witnesses normally react with astonishment or fear. Thus the literary pattern is one of confrontation, expulsion, and reaction. Mark 1:23–28, 5:1–20, and 9:14–29 are stories that focus on this overthrow of demonic power.

2. **A Controversy Story Containing a Miracle.** In this type, Jesus is in conflict with religious leaders over what the Jewish law permits. When challenged by his opponents, Jesus often asks a key question. Following the pattern of a controversy story (or *chreia*), the briefly described exchange between the teacher and the antagonists climaxes in a final saying, sometimes accompanied by an action, that confounds the opponents. If the action

involves a healing or another kind of miracle, this stands as a confirmation of Jesus' argument. Wire labels this type of story "exposé" with the following description of its intent: "The 'ethics' of the story in each case is negative, purgative, in a social sense revolutionary, breaking down the restrictions erected in God's name to maintain order and privilege" (96). Examples are sabbath healing stories (Mark 3:1–6; Luke 13:10–17; 14:1–6), the Beelzebul controversy story (Matt. 12:22–30/Luke 11:14–23 and Matt. 9:32–34), the temple tax miracle (Matt. 17:24–27), and the healing of the paralytic (Mark 2:1–12).

3. **A Story of Healing as Response to a Petitioner.** In this kind of story, a sick person or an intermediary approaches Jesus, directly or indirectly entreating him for help. In some cases, Jesus throws the demand back to the petitioner with a word of rebuke or a question about faith. The story often stresses the hopeless predicament of the sick person. Jesus' authoritative word and/or touch effects the healing, though the story can end by celebrating the faith of the person. The following stories could be profitably analyzed with these motifs in view: Matt. 8:5–13; Mark 1:40–45; 5:21–43; 7:31–37; Luke 7:1–10.

4. **A Provision Story.** What Theissen terms "gift miracles" (103–106), Wire calls "provision stories" (96–99). This type of story depicts Jesus' response to a situation of need, and examples include the feeding miracles in Mark 6:30–44, Mark 8:1–10, and John 6:1–14. Unlike other stories, there is no request for a miracle; Jesus perceives the need and initiates the action. In most cases, Jesus' provision of food symbolizes far more than sustenance for the physical body. Luke 5:1–11 and John 2:1–11 might also represent this type.

5. **A Rescue Story.** A few stories depict situations of distress in which followers of Jesus find themselves. A storm on the lake threatens them (Mark 4:35–41), or imprisonment can be their lot (Acts 12:1ff. and Acts 16:16ff.). Such a story includes some kind of entreaty or prayer by disciples, and frequently there is an epiphany that precedes their deliverance.

6. **An Epiphany.** A few stories concentrate on a divine manifestation of Jesus and describe the strong reactions that these epiphanies evoke in those who witness them. Jesus' appearance on the lake serves as one example of an epiphany (Mark 6:45–

52/Matt. 14:22–33). Another example is the marvelous catch of fish in Luke 5:1–11, which demonstrates Jesus' lordship over the waters and prompts Simon Peter's self-disparaging confession. Moreover, it seems accurate to say that most, if not all, of the "signs" in John have an epiphanal character, manifesting both the glory and power of this figure sent from God.

The Value for Interpretation

Although it is helpful to study miracle stories in light of the above descriptions, the interpreter will gain further insight into each miracle story by analyzing its individualized characteristics and dramatic movement as a brief narrative. This includes gaining an appreciation of the interplay between action and speech in the story. This type of literary investigation can include the following three questions: (1) What characters are included in the story and how do they interact? Hans Dieter Betz reminds the interpreter to take note of the "history" of the characters in the story. A character can be at the fringe of the story, then its center, and then back at the fringe. Or a character can start at center stage and then vanish from the story's action. Betz also speaks of the movement from "mind contact to face-to-face contact" or from "visual to verbal to face-to-face contact" (72). (2) Where does the dramatic stress occur in the story, and what difference does it make? and (3) What role does the miracle itself play in the story?

Sensitivity to these questions may lead to an elucidating analysis of a story, but any comprehensive interpretation must also investigate the role of the miracle story in the entire Gospel and how this story functioned in creating meaning for the earliest Christians.

Two examples—a controversy story reporting a miracle and a healing story involving a response to a petitioner—illustrate an analysis that keeps in mind the three questions noted above and focuses on the individuality of a given miracle story. A detailed outline of the development of the healing story of the person with a withered hand in Mark 3:1–6 follows:

1–4	I.	Opening scene		
1–2		A.	Introduction of characters	
1a			1.	Reference to place and introduction of Jesus
1b			2.	Introduction of sick person (his malady)
2			3.	Introduction of opponents

		a. Their observation of Jesus
		b. Their malevolent intent
3–4	B.	Dialogue initiated by Jesus
3		1. His instruction to the sick person
4ab		2. His question to the opponents
4c		3. Opponents' silence
5	II.	Main scene
5a		A. Jesus' strong reaction to the opponents
5bc		B. Jesus' preparing for the miracle
		1. Jesus' command to the sick person
		2. Sick person's compliance
5d		C. Occurrence of the miracle
6	III.	Concluding scene: description of the opponents' reaction to the miracle

This story contains three characters: Jesus as the teacher and healer, the sick person, and the opponents. Though introduced directly after Jesus appears in the synagogue, the sick person plays only a minor role in the story. The sick person is directed to center stage by Jesus but recedes into the background in the concluding scene. We learn nothing, for example, of his response to the healing. In contrast, the story gives sustained attention to Jesus' interaction with his opponents. The extended opening scene is not incidental; it expresses the purpose of the story. Once Jesus and the sick man are on stage, we immediately learn of the opponents' presence. Unnamed, they lurk in the shadows at this juncture, but the story quickly notes their malevolent intent. Moreover, Jesus' command to the sick man foreshadows his probing question to the opponents. The intended dialogue never ensues because of their menacing silence; perhaps they remain silent because the answer to Jesus' question is so obvious and so contrary to their intentions.

The main scene describes Jesus' strong reaction to his opponents' malevolence and his bold healing of the man's hand on center stage. The final scene, for the audience, brings the opponents' dark intentions out into the light as it reveals their plan to destroy Jesus. By this development, the meaning of the story comes into sharper focus: Jesus' healing constitutes the good and the saving of life he was asking about, whereas the opponents' plan reveals not only their failure to become convinced by Jesus' miracle but also their ironic contravention of the sabbath in their scheming to do that which was evil. In the Markan context, the story offers another illustration of the truth of Jesus' pivotal declaration in 2:27–28: "The sabbath was made for humankind, and not humankind for the sabbath; so the Son of Man is lord even of the sabbath."

An analysis of the healing story of the woman with a hemorrhage (Mark 5:24–34) offers another example:

24–28	I.		Opening scene
24a		A.	Redactional transition from previous story
24b–25a		B.	Introduction of characters
24b			1. Appearance of crowd with Jesus
25a			2. Appearance of sick woman
25b–26		C.	Description of woman's distressing condition
25b			1. Length of problem
26a			2. No help from physicians
26b			3. Depletion of monetary resources
26c			4. Worsening condition
27–28		D.	Woman's approach of Jesus
27a			1. Establishment of mind contact: she hears of Jesus
27b			2. Establishment of physical contact: she secretly touches Jesus' garment
28			3. Her motive for touching Jesus' garment
29a	II.		Main scene: Occurrence of the miracle
29b–34	III.		Concluding scene
29b		A.	Woman's awareness of her healing
30a		B.	Jesus' awareness of departing power
30b		C.	Jesus' question to the crowd
31		D.	Disciples' response
32		E.	Jesus' searching glance for the person
33–34		F.	Face-to-face encounter of woman and Jesus
			1. Woman is drawn from her anonymity
33a			a. In fear and trembling
33b			b. Kneels before Jesus
33c			c. Tells the whole truth
			2. Jesus' final word to her
34a			a. Acknowledges her faith
34b			b. Dismisses her in peace
34c			c. Reconfirms her healing

This healing story includes four characters: Jesus, with his charismatic power to heal; a desperate woman seeking healing; a crowd important to the progress of the story; and disciples who in the concluding scene move from the wings to center stage for a quick response to Jesus' question to the crowd, and then exit again. Because in the Markan sequence this story acts as an interruption in the story of Jairus (Mark 5:21–24a, 35–43), an audience assumes that Jairus accompanies the crowd. Though plainly Jairus plays no explicit part in the inserted story, the episode with the woman affects what happens for him; the delay results in word from the ruler's house of his daughter's death. Moreover, the interrelating of these two stories invites comparisons. The woman has suffered for twelve years, whereas the ruler's daughter enjoyed only twelve years of life. The woman gains her healing by means of faith: Jairus's faith needs strengthening once he receives news of his daughter's death. The woman receives healing power by touching Jesus' garment; Jesus touches the dead girl and raises her to life.

More becomes apparent from the analysis of the narrative development of the story. In contrast to many miracle stories, the closing scene is extended and matches the opening scene in length. Throughout the scenes, the woman and Jesus dominate the action. Most of the opening scene describes the seemingly hopeless plight of the woman. She has been afflicted by a twelve-year menstrual flow, which makes her perpetually unclean according to the Jewish law (Lev. 15:25–30). Not only has she received no help from doctors, but she also has suffered at their hands as they depleted all her financial resources on these efforts to be healed. Now in a worsening state, she makes concealed contact with Jesus' garment, thus exercising her hope to be healed (or, as the Greek word *sōzō* also implies, "to be saved").

The actual healing is reported briefly; power moves from Jesus into the woman's body. The events in the extended concluding scene induce a face-to-face meeting for the woman with Jesus. She is pulled out of her isolation into relationship. Jesus' persistence in seeking to discover who touched him compels the story in this direction. He wants to know the one who touched him, and the woman lets herself be known. She kneels before Jesus, in fear and trembling, and tells him the whole truth. Then, surprisingly, she receives his commendation for her faith. Thus the story concludes not with a chorus word of praise or the woman glorifying God for what has happened to her, but with her life-granting relationship with Jesus. The story moves from hopelessness to wholeness, from a woman's isolation and anonymity to relationship and life. It ends celebrating her faith. Although the miracle itself is the climax of the story, it is not until the denouement that the hearers can discern that the miracle involves far more than physical healing; it includes entry into a "saving" relationship with Jesus himself.

In summary, then, narratives called "miracle stories" actually represent a variety of types and considerable individuality in their telling. A careful analysis of the literary features and movement of each story can be fruitful for the exegete and preacher. Finally, however, categorizations come up wanting, for only a close investigation focuses attention on the nearly unlimited variety of options available for narrating a story involving a miracle. Examinations like the preceding work could be undertaken with each miracle story in the Gospels and Acts. This type of analysis could reveal as well the significance of the Johannine signs. It is important to note that Matthean and Lukan parallels to Markan stories demand careful attention. These reports of a miracle are not merely mechanical repetitions of another story. Instead, each provides its own variety and nuances. Each should be studied on its own terms and in its own literary context.

Selected Bibliography

Berger, Klaus, 1984. "Hellenistische Gattungen im Neuen Testament." In *Aufstieg und Niedergang der römischen Welt*, 1212–1231. II.25,2. Berlin & New York: Walter de Gruyter. This section contains a helpful analysis of miracle stories and aretalogies, illustrating the various ways reports of miracles are used in the ancient world.

Betz, Hans Dieter. 1978. "The Early Christian Miracle Story: Some Observations on the Form Critical Problem." *Semeia* 11, 69–81. Viewing the miracle stories as literary phenomena (following Theissen) leads Betz to offer helps in pursuing an aesthetic description of a miracle story.

Bultmann, Rudolf. 1963. *The History of the Synoptic Tradition*. Translated by John Marsh, 209–244. Oxford: Basil Blackwell. This segment focuses on the development of the miracle story tradition.

Kee, Howard Clark. 1983. *Miracle in the Early Christian World*. New Haven & London: Yale University Press. Employing a socio-historical approach, Kee investigates the significance of miracle as part of the Greco-Roman environment.

Theissen, Gerd. 1983. *The Miracle Stories of the Early Christian Tradition*. Translated by F. McDonagh. Philadelphia: Fortress Press. This important study pursues interrelated approaches for understanding the miracle stories.

Wire, Antoinette Clark. 1978. "The Structure of the Gospel Miracle
Stories and Their Tellers." *Semeia* 11, 83–113. This article, which
investigates the interaction between characters in the miracle story,
categorizes them according to types.

COMMISSIONING STORY

Definition of the Form

A number of stories in the Gospels and Acts resemble the
commissioning or call stories that appear frequently in the Hebrew scriptures. Benjamin Hubbard (104–107) lists twenty-
seven stories of this type in the Hebrew scriptures (e.g., Gen.
11:28–30, 12:1–4a; 17:1–14; Exod. 3:1–4:16; Num. 22:22–35;
Deut. 31:14–15; Josh. 1:1–11; 1 Sam. 3:1–4:1a; Isa. 6; Jer.
1:1–10; Ezra 1:1–5), from which he derives the following characteristic elements: introduction, confrontation, reaction, commission, protest, reassurance, and conclusion. Building on
Hubbard's analysis of Matt. 28:16–20 as a "commissioning
form," Terence Mullins (603–614) uses these typical components to study thirty-seven stories in the Gospels and Acts. Both
he and Hubbard (114–123), who lists only twenty-five New Testament commissioning stories, have discovered that this form
appears most frequently in the Lukan writings. This is not surprising given Luke's dominant interest in the "prophet" paradigm (see Luke 4:16–30; 7:16; 7:39; 13:31–33; 24:19; Acts
3:22; 7:37).

Indispensable to this type of story are the elements (a word,
phrase, or a block of material) of confrontation, commission, and
reassurance. The confrontational component depicts a divine
representative or person who issues an authoritative commission
to someone in the story; the commission is issued to make the
recipient an agent of a higher authority; the reassurance is
apparently designed to eliminate any remaining resistance from
the person being commissioned. In at least nine stories, an introduction, a reaction to the confrontation, a protest to the commission, and a conclusion are also present. Yet in other examples,
one or more of these ingredients are missing, most frequently
the element of reaction or protest.

The Value for Interpretation

An examination of two stories will illustrate the value of recognizing this form for interpreting texts. The first one, the commissioning of Paul in Acts 9:1–9, is an obvious choice. The following outline describes the way Luke has ordered the characteristic elements in this account.

Introduction (1–3a): Saul is on the way to Damascus to suppress "the Way."

Confrontation (3b): There is a sudden appearance of flashing light from heaven.

Reaction (4a): Saul falls to the ground.

Confrontation (4b): A voice addresses Saul with a question.

Reaction (5a): Saul responds with a question.

Commission (5b–6): The Lord responds with a directive to enter the city.

Reaction (7): The speechlessness of Saul's companions is mentioned.

Conclusion (8–9): The blind Saul is led into the city.

In this instance, the protest component is lacking, and perhaps the reassurance one as well. Mullins (606), however, labels v. 6b as the reassurance (". . . and you will be told what you are to do") rather than part of the commission. What follows in Acts 9:10–19 provides the sequel to 9:1–9 and possibly dictates variations in the typical pattern. Though 9:10–19 describes a parallel commission to Ananias, it also brings reassurance and a confirmation of Paul's call (9:17–18). Producing an outline according to the elements of the "commissioning story" does clarify the movement of the narrative.

Stories about the Risen Lord (Matt. 28:1–8; 28:16–20; Mark 16:1–8; Luke 24:36–53) and certain of the infancy stories (see *Stories About Jesus*) also seem to represent this commissioning form. The story of the annunciation to Mary in Luke 1:26–38 is one of the infancy stories:

Introduction (26–27): Gabriel is sent to Mary.

Confrontation (28): Gabriel addresses Mary.

Reaction (29): Mary is perplexed by the angelic greeting.

Reassurance (30): Mary is told not to fear because of God's favor.

Commission (31–33): Mary is to conceive and bear a son, "Jesus."

Protest (34): Mary questions this because of her virginity.

Reassurance (35–37): The angel speaks of the power of the Spirit and the fact of Elizabeth's pregnancy.
Conclusion (38): Mary accepts her role and the angel departs.

As with Acts 9:1–9, Luke 1:26–38 unfolds the pattern flexibly, including two descriptions of reassurance (30 and 35–37), one after Mary's initial reaction and one after her protest. Because the "form" is merely descriptive of the ingredients necessary for this type of story, variation in the order and presentation of these important elements should not surprise the interpreter.

Recognizing the form of the commissioning story allows the interpreter to understand the primary intent of such stories: "to commission someone to carry out a divinely-instigated task" (Hubbard, 123). So, for example, Luke's use of this form to describe the event in Acts 9 tells the astute reader how the evangelist regards the event—not as a "conversion" of Saul in our terms, but as his prophetic call and commissioning. The interpreter knows this not primarily by the express content of the story, or by anything Luke says directly to the reader, but by the form alone.

Additional Examples

Hubbard (122) and Mullins (605–606) largely agree that the following are examples of the "commissioning story": Matt. 28:1–8; 28:16–20; Mark 16:9–20; Luke 1:5–25; 1:26–38; 2:8–20; 24:36–53; John 20:19–23; Acts 9:1–9; 9:10–17; 10:1–8; 10:9–23; 22:6–11; 22:17–21; 23:11; 26:12–20; 27:21–26. Mullins also sees this form as describing various other stories, some of which are typically classified as miracle stories (Matt. 14:22–33 and Luke 5:1–11). He includes as well the Matthean version of transfiguration (Matt. 17:1–8), the Markan story of the entry into Jerusalem (Mark 11:1–10), and a parable like Luke 15:11–31.

Selected Bibliography

Hubbard, Benjamin J. 1977. "Commissioning Stories in Luke-Acts: A Study of Their Antecedents, Form and Content." *Semeia* 8, 103–126. This article investigates the commissioning stories in Luke-Acts in light of stories in the Hebrew scriptures and Ancient Near East.

Mullins, Terence Y. 1976. "New Testament Commission Forms, Especially in Luke-Acts." *Journal of Biblical Literature* 95, 603–614.

Building on Hubbard's analysis of Matt. 28:16–20, Mullins analyzes many more New Testament stories as representative of the commissioning story form.

STORIES ABOUT JESUS

Definition of the Form

Stories that do not fit the categories of pronouncement story and miracle story have typically been classified as "stories about Jesus" by English-speaking scholars. Vincent Taylor (142) suggested this nondescript label for those stories that, in his judgment, "have no common structural form." He did so because he wished to avoid the term "legend" employed by Martin Dibelius (104ff.) and Rudolf Bultmann (244ff.), a term that prejudges the historical worth of these stories for most people. Although Bultmann is skeptical about the historical value of these stories, describing them as "religious and edifying" and "not historical" (244), in a footnote he also acknowledges that "historical happenings may underlie legends" (244–245). In a similar vein, Dibelius (104) uses "legend" to designate a religious story with a mixture of biographical and aetiological (explaining cause or origin) interest designed to provide grounds for the significance of an extraordinary figure it remembers and promotes. Even Taylor (142–146), who seeks to safeguard the historical value of stories, recognizes that these "stories about Jesus" are not biographical in any modern sense but are "self-contained stories" that reflect the needs and interests of the early church.

The Value for Interpretation

Because "stories about Jesus" serve as a category that includes a wide variety of stories, it seems best to discuss the characteristics of these stories according to the following subgroups: public ministry stories, infancy stories, passion stories, and resurrection stories. The defining characteristics of each group of stories and some hints regarding their proper interpretation will be offered.

Public Ministry Stories

Most of the stories that describe episodes in Jesus' ministry focus directly on the issue of Jesus' identity. For example, Mark 6:1–6a describes hometown people's rejection of Jesus as a divinely appointed prophet. In Mark 6:14–16, Herod Antipas gets word of Jesus and wonders if he is a "resurrected" John the Baptist. Mark 8:27–30 treats explicitly the question of Jesus' identity as addressed to his disciples. Furthermore, Mark 11:1–10 depicts Jesus' entry into Jerusalem as the Davidic messiah, and Mark 11:15–18 portrays Jesus' prophetic and provocative activity in the Jerusalem temple.

Interpreters also should note that at least three stories about Jesus incorporate mythic elements. This means that they describe transcendent reality in historical terms. In particular, Mark 1:12–13 depicts the temptation of Jesus as a desert encounter with "Satan"; the longer version in Matt. 4:1–11/Luke 4:1–13 historicizes Jesus' struggle with evil even more completely. The story of Jesus' baptism in Mark 1:9–11 also includes mythic elements—the splitting of the heavens and the voice out of the clouds declaring Jesus to be the beloved Son. Finally, the transfiguration story in Mark 9:2–9 par. offers a manifestation of Jesus' identity as the Son of God and of the nature of his mission. This story possesses a mythic quality in its description of the appearances of Elijah and Moses, the brightness of Jesus' clothes, the heavenly voice, and the cloud.

According to David Aune (270–274), both the story of Jesus' baptism and that of his transfiguration incorporate a brief form called a "recognition oracle." In both instances, the pronouncement is attributed to God and possesses two structural elements: "the primary recognition statement followed by a brief exposition of that statement" (272). In the case of Mark 1:11, the divine oracle of recognition as a quotation of Ps. 2:7 comes first, and then an allusion to Isa. 42:1 follows as the exposition:

> "You are my Son, the Beloved;
> with you I am well pleased."

In Mark 9:7, the recognition oracle in the transfiguration story, the first component, again in the words of Ps. 2:7, is the divine acknowledgment of Jesus' identity; the second element is a command to listen to him. It is noteworthy that the pronouncement now appears in the third person:

"This is my Son, the Beloved;
listen to him!"

In summary, many of the stories about Jesus that depict his ministry concentrate on Jesus' identity and mission, and some do so by incorporating mythic language and a recognition oracle. Undoubtedly, the earliest Christians shaped these stories retrospectively in light of their postresurrection confessions and experience. It is critical for the interpreter to appreciate the confessional and mythic character of such stories.

Infancy Stories

Matthew 1–2 and Luke 1–2 are routinely designated as "birth narratives" or "infancy narratives," even though one Lukan story describes Jesus at age twelve (Luke 2:41–51). Certain characteristics of the infancy narratives will guide exegetes in their interpretation of these stories.

First, it is important for the interpreter to understand that the infancy stories are not factual history in any modern sense. This does not imply, however, the total absence of material of historical value (see Brown 1977, 26–38, 505–533). Most scholars agree that these stories—which do not appear in the earliest Gospel, Mark—emerged late in the pre-Gospel tradition. Raymond Brown explains:

> The earlier one goes, the less emphasis one finds on the birth and family of Jesus. There is no reference at all to the birth in the sermons of Acts, and only one specific reference to it in the main Pauline letters (Gal. 4:4–5). In the early Christian preaching the birth of Jesus had not yet been seen in the same salvific light as the death and resurrection. (28)

As evidence for this, Brown elsewhere observes that the rest of the Gospel shows no awareness of the infancy narrative episodes and that there are no references back to them. For example, in Matt. 2:3 it is stated that Herod and all residents in Jerusalem heard of the birth of Jesus as King of the Jews, but during Jesus' ministry people make no reference to his extraordinary origins (see Matt. 13:54–58). Or, according to Luke 1:39ff., John the Baptist is a relative of Jesus, yet later in Luke 7:18–23 the Baptist inquires about Jesus' messianic identity. These inconsistencies are multiple.

A second point worth noting is that the infancy narratives primarily serve christological purposes, making clear to the audience from the outset something about Jesus' identity. They function as a preface to the Gospel. Similar to the Johannine prologue, the birth narratives anticipate major theological and christological themes that appear in the later Gospel narrative. For example, Herod's threat against the life of the infant Jesus foreshadows Jesus' crucifixion. Or the reference to the Gentiles in Simeon's song in Luke 2:29–32 anticipates the reception of the Gentiles into the church. Hence interpreters do well to interpret and preach a specific infancy story with an eye to how the story crystallizes a christological confession of the early church, how it offers a rich reflection regarding the significance of Jesus' ministry, crucifixion, and resurrection.

Third, some scholars (e.g., Brown and Horsley) point out that certain features of the infancy narratives correspond to those of the infancy stories that appear in Greco-Roman biographies of famous persons. More specifically, Richard Horsley suggests that hearers of the infancy narratives in Matthew and Luke would have been familiar with "features such as dreams, portents, and childhood prodigies from contemporary accounts of important figures, such as the biographies of the Caesars by Suetonius" (170).

Probably more important than these general parallels is the likelihood that the infancy narratives, especially Matt. 1–2, are midrashic in character (see *Midrash*). John Dominic Crossan (18–27) has rather convincingly demonstrated that the Matthean infancy stories echo midrashic accounts of the stories about Moses in Exod. 1–2. Parallels between these stories and Matt. 1–2 abound: in the Moses story a sign comes in the form of a prediction and a dream, and in the Jesus story the sign is a star; Pharaoh and his courtiers fear, and Herod fears; Pharaoh consults with advisers in his court, and Herod consults with priests and scribes; Pharaoh decides to massacre male Hebrew children, and so does Herod; and so forth. If biblical stories—by means of a midrashic version—play an important role in the formation of the Matthean infancy narrative and even the Lukan one (e.g., Mary's song echoes parts of Hannah's song in 1 Sam. 2:1–10), the interpreter must pay close attention to these scriptural themes and how they are adapted. For example, in Matt. 1–2, the stories present Jesus as the "new" Moses but with a twist—"Jesus flees for safety not *from*, but *to* the gentiles (in Egypt)" (Crossan, 27).

Finally, it is important for the interpreter to recognize that the stories in Matt. 1–2 and Luke 1–2 are not the same. They offer two quite different infancy narratives. Rather than neatly harmonize them, the interpreter needs to honor the particularity of each narrative. Unfortunately, "traditional" nativity pageants have largely perpetuated the popular notion that Matthew and Luke offer one chronological, historical sequence for the events surrounding Jesus' birth. By failing to take seriously the character and distinctiveness of these birth stories, Sunday School performances unintentionally domesticate the radical and liberating power of these stories (see especially Horsley).

Passion Stories

In this section, the focus will be on the Markan passion narrative because it is probably the earliest one. Careful study of the other passion narratives (Matt. 26–27; Luke 22–23; John 18–19) would also reveal their own distinctive strategies and themes (see Matera). Most scholars agree that the depiction of Jesus' arrest, trial, condemnation, and crucifixion in Mark 14–15 displays a remarkable inner coherence as a narrative. They differ, however, in their explanations of the origin of this carefully constructed passion narrative. Was Mark 14–15 given its basic shape in the pre-Markan tradition, a position long held by most scholars, or was the author of Mark responsible for creating this tightly plotted narrative drama?

George Nickelsburg (153ff.), who alone seems to have addressed the question of genre regarding the Markan passion narrative, proposes that the model for Mark 14–15 is to be found in certain Jewish writings (the Joseph narrative in Gen. 37ff., the story of Ahikar, the book of Esther, Dan. 3 and 6, Susanna, and, at least in part, Wisd. Sol. 2, 4–5) that develop a common theme—"the rescue and vindication of a persecuted innocent person or persons" (156). From these Jewish writings, Nickelsburg detects a number of narrative components that, when applied to Mark 14–15, reveal the following pattern (164–166): provocation (11:15–17); conspiracy (11:18; 12:12, 13; 14:1–2); provocation (14:3–9); conspiracy (14:10–11); trial and accusation (14:53–64); choice, trust, obedience (these are not explicit, but see 14:60–62); reaction (14:63); condemnation (14:64); rescue, exaltation, and vindication (these are not explicit, but see 14:62); trial and accusation (15:1–15); reaction (15:5); assistance (15:9–14); condemnation (15:15); investiture and acclamation (15:16–20); acclamation (15:26); ordeal (15:29–32); prayer (15:34); ordeal (15:36); death (15:37); vindication (15:38); acclamation (15:39).

There are some problems with this analysis. For example, some Markan texts are omitted in the outline, there are many doublets, and vindication certainly comes with Mark 16:1–8. It does seem reasonable, however, that a narrative describing the accusation, trial, and condemnation of a righteous one would include certain common components. Whether or not this narrative pattern provided guidance for the composition of Mark 14–15, there are definite characteristics of the passion narrative that might be helpful to the interpreter to observe.

First, the stories are tightly interwoven. This means that the interpreter needs to study each story with an eye to its role in the passion narrative as a whole. For example, in 15:29 those who taunt Jesus on the cross refer to his claim that he will destroy the Temple and rebuild it in three days, an accusation issued in the trial and labeled by the narrator as false (14:57–59).

Second, the stories in the passion narrative take up themes and motifs that have previously surfaced in Mark 1–13. Werner Kelber (153–159) notes this as a telling point of intersection of the work of various scholars on the separate stories in the Markan passion narrative:

> *Virtually all major (and a multiplicity of minor) Markan themes converge in Mk. 14–16.* The major ones are: passion Christology, meal Christology, titular Christology, Messianic Secret, Temple theology, Kingdom eschatology, discipleship failure, Petrine opposition, anti-Jerusalem theme, Galilean thesis, the leitmotif Gospel, as well as a christological, eschatological undercurrent. (Kelber, 156–157)

In light of this, understanding of a particular story in the passion narrative is obviously enriched when it is seen as part of the entire Markan tapestry of themes.

Third, interpreters do well to remember that the Markan passion narrative is permeated with quotations and allusions from the Hebrew scriptures. Here again this might be the result of a type of midrash. For the description of Jesus' crucifixion in 15:25–39, for instance, the narrative contains at least six quotations and allusions (Ps. 22:7 in v. 29; Ps. 69:8 in v. 32; Amos 8:9 in v. 33; Ps. 22:1 in v. 34; Ps. 69:21 in v. 36; Exod. 26:31ff. in v. 38). This scriptural substratum for the Markan passion narrative assured the earliest Christians that everything done to Jesus, even the most appalling and shameful acts, happened according to God's will. Mark 14–15 demonstrates the truth of the creedal statement that "Christ died for our sins in accordance with the scriptures" (1 Cor. 15:3).

Finally, the passion stories, unlike other stories about Jesus, are quite realistic and do not offer us a great deal of mythic material (that is, the description of transcendent realities in historical terms). As Burton Mack has noted: "The account is certainly not devoid of reference to the transhistorical significance of the event it relates, but there is far less manifestation of the transcendent in this merger of myth and history than one might expect" (249–250). Apart from the scriptural references, the stories only seldom offer the hearers glimpses of the divine will—in the uncommon "darkness" (15:33) and remarkable rending of the temple curtain (15:38). Otherwise, the stories are rooted in the reality of human decisions and interactions.

Resurrection Stories

In contrast to the passion stories, the resurrection stories embrace mythic language far more eagerly, because they seek to describe in narrative form the divine activity that gave birth to the Christian movement and was confessed in 1 Cor. 15:4–5: " . . . that he was buried, and that he was raised on the third day in accordance with the scriptures, and that he appeared to Cephas, then to the twelve." So it is not surprising to discover stories depicting an earthquake, an angel with radiant appearance who rolls back the gravestone and speaks to the women's fear, a sudden appearance of the risen Jesus with a charge to the women, and a climactic encounter of the risen Jesus with his eleven disciples on a Galilean mountain (see Matt. 28:1–20). Mythic language is required to give expression to the extraordinary apocalyptic claim: Jesus' resurrection initiates a "new age" in which the Christian mission is to give witness in the presence of all peoples.

In the resurrection narratives, two types of stories can properly be distinguished: empty tomb stories (Mark 16:1–8; Matt. 28:1–7; Luke 24:1–11) and appearance stories (Matt. 28:8–10, 16–20; Luke 24:13–35, 36–49; John 20:1–2, 11–18, 19–29; 21:1–24. See also Acts 1:1–11). The three empty tomb stories, though not identical in all details, revolve around women arriving at Jesus' burial place and discovering the tomb empty. All three describe the presence of one or two messenger figures with words addressed to the women; only the Matthean account adds an appearance of Jesus to the women themselves (Matt. 28:9–10). All three stories depict the women's experience of the angelic figure(s) and the empty tomb as a wondrous event for them, but Matthew in particular heightens the event's awesomeness by his description of the earthquake, the angel's appearance and activity of moving the stone, and the fearful reaction of the guard (Matt. 28:2–4; see also Luke 24:4–5).

On the other hand, most of the appearance stories can be classified as commissioning stories (see *Commissioning Story*). As a full form, such a story includes the following:

1. Introduction that describes the setting;
2. Confrontation in which a divine messenger confronts a human or humans who are to be given a task, which in turn prompts a fearful response followed by the reassurance "Do not fear . . .";
3. Commission is given;
4. Objection might be uttered by human recipient(s) of the commission, which leads to another reassurance and sign of proof;
5. Conclusion, where the messenger departs (see Neyrey, 25–29).

Matthew 28:16–20, as an example, exhibits this pattern as follows: introduction (28:16), confrontation (28:17a), reaction (28:17b), reassurance (28:18a), commission (28:18b–20), and sign (28:20b). In this particular story, there is neither an objection nor a conclusion. The obvious value for interpreters in recognizing the story's form is the understanding that Jesus' appearance meant the commissioning of disciples and the confirming of their mission. Of all the appearance stories, only Luke 24:13–35 does not correspond to the form of the commissioning story. According to Jerome Neyrey (38–44), Luke 24:13–35 is cast in a chiastic form (see *Chiasm*) whose structure has at its center an emphasis on Jesus' initiative in teaching and feeding the disciples. Teaching and the Meal, both crucial to the life of the Christian community, stand in the spotlight.

The resurrection stories, like all other "stories about Jesus," are primarily vehicles of the proclamation about Jesus who—in accordance with the scriptures—was crucified, buried, raised from the dead, and appeared to many. These stories were rooted in the experience and confession of the earliest Christians and were designed to address their continuing needs as community.

Selected Bibliography

Aune, David E. 1983. *Prophecy in Early Christianity and the Ancient Mediterranean World*. Grand Rapids: Wm. B. Eerdmans. This volume contains a discussion of prophetic forms used in the New Testament.

Brown, Raymond E. 1977. *The Birth of the Messiah*. Garden City, N.Y.: Doubleday & Co. This book is an indispensable resource on the infancy narratives.

———. 1986a. "Gospel Infancy Narrative Research from 1976 to 1986: Pt. I. (Mt.)." *Catholic Biblical Quarterly* 48, 468–483.

———. 1986b. "Gospel Infancy Narrative Research from 1976 to 1986: Pt. II (Lk.)." *Catholic Biblical Quarterly* 48, 660–680.

These articles annotate an immense number of studies on the infancy narratives as well as summarize the major conclusions of this scholarship.

Bultmann, Rudolf. 1963. *The History of the Synoptic Tradition*. Translated by John Marsh, 244–317. Oxford: Basil Blackwood. This classic book on form criticism discusses "Historical Stories and Legends."

Crossan, John Dominic. 1986. "From Moses to Jesus: Parallel Themes." *Bible Review* 2, 18–27. This article compares Matt. 1–2 to midrashic stories in the Jewish tradition on Exod. 1–2.

Dibelius, Martin. 1971. *From Tradition to Gospel*, 104–132, 178–219. 2d. ed. Cambridge & London: James Clarke & Co. Ltd. First published in 1919, this book discusses "Legends" and "The Passion Story."

Fuller, Reginald H. 1971. *The Formation of the Resurrection Narratives*. New York: Macmillan Co. This book offers a comprehensive study of the resurrection narratives.

Horsley, Richard A. 1989. *The Liberation of Christmas: The Infancy Narratives in Social Context*. New York: Crossroad. Horsley undertakes a sociological study of the infancy narratives.

Kelber, Werner H., ed. 1976. *The Passion in Mark*. Philadelphia: Fortress Press. Especially helpful are the introduction by Donahue and the summary by Kelber.

Mack, Burton L. 1988. *A Myth of Innocence*, 247–312. Philadelphia: Fortress Press. Mack's book contains an important discussion on the character and development of the Markan passion narrative.

Matera, Frank J. 1986. *Passion Narratives and Gospel Theologies.* New York: Paulist Press. The book provides interpretations of the Synoptics in light of their passion narratives.

Neyrey, Jerome H. 1988. *The Resurrection Stories.* Wilmington, Del.: Michael Glazier. This work includes a useful discussion on the structure and form of the resurrection stories.

Nickelsburg, George W. E. 1980. "The Genre and Function of the Markan Passion Narrative." *Harvard Theological Review* 73, 153–184. Nickelsburg investigates the generic identity of the Markan passion narrative.

Taylor, Vincent. 1935. *The Formation of the Gospel Tradition,* 44–62 and 142–167. 2d ed. London: Macmillan and Co. This British work on form criticism includes chapters on "The Passion Narratives" and "The Stories About Jesus."

MIDRASH

Definition of the Form

By the first century C.E., the term "midrash," derived from a Hebrew verb *drs,* had acquired the technical meaning of "investigation" or "interpretation" of a scriptural text. Fundamental to all midrashic interpretation is the canonical or sacred status of the written text or texts being commented upon. The midrashist attempts to demonstrate both the authority and the relevance of the scriptural passage for the community in its present situation.

Clearly, postbiblical Judaism developed a number of literary forms that can be legitimately classified as midrash (see Porton, 70ff.). First, there are translations, such as the Septuagint and Aramaic targums, which made the scriptures accessible to believers who no longer knew Hebrew. Second are rewritings of the scriptures, which characteristically included elaborations of the biblical narrative and other contemporizing interpretations (e.g., *Genesis Apocryphon,* which was discovered in Cave I at Qumran and includes a lively retelling of episodes in Gen. 12–14). Third are *pesher* interpretations, used in the Qumran documents, which are identified by the appearance of the Hebrew word *pesher* (meaning "to interpret") after a quotation of a scriptural passage. This method applied the text to the events of this community with its eschatological perspective. And fourth is rabbinic midrash, which characteristically included comments attributed to named rabbis on biblical units, often topically arranged, or on subjects prompted in some way by the biblical segments, for example, Genesis Rabbah and Leviticus Rabbah. To this list we can add a fifth form of midrash, which pursues an allegorical interpretation. This form cites persons and features in the biblical account as representing a higher reality (e.g., Philo introduced considerable allegory in his interpretation of the scriptures).

Of the forms of midrash developed in postbiblical Judaism mentioned above, the use of the Hebrew scriptures in the New Testament writings resembles basically the pesher interpretation practiced at Qumran, although there are a few examples of allegorical interpretations in Paul (see *Midrash* in the Pauline Tradition section of this volume). Like the Qumran community, the Christians quoted and interpreted passages in the sacred scriptures retrospectively in light of what they were convinced was God's new revelatory activity and in the firm conviction that they were living in the end-times. Unlike Qumran, however, the Christians believed their leader, Jesus, to be the promised messiah. Accordingly, they looked to the scriptures for confirmation that Jesus' activities, crucifixion, and resurrection made sense christologically (see Luke 24:44).

What is of special interest are the ways in which the Gospel writers use the Hebrew scriptures and how these correspond to Jewish midrash. To label the evangelists' frequent use of the Hebrew scriptures as examples of midrash seems accurate, but it is more difficult to classify these various uses. They represent at least two subforms of midrash: (1) pesherlike or prophecy interpretation and (2) typological interpretation.

Pesherlike or Prophecy Interpretation

In the strictest sense, the Gospel writers' uses of scriptural passages do not correspond to the pesher form employed in the Qumran writings, because these do not typically involve a quotation of a scriptural text followed by a clear "interpretation" that applies this text to the Christian community. Perhaps Luke 4:16–21 comes closest to this pattern, where Jesus quotes Isa. 61:1–2 and 58:6, sits down (as a sign of teaching authority), and declares, "Today this scripture has been fulfilled in your hearing." Many, if not most, of the evangelists' quotations of scripture are nonetheless like the pesher interpretation in their retrospective character because the Gospels use texts to legitimate and illuminate the events surrounding Jesus and the early church.

Jacob Neusner (31–40), for instance, suggests "prophecy midrash" as the term to include both the pesher-midrash practiced at Qumran and the midrash used in Matthew. In both cases, "scripture was taken to provide an account of the present and near-term future" (1). But the Matthean pattern is different: after a story is told or words are spoken that relate to Jesus or another figure, a scriptural text is quoted to disclose the divine meaning and purpose of what has been narrated. For example, Matt. 4:12–13 narrates that Jesus, at the news of John's arrest, withdraws to Galilee and makes his home in Capernaum in the territory of Zebulun and Naphtali. Immediately following this brief narrative, Matthew affixes the words "so that what had been spoken through the prophet Isaiah might be fulfilled" (4:14) as a lead-in to a quotation of Isa. 8:23–9:1 (4:15–16). This links Jesus' ministry in Galilee to the place of the Gentiles. Matthew 8:16–17 provides another example of this same pattern:

> *Narrative:* That evening they brought to him many who were possessed with demons; and he [Jesus] cast out the spirits with a word, and cured all who were sick.

> *Fulfillment Formula:* This was to fulfill what had been spoken through the prophet Isaiah,

> *Scriptural Quotation* (Isa. 53:4): "He took our infirmities and bore our diseases."

Though without the same formalized pattern used in Matthew, other Gospel writers use the Hebrew scriptures as "prophecy" that offer divine proof for Jesus' activities and even his manner of death and his resurrection. This is especially apparent in the speeches in Acts where Luke employs scriptural texts to make sense of Jesus' crucifixion and resurrection. For instance, in Peter's speech in Acts 2:22ff., Luke first depicts Jesus as "a man attested to you by God with deeds of power, wonders, and signs," yet crucified by those outside the law and then raised up by God. In this summary, the author of Acts alludes to a phrase in Ps. 16:8–11, which he then quotes in full. Furthermore, Luke argues on the basis of the psalm that David foretold the messiah's resurrection when he, as the psalmist, declared: "You will not abandon my soul to Hades, or let your

Holy One experience corruption." Luke has Peter end his argument from scripture for Jesus' resurrection by quoting Ps. 110:1 to show that "God has made him both Lord and Messiah, this Jesus whom you crucified" (Acts 2:36). In sum, the midrashic pattern here is (1) narration, (2) scriptural quotation, (3) commentary on scripture, and (4) culminating scriptural quotation with concluding declaration. For another example, see Paul's speech in Acts 13:16–41.

Typological Interpretation

A typological interpretation of a scriptural text discovers in it a foreshadowing of some later event or person; for the church this meant the foreshadowing of Jesus as the Christ and his work. Seldom do the evangelists explicitly draw this typological connection with a scriptural text, but there are a few examples. Matthew 12:39–40 understands Jonah's three days and three nights in the belly of the sea monster as foreshadowing Jesus' three days and three nights in the heart of the earth. And the familiar passage in John 3:14 interprets the bronze serpent on a pole in the wilderness (Num. 21:9) as an anticipation of Jesus' cross.

More often, the typological interpretation is more subtle, yet nonetheless discernible by early Jewish Christians who were acquainted with the scriptural stories. The stories in Matt. 1–2 depicting episodes surrounding Jesus' birth are likely the result of Christian midrashic exegesis of scriptural texts and themes. For example, does not Matt. 2:13–15, with its culminating quotation of Hosea 11:1, seek to make a typological link between the historical Israel, as God's son, and Jesus as the "new Israel"? As another example, John 6 shows evidence of a midrashic pattern at work that interprets the story of Jesus' feeding of the five thousand in light of the Exodus narrative of Moses with Israel and manna in the wilderness. In John, Jesus is the "new Moses" as well as the "bread that came down from heaven."

The Value for Interpretation

It is important for the interpreter to realize how frequently and freely the New Testament writers make use of the Hebrew scriptures. The Gospels and Acts are no exception in this regard, for scriptural quotations and allusions are in evidence throughout. In Mark 11–16 alone, for example, one scholar counted 57 scriptural quotations and approximately 160 allusions to scripture. This frequent appeal to the Hebrew scriptures demonstrates that first-century Christians sought warrant for and confirmation of their faith in Jesus as the Christ in what for them were the sacred writings. The God of the Torah, Prophets, and Psalms was for them the same God they experienced in the event of Jesus Christ.

Second, the interpreter should seek to understand the early Christians' appeal to the Hebrew scriptures and their interpretive patterns as part of a larger Jewish interpretive tradition called "midrash." As we have seen, the New Testament's use of the Hebrew scriptures shares most in common with the use of the scriptures in the Qumran writings. Both communities had an eschatological orientation and believed that God had acted decisively for Israel in their founding figures. All this allowed their interpreters to study the sacred writings to discover how the events in which their communities were involved fulfilled previous divinely given prophecy. In the case of the early Christians, it is this retrospective and christological orientation that provides the clue for the contemporary interpreter to make sense of why, for example, Luke can have Peter exegete Ps. 16 as he does in Acts 2:22ff. Although we might not judge midrashic methods appropriate for interpreting the Hebrew scriptures today, it is also not appropriate for us to judge the New Testament authors too harshly. Rather, we need to understand their interpretive methods and their reasons for applying them.

Selected Bibliography

Fitzmyer, Joseph A. 1960–61. "The Use of Explicit Old Testament Quotations in Qumran Literature and in the New Testament." *New Testament Studies* 7, 297–333. Fitzmyer discovers parallels between the Qumran and New Testament writings in the ways that both render quotations from the Hebrew scriptures.

Juel, Donald. 1988. *Messianic Exegesis: Christological Interpretation of the Old Testament in Early Christianity.* Philadelphia: Fortress Press. The second chapter on "Biblical Interpretation in the First Century C.E." is a helpful introduction to the subject.

Kugel, James L., and Rowan A. Greer. 1986. *Early Biblical Interpretation,* esp. 126–154. Philadelphia: Westminster Press. Note the helpful chapter on "Christian Transformations of the Hebrew Scriptures."

Lindars, Barnabas. 1961. *New Testament Apologetic.* London: SCM Press. This widely used book provides a detailed study of how the early church used the Hebrew scriptures in formulating its doctrinal understandings.

Neusner, Jacob. 1987. *What Is Midrash?* Philadelphia: Fortress Press. This offers a useful introduction to midrash, including examples of the various types of midrash.

Porton, Gary G. 1981. "Defining Midrash." In *The Study of Ancient Judaism,* Vol. 1. Edited by Jacob Neusner, 55–92. New York: KTAV. This oft-cited article provides definitional clarity about midrash.

HYMN

Definition of the Form

The Gospels include several hymns. The most obvious examples are the canticles in Luke 1–2: the song of Mary (1:46–55), the prophecy of Zechariah (1:68–79), the song of the angels (2:13–14), and the song of Simeon (2:29–32). The early church recognized the hymnic character of these Lukan segments and made liturgical use of them, designating them by their initial words in Latin—the Magnificat, the Benedictus, the Gloria in Excelsis, and the Nunc Dimittis. For this reason, most contemporary worshipers show little resistance to the scholarly conclusion that these canticles, with the possible exception of the song of the angels, were used among Jewish Christians prior to their incorporation in the Gospel of Luke (see Brown 1977, 346–355). Luke's use of them can be likened to a preacher including a well-known hymn in his or her sermon.

In addition to these most familiar hymns in the Gospels, two other passages should be mentioned. First, the Johannine prologue (John 1:1–18) has the character of a poetic hymn, exhibiting a "staircase" parallelism whereby a prominent word in one line then appears in the next line (see Brown 1966, 19). Second, a number of texts quote verses from the Hebrew psalms, but in particular Mark 11:9–10 and par., with its quotation of Ps. 118, represents in the narrative a song of praise as the pilgrims enter Jerusalem:

> Hosanna!
> Blessed is the one who comes in the name of the Lord!

Blessed is the coming kingdom of our ancestor David!
Hosanna in the highest heaven!

Although certain scholars draw attention to similarities between New Testament hymns and pagan hymns in the Hellenistic world (see Berger, 1149–1169), most agree that the Lukan
canticles are best understood in light of the psalms of praise in
the Hebrew tradition (Pss. 33, 47, 48, 113, 117, 135, 136). Hymns
in the Hebrew tradition exhibit the characteristics of poetry:
figurative language with vivid images and various patterns of
rhythm and repetition. Most characteristic in Hebrew poetry is
parallelism, the practice of paralleling a second line to reinforce
or reverse the meaning of the first line. Most often this involves
what is termed *synonymous parallelism* (a pattern in which a
second line imitates the structure of the first one while repeating
its content in different words), *antithetical parallelism* (a structural repetition in which the second line offers a contrasting
meaning to the first one), or *synthetic parallelism* (a pattern in
which the second line completes or expands the meaning of the
first one). For examples of these patterns and further explanation of Hebrew poetry, see *Poetry and Hymn* in the Pauline
Tradition section of this volume.

By focusing on the Lukan canticles, more can be determined
about their form. Claus Westermann (34–35) distinguishes between two types of psalms of praise: *declarative praise*, which
is more spontaneous and joyous and extols God for a specific and
recent act of deliverance (e.g., the Song of Miriam in Exod.
15:21), and *descriptive praise*, which is more exegetical and
speaks of God's being and action as a whole (e.g., Ps. 33). This
latter type is a development of the former.

In the New Testament, Westermann (115) cites Luke 1:68–75
as an example of "declarative praise of the people" and both
1:46–55 and 2:29–32 as examples of "declarative praise of the
individual." Though these Lukan canticles fit the pattern only in
general, each begins with the characteristic word of praise and
the reason for it:

My soul magnifies the Lord,
    and my spirit rejoices in God my Savior,
for (hoti) he has looked with favor on the
    lowliness of his servant. (1:47–48a)

> Blessed be the Lord God of Israel,
> *for* he has looked favorably on his people
> and redeemed them. (1:68)

> Master, now you are dismissing your servant in peace,
> according to your word;
> *for* my eyes have seen your salvation. (2:29–30)

A closer analysis of any of these Lukan canticles yields helpful insights for the interpreter. Robert Tannehill, in particular, has analyzed the rhetorical strategies at work in the Magnificat. For instance, he calls attention to the effect on the hearers of the hymn's use of repetition.

> The simple device of saying things twice involves a retardation of the forward movement of thought which gives place to deeper meaning, including the felt meanings which are important to our total humanness.(266)

For example, by means of the synonymous parallelism in Luke 1:47, the meaning of the first line ("My soul magnifies the Lord") is reinforced and even expanded by the second ("and my spirit rejoices in God *my Savior*"). Together these paralleled lines add force and import to its introductory statement of praise. When heard, these words gathered one up in the excitement of praising God. Luke 1:71, 72, and 79 in the Benedictus offer other examples of synonymous parallelism, each second line not merely repeating but enriching the meaning of the first.

In his analysis of the Magnificat, Tannehill (266–267) also speaks of the process of "coupling." Particular words in this poetic hymn interact for the hearer with other words. "Lowliness" in v. 48 initially strikes the hearer as being ambiguous, yet immediately v. 49a indicates that God has done "great things" for this lowly servant girl. Then in v. 52 there is a second reference to "lowly," but this time it is linked with "the powerful." Further, the Greek word for "the powerful" *(dynastas)* recalls the title for God in v. 49 *(ho dynatos)*, thus setting up "a basic triangular tension, with the humble, the mighty God, and the oppressive rulers of the world forming the three corners" (267). What is surprising about the triangle is that God is not aligned with the powerful as expected in the ancient world, but with the powerless.

Moreover, the form of vs. 52–53 mirrors the actual tension involved in the struggle between the powerful and the power-

less. These words form a chiastic structure (A B B′ A′) that
functions to set up an antithesis between the two groups, with
the powerful depicted as the rich and the lowly as the hungry
(see *Chiasm*).

God has brought down	the *powerful*	(A)	from their thrones,
and lifted up	the *lowly*	(B)	
God has filled	the *hungry*	(B′)	with good things,
and sent	the *rich*	(A′)	away empty.

Finally, it is worth noting that the song of Mary and the other
Lukan canticles echo traditional language used in Israel, thereby
awakening hearers to past meanings. For example, the song of
Mary recalls phrases from the song of Hannah in 1 Sam. 2:1–10
and motifs of Ps. 113. Both texts link the incomparability of God
with divine advocacy for the powerless, which can involve making the barren woman a mother (Brown 1977, 361, suggests that
Mary's virginity might have been viewed like Elizabeth's bar-
renness as an obstacle that God must overcome). Raymond
Brown has listed all the scriptural allusions in the Magnificat
(1977, 358–359), the Benedictus (1977, 386–389), and the Nunc
Dimittis (1977, 458).

The Value for Interpretation

Sensitivity to the poetic quality and structure of hymns can
lead the interpreter to investigate various features. With the
Magnificat as an example, it is possible to see how attention to
patterns of repetition, interaction of words, and use of traditional language all contribute to a deeper appreciation of the text
and its effect on hearers. Noting other features such as word
order, the subjects and objects of the clauses, and the tense and
voice of the verbs could produce further insights. It is striking,
for example, that in Luke 1:48–55, ten aorist active voice verbs
depict God as the one who has acted.

Because hymns use patterns of repetition known as parallelism, it is particularly important to ponder how words, lines, and
even segments of the text interact. For instance, the chiasm of
Luke 1:52–53 invites us to understand that "the powerful" are
"the rich," whereas "the lowly" (oppressed) are "the hungry."
An outline of the overall structure of the Magnificat might reveal
a larger repetitive pattern. Twice the Magnificat voices a *hoti*
clause that presents the reason for Mary's rejoicing, but what is
mentioned in v. 48a is expanded in vs. 49–53. God's action in

behalf of Mary, the lowly servant girl, becomes inextricably connected with God's reversal of the fortunes of the powerless and the powerful. Clearly, the repetition in the hymn invites hearers to understand more than the surface and conventional meanings of the words. Repetition offers second and even third opportunities to ponder and make connections.

In the Gospels, each hymn is placed in the narrative. The interpreter needs to think about this interplay between narrative prose and poetry. What is only hinted at in the narrative is often explicitly expressed in the poetic piece. In the Lukan narrative, for example, the Magnificat functions as a response to Elizabeth's greeting, which calls Mary "blessed." It is Mary's song, not the narration itself, that enunciates the revolutionary notion that her blessedness results from God's characteristic yet incredible action—God's intentional reversal of the plight of the powerful and that of the powerless. In general, it can be said, the Lukan canticles announce themes important to the rest of the Lukan Gospel. In a similar manner, the poetic hymn in John 1:1–18 functions to anticipate themes crucial to the fourth Gospel (e.g., the dialectic of light and darkness, life and death, and faith and unbelief).

Lastly, hymns use poetic language of worship. It is not a linguistic world of explanation but one of exaltation; not of practical reason, but of lament and praise. Even an interpreter only remotely aware of the potential of worship will appreciate the use of hymns by the church as a daring act of worship that shatters conventional patterns of viewing the world.

Selected Bibliography

Berger, Klaus. 1984. "Hellenistische Gattungen im Neuen Testament." In *Aufstieg und Niedergang der römischen Welt*, 1149–1169. II.25,2. Berlin & New York: Walter de Gruyter. Berger describes the structure and use of hymns in the Hellenistic world, noting their similarities to hymns in the New Testament.

Brown, Raymond E. 1966. *The Gospel According to John* (i–xii). Vol. 1, pp. 1–37. Garden City, N.Y.: Doubleday & Co. This section of the commentary treats the Johannine prologue as hymn.

———. 1977. *The Birth of the Messiah*, 339–479. Garden City, N.Y.: Doubleday & Co. These pages provide a detailed exegesis of the Lukan canticles.

Farris, Stephen. 1985. *The Hymns of Luke's Infancy Narratives. Journal for the Study of the New Testament.* Suppl. Series 9. Sheffield, Eng.: JSOT Press. Farris undertakes a detailed study of the origin, meaning, and significance of the Lukan hymns.

Horsley, Richard A. 1989. *The Liberation of Christmas: The Infancy Narratives in Social Context*, 107–123. New York: Crossroad. Horsley contends that serious attention to social context reveals the Lukan canticles to be "revolutionary songs of salvation," not simply "pious prayers."

Tannehill, Robert C. 1974. "The Magnificat as Poem." *Journal of Biblical Literature* 93, 263–275. This insightful article illuminates features of the rhetoric in the Magnificat.

Westermann, Claus. 1985. *Praise and Lament in the Psalms*, 15–35, 52–162. First translated by K. R. Crim and R. N. Soulen in 1965 from the 1961 German ed. Atlanta: John Knox Press. This important work, which describes praise and lament as the two major types of prayer in Israel, includes a discussion of declarative and descriptive praise.

SPEECH (ACTS)

Definition of the Form

Speeches play a prominent role in the book of Acts, an observation already made earlier this century by Henry Cadbury (1933, 402–427) and Martin Dibelius (138–185). According to Cadbury (1933, 402–403), speeches occupy about one-fifth of the Acts narrative and include twenty-four principal ones—eight attributed to Peter, two to James, one to Stephen, nine to Paul, and four to non-Christians.

Such attention to "speech" as well as "action" is not unusual in the ancient writing of history. Already in the fifth century B.C.E., a time when oratory was gaining importance in Athens, the historian Thucydides enhanced the artistic use of speeches in the writing of history. Often possessing few if any accurate sources of actual speeches, Thucydides and succeeding historians learned to fashion speeches that were "in character" with the speaker and appropriate to the narrative context. As rhetorical creations, these speeches functioned to convey the significance of the historical events under consideration. Ancient historians inserted speeches not only to enlighten the narrative and to make it more interesting for the readers, but also to achieve more specific aims. A speech might provide commentary on the event just related in the narrative, offer insight into the character of the speaker, or further the narrative action itself (Dibelius, 139–140).

Because scholars agree that the speeches in Acts clearly reflect the literary style and themes of Luke, much attention has been devoted to the function of the speeches in the narrative. The speeches are indispensable to the story itself; they give voice to Lukan proclamation of the gospel. Paul Schubert comments, "Without them the Book of Acts would be a torso consisting chiefly of a miscellany of episodes and summaries" (16).

The speeches in Acts vary considerably in content and form. Those in the early chapters are primarily evangelistic in character, whereas most in chs. 22–26 represent "defense speeches" of Paul.

According to Eduard Schweizer (208–216), the evangelistic speeches exhibit an identifiable pattern: direct address, appeal for attention, mention of a misunderstanding, initial scriptural quotation, witness to Jesus Christ, proof from scripture, announcement of salvation, and direct invitation to the audience to repent and believe. However, this common pattern is more detectable in the six speeches addressed to Jewish audiences (Acts 2:14ff.; 3:12ff.; 4:8ff.; 5:29ff.; 10:34ff.; 13:16ff.). The two speeches of Paul before Gentile audiences (Acts 14:14ff. and 17:22ff.) reveal one characteristic difference: the witness about Jesus Christ is replaced by a more general testimony to God's presence in creation (14:16–17 and 17:24–27 with the proof from scripture taken from the Greek poets in 17:28).

In more recent years, scholars have evaluated speeches in the New Testament to determine if some or all fit the rhetorical patterns developed and employed in the Greco-Roman world. By the first century C.E., three types of rhetorical strategy for speeches were well established: judicial, deliberative, and epideictic (for a full explanation of Hellenistic rhetoric, see *Forms of Argumentation*).

One of the evangelistic speeches noted by Schweizer, Paul's speech in Pisidian Antioch in Acts 13:16–41, can serve as an example. Clifton Black (8–11) has advanced the brief analysis of George Kennedy (124–125) to show how this speech conforms to the rhetorical pattern of exordium, narration, proposition, proof, and epilogue. Paul's initial words in 13:16b constitute the *exor-*

dium ("You Israelites, and others who fear God, listen"), the introductory section that Schweizer (210) divides into "direct address" and "appeal for attention." Paul's speech immediately offers a recital of God's salvific acts in Israel's history as the *narration* (13:17–25), that is, as the background needed to prepare the audience to make a judgment about what follows. Black then labels 13:26b as the *proposition* (". . . to us the message of this salvation has been sent"), the major point in the speech that asserts the present relevance of that salvific activity of God. Acts 13:27–37 then follows with the *proof* of this assertion by demonstrating "that the significance of Jesus, formerly ignored by the inhabitants of Jerusalem and their rulers, has been vindicated by the resurrection and corroborated by Scripture" (Black, 9). It is at this point that Black (9) amplifies Kennedy's brief suggestion by contending that the proof in 13:27–37 employs four types of a priori "probabilities" recognized by the classical rhetoricians: (1) things perceived by the senses—the risen Jesus seen by reliable witnesses (13:30–31); (2) matters about which there is general agreement—the power of God to fulfill promises (13:32–33, 37); (3) matters that are confirmed by law—the fulfillment of scripture (13:27, 29, 33–35); (4) matters relating to the issue that would be conceded by all parties involved—the innocence of Jesus and his sentencing by Pilate (13:28) and the death and burial of both Jesus and David (13:29, 36). Finally, 13:38–41 comprises the *epilogue*, which includes an attempt to gain the sympathy of the hearers and their opposition to scoffers of the gospel (13:38, 41), a focus on the principal reality that involves the forgiveness of sins (13:38), a summary of the basic argument (13:38b–39), and an evocation of the hearers' emotions (13:40–41).

Thus the study of Acts 13:16–41 according to the canons of classical rhetoric adds precision to Schweizer's description by disclosing a pattern of argumentation. Opinions differ, however, on the type of speech represented by 13:16–41. Black classifies it as either judicial or deliberative, whereas Kennedy suggests that it is epideictic. Most of the evangelistic speeches should fit the deliberative categories of rhetoric because they are urging the hearers to future decision and action. All this suggests that these distinctions may sometimes be hard to apply to New Testament material.

As already noted, the speeches in chs. 22–26 relate to the trial of Paul and best correspond to judicial rhetoric. Judicial speech has two subtypes: accusation and defense, and Paul's speeches in these late chapters represent the latter (Acts 22:1–21; 23:1, 6; 24:10–21; 26:2–23), though not fully, as David Aune notes (126). On the basis of an extensive sample in Greco-Roman literature, Fred Veltman (251–253) lists the following elements as frequently appearing in the "defense speech":

1. Opening narrative framework: trial scene is described, charges are mentioned, defendant is described, speech is identified as an apology, and defendant speaks on his own initiative.
2. Introduction of the defense speech: uses term of address, and speech is identified as an apology.
3. Body of the defense speech: opens with mention/refutation of charges, clearly treats the charges, asks rhetorical questions, and claims innocence.
4. Conclusion of the defense speech: uses term of address, claims innocence; speech is sometimes interrupted.
5. Closing narrative framework: trial scene is described and verdict revealed.

After comparing three episodes in Acts (21:27–22:29; 24:1–23; 25:23–26:32), Veltman concludes that the elements in the narrative framework as well as in the introduction and body of the Pauline speeches correspond to the "defense speech" model. On the other hand, the conclusions cannot be compared because the speeches in Acts are usually interrupted before completed.

In a separate study, Jerome Neyrey (210–224) notes how the opening words of these speeches (part of the exordium) function to win the audience to Paul's side by vouching for his own character or ethos (22:3 and 26:5—reared in Jerusalem and educated by Gamaliel; 26:5—lived as a Pharisee; 22:5 and 26:9–12—acted as a zealous Jew authorized by the Jewish authorities in Jerusalem; 22:7–8 and 26:14–15—experienced a definite change of view and met hostility because of it).

Neyrey also detects in the Acts speeches another element of the traditional defense rhetoric. The defendant characteristically attempts to establish before the judges what is actually at issue. For Paul, this involves the resurrection rather than the charges brought against him (see 23:6; 24:20–21; 26:6–8). Neyrey suggests that the proofs enumerated by Paul to support this main contention correspond to those types of proof considered convincing in a defense speech: that of "witness" (22:15 and 26:16), that of "irrefutable and necessary proof" in his Damascus experience of the risen Lord (22:6–10 and 26:12–18), that of "confirmatory evidence" in signs (22:6, 9, 11, 13; 26:13), and that of "corroborating witnesses" (22:5, 12–15; 26:5, 12–13).

The Value for Interpretation

Awareness of the rhetorical and literary conventions that likely influenced the author of Acts helps exegetes interpret the speeches more adequately. It reminds modern interpreters of the import ancient historians assigned to speech in the narrative. For them, speech was the natural complement to action (Dibelius, 139) and possessed wide-ranging potential to reveal why people act as they do. It explained the speaker's actions, interpreted a complex of events, or foreshadowed coming events. No matter how speeches functioned for an author in the narrative, they were invariably used to address the hearers directly as a means to motivate their actions or shape their beliefs.

When considering conventions, it is critical to appreciate the difference between ancient and modern views toward the use of speech in the writing of history. Because we have the technology to reproduce verbatim recordings, we in the modern world highly prize factual accuracy in reporting celebrated speeches. We often fail to recognize that quite a different set of factors were at work in the ancient world. It was then commonly understood that the historian was free to exercise his imagination, not only in creating speeches for prominent historical figures, but also in employing these speeches to weave together themes disclosing the deeper significance of the historical events. Thus, although we cannot judge the factual veracity of the speeches in Acts, knowledge of the function and form of speeches in antiquity can alert us to the larger, recurring themes that the Acts speeches convey. These speeches communicate the message about Jesus as the Word of God and present the events as unfolding according to the divine purpose of God.

The recognition among scholars that the author of Luke-Acts knew and used literary conventions practiced by ancient Greco-Roman biographers and historians also allows interpreters to determine more precisely how ancient rhetoric informed and shaped at least some of the speeches in Acts. The obvious advantage of such study is that they come to understand the argument of a specific speech more precisely.

Finally, as with every form, interpretation is enriched when investigators carefully study not only the form of the speech but also its interplay with its narrative context. For this reason, it is also important to examine closely the narrative framework for each speech. These crafted speeches in Acts become articulated responses to conflicts and activities in the narrative. They set into motion a new course of events, often precipitating negative as well as positive reactions from the parties who carry the narrative action. But above all, in Acts the speeches make clear that divine action drives the plot.

Additional Examples

In addition to the speeches in Acts mentioned above, see Acts 1:16–22; 7:2–53; 11:5–17; 15:7–11; 15:13–21; 24:2–8; 25:14–21; 25:24–27; 28:17–20; 28:25–28. Moreover, there are major sections of sayings in the Synoptics presented as extended speeches of Jesus (Luke 6:20–49; Matt. 5:3–7:27; 10:5–42; 23:1–39), yet their use of traditional sayings-material would necessitate a somewhat different type of analysis from that used for the speeches in Acts.

Selected Bibliography

Aune, David E. 1987. *The New Testament in Its Literary Environment*, 91–93, 124–128. Philadelphia: Westminster Press. These sections describe Luke's use of speeches in Acts.

Black, C. Clifton, II. 1988. "The Rhetorical Form of the Hellenistic Jewish and Early Christian Sermon: A Response to Lawrence Wills." *Harvard Theological Review* 81, 1–18. This carefully reasoned article applies ancient rhetoric to certain speeches in the New Testament.

Cadbury, Henry J. 1933. "The Speeches in Acts." In *The Beginning of Christianity*. Pt. 1, 402–427. London: Macmillan & Co.
———. 1958. "Speeches, Letters and Canticles." In *The Making of Luke-Acts*, 184–193. London: SPCK.
    Cadbury's foundational studies of Luke-Acts demonstrate how the evangelist's literary style and purpose influenced the speeches.

Dibelius, Martin. 1956. "The Speeches in Acts and Ancient Historiography." In *Studies in the Acts of the Apostles*, edited by H. Greeven, 138–185. New York: Charles Scribner's Sons. This essay was most influential in leading scholars to see the affinities between the speeches in ancient historiography and the book of Acts.

Kennedy, George A. 1984. *New Testament Interpretation Through Rhetorical Criticism*, 114–140. Chapel Hill: University of North Carolina Press. Kennedy offers a suggestive analysis of the speeches in Acts in light of Greco-Roman rhetoric.

Neyrey, Jerome H. 1984. "The Forensic Defense Speech and Paul's Trial Speeches in Acts 22–26: Form and Function." In *Luke-Acts*, edited by C. H. Talbert, 210–224. New York: Crossroad. This article examines Paul's speeches as traditional defense speeches.

Schubert, Paul. 1968. "The Final Cycle of Speeches in the Book of Acts." *Journal of Biblical Literature* 87, 1–16. Schubert investigates how the speeches serve the theological themes in Acts.

Schweizer, Eduard. 1966. "Concerning the Speeches in Acts." In *Studies in Luke-Acts*, edited by L. E. Keck and J. L. Martyn, 208–216. Nashville and New York: Abingdon Press. This article analyzes the missionary speeches in Acts.

Veltman, Fred. 1978. "The Defense Speeches of Paul in Acts." In *Perspectives on Luke-Acts*, edited by C. H. Talbert, 243–256. Edinburgh: T. & T. Clark. Veltman compares Acts speeches to a "defense speech" model.

JOHANNINE DISCOURSE

Definition of the Form

The speech attributed to Jesus in the fourth Gospel exhibits a character and tone far different from the terse sayings and parables of Jesus in the Synoptics. Even though Jesus' sayings in the Synoptics sometimes comprise longer discourse segments, as in Matt. 23 or Mark 13, these consist essentially of smaller saying units that are pieced together. In contrast, Johannine discourse sections display a more sustained and unified character, presenting extended dialogues and monologues as literary wholes. Moreover, because the speech in John reveals a speaker explicitly aware of his divine nature and mission, most scholars agree that this discourse, cast as the revelatory speech of Jesus as the divine Son, reflects the confessional and homiletical language of the Johannine community. The history of this community probably involved a long and painful struggle over how Jesus was to be understood and confessed, not only among groups within its circle but, beyond itself, with Jews who viewed the community's confession of Jesus as blasphemy.

Because the Johannine Jesus speaks as the divine Revealer, his discourse assumes a somewhat different content from the speech of Jesus in the Synoptics. In the Synoptics, for example, Jesus engages in realistically depicted debates and exchanges with individuals and groups concerning matters of the Torah and ethics. Jesus' discourse in John, on the other hand, predictably concentrates on christological and faith issues: who Jesus is as the one sent from the Father and what it means to believe in him as the divine Son. It is for this reason that the speech of the Johannine Jesus characteristically involves double meaning and irony, features that prompt misunderstanding or puzzlement on the part of Jesus' questioners (John 2:20; 3:3–4; 4:10–12; 4:32–33; 6:32–34; 7:33–36). For John, it is fundamentally ironic that the divine Word (*ho logos*) appears as the incarnate one. Throughout the Johannine narrative, Jesus as the incarnate one engages individuals and groups in dialogue (e.g., Nicodemus, the Samaritan woman, the disciples, the Pharisees, the Jews), yet they seem to comprehend, at least at first, only the surface meaning of his words. As the dialogue proceeds, sometimes changing into a monologue, the alternative and more profound significance of Jesus' words is disclosed. John's hearers and readers are to grasp this divinely revealed meaning.

The first story to illustrate this pattern is Jesus' exchange with Nicodemus in John 3:1–21. It can be outlined in the following way:

vs. 1–2a: Nicodemus is introduced and the scene established.

v. 2b: Nicodemus's statement indicates the dialogue: "Rabbi, we know that you are a teacher who has come from God; for no one can do these signs that you do apart from the presence of God."

v. 3: Jesus offers a somewhat puzzling answer: "*Very truly, I tell you,* no one can see the kingdom of God without being born from above."

v. 4: Nicodemus responds with a double question: "How can anyone be born after having grown old? Can one enter a second time into the mother's womb and be born?"

vs. 5–8: Jesus next proffers a more elaborate answer in which he links "being born from above" with the Spirit: "*Very truly, I tell you,* no one can enter the kingdom of God

without being born of water and Spirit. . . . So it is with
everyone who is born of the Spirit."

v. 9: Nicodemus poses yet another question: "How can these
things be?"

vs. 10–21: Jesus' final answer develops into a lengthy monologue that becomes explicitly christological and calls for
belief in himself as God's only Son: *"Very truly, I tell you,
we speak of what we know and testify to what we have
seen. . . ."*

This first example of Johannine discourse has a discernible
design. It involves a question and answer form similar to certain
Hellenistic literature (e.g., Corpus Hermeticum). In this dramatic dialogue, Nicodemus speaks three times (vs. 2b, 4, 9), the
last two being explicit questions and the first being treated as an
implicit one. Each time Jesus' answer begins with the solemn
phrase "Very truly, I tell you" *(Amēn, amēn, legō soi)*; moreover, the answers become progressively longer (in Greek, first
there are 16 words and then 70 words and finally 221 words).
Clearly, Jesus' discourse dominates the conversation with Nicodemus and moves toward monologue; Nicodemus's questions
act primarily as prompters for the next segment of Jesus' extended speech. Nicodemus asks questions, and Jesus as the Revealer offers answers that possess the character of divine
revelation.

Another finding seems relevant to what has thus far been
demonstrated. According to J. P. Louw (10), a close investigation of the syntax of discourse sections in John reveals that the
Greek phrases typically tend to lengthen as a specific discourse
unfolds. This observation fits what has already been noted; that
is, that in John the discourse of Jesus is noticeably stretched from
short to far more extended and elaborated segments of speech.
Moreover, as the syntax and speech lengthen in the Johannine
discourse, Jesus' words become more self-revealing and theologically profound.

Because the Johannine Jesus speaks as the Son who is sent
from God and who is aware of all things, it is not surprising that
his message is symbolic and polyvalent, operating at more than
one level. Indeed, there is a variety of ways Jesus' speech,
though deceptively simple in vocabulary, plays with levels of
meaning. For instance, his words make frequent use of ambiguity, double meaning, and irony. Because of this subtle and sup-
ple use of language, Jesus' interlocutors in dialogue constantly

appear confused, often misunderstanding what Jesus means. It is often this very misunderstanding that propels the Johannine discourse forward.

The Nicodemus dialogue in John 3 provides an illustration of these techniques. In his first response to Nicodemus (3:3b—"no one can see the kingdom of God without being born *from above*"), Jesus employs the word *anōthen*, which is ambiguous and has a double meaning—either "again" or "from above." Nicodemus's questions in 3:4 assume that Jesus is talking about a second physical birth rather than a spiritual birth "from above." It is this misunderstanding that causes Jesus to explain more in vs. 5–8. Then another uncomprehending question in v. 9 prompts an ironic question from Jesus in v. 10 ("Are you a teacher of Israel, and yet you do not understand these things?") and further revelation in vs. 11ff. The irony surrounds the fact that Nicodemus, who had come at night, is still "in the dark," and that Nicodemus, who is a leader and teacher of Israel, fails to understand Jesus' words even after several revealing pronouncements (Duke, 45–46).

A variation of the above pattern begins with a healing story, which itself contains dialogue, and then issues into a dialogue that subsequently gives way to a monologue by Jesus. Often this is followed by an epilogue offering a recapitulation of the leading ideas of the section. C. H. Dodd comments on the interpretive significance of this interlacing of narrated story and Jesus' discourse:

> The incidents narrated receive an interpretation of their evangelical significance in the discourse; or, to put it otherwise, the truths enunciated in the discourses are given dramatic expression in the actions described. Act and word are one. . . ." (384)

John 4:46–5:47 offers an example of this pattern. Two stories (4:46–54 and 5:1–9a) begin the Johannine sequence; the charge regarding the illegal character of the sabbath healing precipitates a dialogue between Jesus and the Jews (5:10–13). After a transitional section (5:14–18), Jesus pursues uninterrupted speech (5:19–47). Here again, although the entire discourse was launched out of a healing story, Johannine dialogue changes to monologue.

A variation of this pattern unfolds in ch. 6. Here the stories of the feeding miracle (6:1–14) and of Jesus' appearance on the water (6:16–21) prompt a dialogue between Jesus and the people who chase after him (6:25ff.). This dialogue then changes imperceptibly, from an exchange between Jesus and Jews who object to what he is saying to a conversation between Jesus and his disciples. In this chapter-long dialogue, the extent of Jesus' separate speeches tends to increase and then decrease.

Finally, it is important to note that Jesus' revelatory discourse in the Gospel of John contains "oracles of self-commendation." This type of pronouncement normally begins with the phrase "I am" and is used by a speaker to legitimate himself or herself as a divine spokesperson. David Aune (70–72) cites examples of the oracle of self-commendation in the pagan world (e.g., "I am the new Asklepios"), but he also notes its appearances in the Gospels. Clearly, the fourth Gospel develops most fully this "I am" revelatory speech, often incorporating these declarations into Jesus' more extended discourse (e.g., during the dialogue in ch. 6 Jesus announces in 6:35, "I am the bread of life"). In John, Jesus' "I am" sayings sometimes occur with no predicate (6:20; 8:24; 8:58; 13:19; 18:5), but they also appear with a predicate nominative (8:12; 10:7, 9; 10:11, 14; 11:25; 14:6; 15:1, 5). In every instance, the "I am" revelations suit the character of Jesus' speech in the fourth Gospel, as he repeatedly discloses his divine identity and mission (see Brown, 533–538).

The Value for Interpretation

First, it is important for interpreters to recognize that the Johannine Jesus speaks in a manner quite different from that of the Jesus of the Synoptics. In contrast to the Synoptics' brief and crisp sayings of Jesus, the Johannine discourse presents Jesus' words as extended speech and as transparently revelatory of the community's hard-earned confessional understandings of Jesus as the divine Son. Realizing this fact, interpreters should approach Johannine discourse and narration as embodying rich theological and christological meaning resulting from concrete struggles in the life of the Johannine community. The Johannine Gospel offers far more profound levels of truth than simply a historically factual one.

As a related point, it needs to be stressed that the oratorical style of the Johannine Jesus is that of a revealer. In many respects, he is an alien figure who, when he speaks, constantly probes beyond surface meanings to the more profound significance latent in words. Because of this, it is important for interpreters to trace with care the development of Jesus' speech in John, analyzing his rhetorical moves both in the dialogues and monologues. This involves both examining the quantity and character of Jesus' speech, and also noting how the questions and statements of his dialogue partners play their part in a particular discourse.

Finally, interpreters should be sensitive to the nuanced ways in which the Johannine Jesus uses language. In John, Jesus' words do not always mean what they first appear to mean. His words confront and challenge; they can surprise and be offensive; they often flirt with double meaning; they explore and expand symbolic significance; and they create irony leading the readers of the Gospel to assume that they understand what characters in the narrative do not. Preachers today do well if they allow the Johannine language to be ironic and puzzling as its way of revealing more deeply the significance of Jesus as "the way, and the truth, and the life" (John 14:6).

Additional Examples

John 3:22–36; 4:7–42; 7:1ff.; 8:12–59; 9:1–41; 10:1–21; 10:22–39; 12:20–36; 13:1–17:26 (the farewell discourses).

Selected Bibliography

Aune, David E. 1983. *Prophecy in Early Christianity and the Ancient Mediterranean World,* 70–72. Grand Rapids: Wm. B. Eerdmans. These pages explain the "oracle of self-commendation."

Brown, Raymond E. 1966. *The Gospel According to John* (i–xii). Vol. 1. Garden City, N.Y.: Doubleday & Co. This commentary offers helpful outlines and explanations of the discourses.

Dodd, C. H. 1953. *The Interpretation of the Fourth Gospel,* 297–423. Cambridge: Cambridge University Press. Dodd analyzes the interplay between narrated episodes and discourse in John.

Duke, Paul D. 1985. *Irony in the Fourth Gospel.* Atlanta: John Knox Press. This book is an intriguing study of the multiple uses of irony and misunderstanding in John.

Louw, J. P. 1986. "On Johannine Style." *Neotestamentica* 20, 5–12. Louw analyzes John's use of synonyms, contrasting meanings, and features of the discourse sections.

O'Day, Gail R. 1987. *The Word Disclosed.* St. Louis: CBP Press. As an aid for preachers, O'Day investigates five Johannine texts (3:1–15;

4:4–42; 9:1–41; 11:1–53; 20:1–18) with a keen sensitivity to their use of language and dialogue.

CHIASM

Definition of the Form

Chiasm is a literary form that appears frequently throughout the Bible. Sometimes known by other names, such as "introverted parallelism" or "concentric pattern", "chiasm"—taken from the design of the Greek *Chi* (X)—is normally the term used to designate this rhetorical pattern. Nils Lund, who published the first comprehensive study of chiasm, defined it as "a literary figure, or principle, which consists of 'a placing crosswise' of words in a sentence. The term is used in rhetoric to designate an inversion of the order of words or phrases which are repeated or subsequently referred to in the sentence" (31). An even simpler definition describes chiasm as "a stylistic literary figure which consists of a series of two or more elements followed by a presentation of corresponding elements in reverse order" (Man, 146).

A chiastic form can appear in poetry or prose and can include a single verse, an entire passage, or a more extended section. In a short sentence, a chiasm normally has four terms or members wherein the first is paralleled by the fourth and the second by the third (A B B′ A′). Certain sayings of Jesus show this chiastic design. Mark 2:27 is one example:

> The *sabbath* (A) was made for *humankind* (B),
> and not *humankind* (B′) for the *sabbath* (A′).

Chiasms as single verses can be readily recognized, but more complex ones are less apparent to most readers or hearers because the chiastic structure is often dependent on similarities in content as well as in language and form. For example, Mark 2:27, quoted above, uses two key words (in Greek, *to sabbaton* and *ho anthrōpos*) and an inverted order to fashion its chiasm. Matthew 7:6, another oft-cited example, is a verse whose chiastic form depends somewhat on content in addition to key words and form:

A   Do not give what is holy to dogs;
   B   and do not throw your pearls before swine,

B′   or they will trample them under foot
A′   and turn and maul you [tear you into pieces].

Here the inverted parallelism makes clear that line B′ is describing the destructive action of swine, whereas A′ is depicting the vicious behavior of dogs. In this case, it is the content of the final two lines, not just key words, that mirrors the earlier two lines.

Although interpreters would undoubtedly agree that Matt. 7:6 is a chiasm, they might not always agree when it comes to extended passages because it is often one's assessment of content that determines whether or not one finds a chiastic pattern. For example, not all interpreters would agree with Ronald Man (149–150), who has discovered the following chiastic design in Luke 1:6–25:

A   Godliness of Zechariah and Elizabeth (v. 6).
  B   Elizabeth barren (v. 7).
    C   Zechariah's priestly service (v. 8).
      D   Zechariah enters the Temple (v. 9).
        E   The people outside (v. 10).
          F   Angel standing (*hestōs*) (v. 11).
            G   Zechariah's fear (v. 12).
              H   The Annunciation (vs. 13–17).
            G   Zechariah's doubt (v. 18).
          F′   Angel who stands (*parestēkōs*) (vs. 19–20).
        E′   The people outside (v. 21).
      D′   Zechariah exits from the Temple (v. 22).
    C′   Zechariah's priestly service (v. 23).
  B′   Elizabeth pregnant (v. 24).
A′   God's favor on Elizabeth (and Zechariah) (v. 25).

If Luke 1:6–25 was deliberately fashioned by Luke (or perhaps someone before him who shaped the birth narrative) as a chiasm, then the balanced form of the text not only pleases aesthetically but also directs attention to the Annunciation as the central event of the story. Thus the chiastic design of an entire passage illustrates the critical characteristics of *balance* and *inversion* as well as focuses on the *central verse or verses* as the important turning point in the events.

John Welch (238) provides another good example of the fact that recognizing the center of the chiasm provides a key to interpreting the text (in this case, Matt. 13:24–30):

A   A man sowed good seed in his field (v. 24).
  B   The enemy comes and sows tares (v. 25).
    C   *Crisis:* Bad fruit is discovered among the good
          and the servants doubt the master (vs. 26–27).
  B' The enemy is exposed and the tares left to grow (vs. 28–29).
A' The good seed is ultimately harvested safely (v. 30).

In light of this chiastic design, the central crisis in this parable is
not the master's decision to allow the weeds and the wheat to
grow side by side, but rather the servants' doubt of the master.

Interpreters have detected chiastic arrangements in groups of
texts as well. Joanna Dewey has argued for such an arrangement
for the controversy stories in Mark 2:1–3:6. She suggests the
following concentric and chiastic pattern, wherein A' parallels
A, B' parallels B, and C stands as the centerpiece in the middle.
Listed with each text are most of the similarities mentioned by
Dewey.

A   *2:1–12 Healing of the Paralytic*
  Setting: Indoors (in a house).
  Pattern: Miracle initiated–debate–miracle completed.
            Counter question used (2:9).
            Opponents do not openly state opposition.
            Observer reaction positive (2:12).
  Catchwords: *kai eiselthōn palin eis* (2:1).
            legei tō paralytikō (2:5, 10).
            kardia (2:6, 8).
  B   *2:13–17 Call of Levi/Eating with Sinners*
    Setting: Outdoors (beside the sea).
            Jesus enters house of Levi.
    Pattern: Action–objection–vindication.
            No miracle.
            Closes with proverb (2:17).
            Emphasis on eating.
    Catchwords: *esthiō* (2:16).
            chreian echō (2:17).
    Theology: Implied Christology.
    C   *2:18–22 Question of Fasting and of the Old and New*
      Setting: None.
      Pattern: Divides into two parts (not three).
              No miracle.
              Opponents not specified.
      Theology: Contrast time before and after
              Jesus' death.

B′   2:23–28 *Plucking Grain on the Sabbath*
Setting: Outdoors (in the fields).
David enters the house of God.
Pattern: Action–objection–vindication.
No miracle.
Closes with proverb (2:27).
Emphasis on eating.
Catchwords: *esthiō* (2:26).
chreian echō (2:25).
Theology: Explicit Christology
A′   3:1–6 *Healing on the Sabbath*
Setting: Indoors (in the synagogue).
Pattern: Miracle initiated–debate–miracle completed.
Counterquestion (3:4).
Opponents do not openly state opposition.
Observer reaction negative (3:6).
Catchwords: *eisēlthen palin eis* (3:1).
legei tō anthrōpō (3:3, 5).
kardia (3:5).

Dewey bases her analysis of the chiastic design on paralleling patterns and details of content, form, and word repetition. Recognition of this concentric pattern in Mark 2:1–3:6, Dewey contends, helps the interpreter understand both the individual elements in the stories and the larger themes developed in the entire section. The symmetry of the stories, for example, illumines two themes: healing–eating–eating–healing (A B B′ A′), activities of Jesus that become major contentions with his opponents; and the death versus life reflected in A C A′. In Mark 2:18–22, the center of the chiastic structure, Jesus speaks of his own death and the new life already present, thus providing the focal point in contrast to the opponents' threat of death (especially in 3:6).

The Value for Interpretation

As we have seen, a single verse, an entire passage, or even a series of stories can exhibit a chiastic design. Some interpreters have proposed a chiastic structure for an entire gospel, for example, Matthew. Although the chiasm of a single verse is best described as a rhetorical device, chiasm used in longer passages can properly be judged a literary form, because an author has to develop an extended pattern of paralleled and inverted elements, often with a deliberate focus on the central segment (e.g., A B C B′ A′).

Detection of chiastic patterns in single verses and especially in longer segments facilitates better interpretation of texts. It is important, then, that the interpreter first give close attention to the wording and structure of texts as well the arrangement of texts in larger sections. This is best done by lining out the text by semantic units in Greek, which allows the interpreter to discover the symmetry and inverted pattern of the text or texts. Often the chiasm is not apparent in the English translation (e.g., John 17:1–5; see Man, 150f.).

Awareness of the chiastic form of verses or texts aids interpretation, as has already been illustrated. The interpreter often discovers meaning by noting the interplay of the balanced elements (e.g., A and A′) and the mechanism of inversion at work at the pivotal point of the chiasm. Often, though not always, the verse or passage at the center of the chiastic pattern receives the stress or offers a theme key to the whole.

Chiasms offer us a glimpse into the patterns of thought of ancients. Relatively unconcerned about a linear and logical flow of ideas, biblical communities relished sayings and stories that were memorable, and they thus appreciated repetition that we might consider redundant. Much more in accord with the needs of oral communication, as Welch (12) reminds us, chiasms and chiastic patterns of stories served both pedagogical and liturgical purposes. A chiasm like Mark 2:27 or Matt. 7:6 could be remembered by hearers and subsequently pondered; a more extended chiastic design could provide the structure for recalling a longer sequence of verses or stories. In a worship setting, separate groups in the choir or congregation could recite the contrasting parts. So, for ancients the chiasm was not only aesthetically valued but also practically functional. In an increasingly "postliterary" environment, it might be critically important for us in the church to become more sensitive to the rhetorical dynamics of the chiastic form and its implications for our actual practice in worship and scriptural transmission.

Additional Examples

Angelico Di Marco (1976, 37–85, and 1979, 3–7) provides a nearly exhaustive list of chiasms in the Gospels and Acts. The following is a limited selection for each book: Matt. 3:14; 3:8–10; 5:43–47; 6:9–13; 10:28; 11:4–5; 17:25–26; 23:16–22.

Mark 1:19–20; 2:14–16; 8:27–10:52; 13:28–36. Luke 4:16–21a; 6:44; 8:40–56; 16:25; 23:2–25. John 1:1–18; 5:19–30; 8:31–41; 13:1–35; chs. 15–17. Acts 1:4–8; chs. 3–28; 11:19–15:40; 20:18–35; 28:26–27.

Selected Bibliography

Dewey, Joanna. 1980. *Markan Public Debate,* 109–130. SBL Dissertation Series No. 48. Chico, Calif.: Scholars Press. Mark 2:1–3:6 and other Markan units are interpreted as chiastic patterns.

Lund, Nils Wilhelm. 1942. *Chiasmus in the New Testament: A Study in Form Geschichte.* Chapel Hill: University of North Carolina Press. This is the earliest study devoted exclusively to the study of the chiasm.

Di Marco, Angelico. 1976. "Der Chiasmus in der Bibel" (3. Teil). *Linguistica Biblica* 39, 37–85.
———. 1979. "Der Chiasmus in der Bibel" (4. Teil). *Linguistica Biblica* 44, 3–7.
These articles provide extensive lists of chiasms in the New Testament.

Man, Ronald E. 1984. "The Value of Chiasm for New Testament Interpretation." *Bibliotheca Sacra* 141, 146–157. This article, which discusses the characteristics of the chiasm, suggests ways in which knowledge of the form enriches interpretation.

Talbert, Charles H. 1970. "Artistry and Theology: An Analysis of the Architecture of Jn. 1,19–5,47." *Catholic Biblical Quarterly* 32, 341–366. This article analyzes the chiastic pattern of John 1:19–5:47, suggesting its implications for the theological meaning of the section.

Welch, John W. 1981. *Chiasmus in Antiquity.* Hildersheim: Gerstenberg Verlag. The Introduction and the chapter "Chiasmus in the New Testament" are both directly pertinent.

GENEALOGY

Definition of the Form

In its simplest form, a genealogy involves a list or narrative that traces a line of descent from an ancestor or ancestors for a person or group. Without exception, genealogies in the Bible are patrilineal. They vary in scope, from only a few generations (Gen. 19:36–38) to numerous generations (Luke 3:23–38), and follow either a *linear* pattern, which records descent through two or more generations, or a *segmented* (branched) one, which lists two or more lines of descent for the key figure in the genealogy. For example, Gen. 11:10–26 is a linear genealogy (except for the last generation that is segmented) in narrative form, whereas Gen. 36:20–28 contains a segmented genealogy in list form.

Genealogies served important purposes for people in biblical times. Some functioned to establish kinship, yet at the same time conferred distinction between Israel and its neighbors while nevertheless linking both to a common ancestor (Gen. 19:36–38; Gen. 25:1–6; Gen. 25:12–16; Gen. 36). Genesis 10 sets the Israelites in the panorama of all the nations of the earth. In addition, in the postexilic period, genealogies were largely used to prove purity and preserve ethnic homogeneity of the Jewish people in Jerusalem (Ezra 2:1–63; Neh. 7:6–65). Some scholars, however, argue that the book of Ruth, with its genealogy in the final verses, provides a protest against the harsh decrees of Ezra and Nehemiah, which required all Hebrew men to divorce foreign wives. The Ruth genealogy (4:18–22) points out the irony of postexilic Hebrews' proudly claiming David as their heralded ancestor and king, when the great grandmother of David himself was a foreigner. Nonetheless, during Hellenistic times, when Jews continued to face an alien culture and the threat of assimilation, the concern for genealogical purity became even more pronounced, especially among the priestly families. Josephus's words make this clear:

> They took precautions to ensure that the priests' lineage should be kept unadulterated and pure. A member of the priestly order must, to beget a family, marry a woman of his own race, without regard to her wealth or other distinctions; but he must investigate her pedigree, obtaining the genealogy from the archives and producing a number of witnesses. (*Against Apion* I, 30–32)

In the first century C.E. itself, the entire Palestinian Jewish society seems to have assumed a genealogical character; all persons and groups were evaluated according to purity criteria (see Jeremias, 271–274). This same concern for genealogical purity is evident among the rabbis. The rabbis also speculated about the precise ancestry of the expected messiah (Johnson, 85–138). Because of the difficulty in dating rabbinic material, it is uncertain how much of this messianic speculation was current in the first century. Nonetheless, certain texts at Qumran, Psalms of Solomon, and Christian writings themselves suggest that debate about the messiah's origins cannot be ruled out.

Two genealogies appear in the Gospels (Matt. 1:1–17 and Luke 3:23–38). Each in a different way makes claims about the ancestry of Jesus as the messiah. The only other references to genealogies in the New Testament occur in 1 Tim. 1:4 and Titus 3:9, where Christians are exhorted to avoid "genealogies" as dangerous to their faith. Perhaps certain Christians were being attracted to the genealogical speculations of gnostic-type groups.

The Value for Interpretation

Knowledge of the language and form of genealogies proves useful in determining a biblical author's purpose for including a specific genealogy in the narrative. In the case of Matt. 1:1–17 and Luke 3:23–38, understanding is also furthered by simply comparing the design of these two genealogies of Jesus.

First, it is revealing to see how Matt. 1:1–17 and Luke 3:23–38 actually develop the form. Both genealogies employ the *list* type in a *linear* pattern; both span a large number of generations, forty-two included in Matthew and seventy-seven in Luke. Yet the two lists move in opposite directions: Matthew begins with Abraham and ends with Jesus, whereas Luke starts with Jesus and traces his ancestry back to Adam, who is designated "son of God." Luke expresses this ascending order, a form more widespread in the Hellenistic period (Kurz, 169–170), by introducing Jesus as the "son of Joseph" and then simply adding the genitive form of the article before the name of each succeeding ancestor. Matthew constructs a descending order by using a past tense of the verb "to beget" or "to father": "A fathered B, B fathered C, C fathered D," and so on. Furthermore, the two lists are not identical where they overlap. Unlike Matthew, Luke does not trace Jesus' Davidic descent by way of Solomon and the royal line; instead, he traces Jesus' descent through David's son Nathan (see 2 Sam. 5:14 and 1 Chron. 14:4). These differences probably provide clues to understanding both the Matthean and Lukan purpose for including the genealogy. One certain conclusion is that Matthew is concerned about presenting Jesus as the messiah who is "son of David" and "son of Abraham" (see Matt. 1:1), whereas Luke sees significance in associating Jesus with Adam, who is "son of God."

It is also helpful to note what, if any, elaboration there is to the simple genealogical list. Noteworthy, for example, are the expansions in Matt. 1:3, 5, 6 ("by Tamar," "by Rahab," "by Ruth," and "by the wife of Uriah"). This unanticipated mention of the four women interrupts the all-male pattern and calls for explanation. By these additions, Matthew was undoubtedly communicating something of import to his audience. But what? Various explanations have been suggested by interpreters. Perhaps all four women were Gentiles whose presence in Jesus' lineage foreshadowed his concern for the Gentile world; and/or perhaps all four women were involved in somewhat irregular relationships that made them subjects of controversy in the later Jewish tradition (see Johnson, 152–179, and Brown 1977, 71–74). Though much more may be intended, at least the Matthean genealogy is claiming that God has encompassed surprising, if not scandalous, events in the history that leads to the promised messiah (Brown 1977, 74). All this prepares for the final reference in Matt. 1:16 to another unexpected event, that of the birth of Jesus the messiah to Mary—wife of Joseph, yet one who conceived as a virgin. This indeed offers an implicit challenge to any patriarchal notion that only the men are crucial to the messianic tradition, especially if the four women are included, because each one advanced God's plan by acting daringly. As does the genealogy in Ruth, the Matthean genealogy protests against narrow ethnocentric concerns.

Yet another way to interpret a biblical genealogy is to discern how it fits its narrative context "in regard to language, structure, and theology" (Johnson, 253). Matthew begins his Gospel with the genealogy, a clear sign of its role in establishing the identity of Jesus; his introductory verse (1:1) heralds Jesus the Christ as son of David and son of Abraham. More than any other Gospel, Matthew grants prominence to the title Son of David (9:27; 12:23; 15:22; 20:30; 22:41–46), but the meaning of his emphasis on Jesus as "son of Abraham" is more subtle. What Matt. 1:17 does make clear is that the birth of Jesus Christ happens as the culmination of a divinely ordered history in which Abraham is the beginning, and both the Davidic reign and the Babylonian deportation represent momentous times.

In contrast, Luke places his genealogy directly after the baptism, with its heavenly declaration of Jesus as God's beloved son, and before the story of the temptation. This placement in the Lukan narrative hints at the evangelist's reason for tracing Jesus' ancestry back to Adam, son of God. He likely intends the genealogy to reconfirm and perhaps even to redefine Jesus as the Son of God. Placing the genealogy at this point in the Lukan Gospel, moreover, might intentionally associate Jesus with Moses, a paralleling that the evangelist clearly makes in Acts 7:18–37 (Kurz, 172–175).

> In relationship to the overall stories of Moses in Exodus and Jesus in Luke, the genealogies occur in almost the same relative positions. They are preceded by preliminary accounts of birth, youth, and commissioning, and they are followed by detailed narratives of Moses' and Jesus' main missions. (Kurz, 173)

The above comparison makes apparent that the two genealogies in Matthew and Luke cannot be neatly harmonized. Rather, they represent two ways to interpret the messianic history. Both are used to make claims about Jesus' identity. Each introduces theological themes important to its respective Gospel. These findings agree with a virtual consensus among contemporary scholars (Johnson, 253–256; Brown 1977, 64–65; and Fitzmyer, 497–498) that the biblical genealogies offer data of only limited use in constructing an actual reliable record of the biological history of any biblical figure, including Jesus. They were designed instead to interpret Israel's history and establish the significance of its key figures, especially the messiah.

Selected Bibliography

Brown, Raymond E. 1976. "Genealogy (Christ)." *Interpreter's Dictionary of the Bible*. Suppl. vol. Nashville: Abingdon Press.
———. 1977. *The Birth of the Messiah*, 57–95. Garden City, N.Y.: Doubleday & Co. This book offers a comprehensive treatment of the Gospel infancy narratives.

Fitzmyer, Joseph A. 1979. *The Gospel According to Luke I–IX*. Vol. 1, 488–505. Garden City, N.Y.: Doubleday & Co. The commentary provides a helpful exegetical study of the Lukan genealogy.

Jeremias, Joachim. 1969. *Jerusalem in the Time of Jesus*, 269–376. Eng. trans. by F. H. Cave and C. H. Cave. 3rd ed. London: SCM Press. Part 4 discusses concerns over racial purity in first-century Judaism.

Johnson, Marshall D. 1988. *The Purpose of the Biblical Genealogies*. 2d ed. Cambridge: Cambridge University Press. As an investigation of the purposes of genealogies in the Hebrew scriptures, Judiasm, and the Gospels, this edition includes an update of the research on genealogies since 1969 (date of first publication).

Kurz, William S. 1984. "Luke 3:23–38 and Greco-Roman and Biblical Genealogies." In *Luke-Acts: New Perspectives from the SBL Seminar*, edited by C. H. Talbert, 169–187. New York: Crossroad. This is an important study that interprets Luke 3:23–38 in light of biblical and Hellenistic genealogies.

OTHER
NEW TESTAMENT
WRITINGS

THE SERMON: HEBREWS

Definition of the Form

Even though the so-called letter to the Hebrews concludes with exhortations, greetings, and a grace benediction, the absence of a typical opening (a statement of sender/recipient, a salutation or greeting, and a thanksgiving) indicates that it is not a real letter. It was common for first-century writers to attach elements of the letter to various types of material (see *General Letters*). A more significant clue concerning the literary form of the book comes in what scholars have often identified as the alternation of *exposition* and *exhortation* in Hebrews. The author expounds a theological truth, usually on the basis of scripture, and then exhorts his hearers, repeating this process over and over again. Because of the alternation of exposition and exhortation or paraenesis, and because of the presence of sophisticated rhetorical elements, Hebrews has often been called a sermon or homily.

A study by Lawrence Wills has sharpened our understanding of the sermon as a first-century literary form (see also Swetnam's summary of the work of Hartwig Thyen, *Der Stil der jüdisch-hellenistischen Homilie*). Wills notes that in many of the rhetorical units found in first-century Christian and Jewish literature, especially in those that are obviously intended to be sermonic, there is an emphasis upon theological and scriptural "exempla" and upon exhortation. In several of the sermons in Acts, for instance, Wills identifies what he sees as a three-part structure: (1) "exempla," theological and scriptural examples or proofs; (2) a conclusion based upon this evidence; (3) an exhortation. Acts 13:16b–41 (which is, it is interesting to note, called a "word of exhortation" in 13:15) illustrates this structure well. According to Wills, Acts 13:16b–37 forms the exempla; 13:38–39, introduced by the particle *oun* ("therefore"), is the conclusion; and 13:40–41, with its shift to the imperative mood, is the exhortation (cf. Acts 2:14–40; 3:12–26; 20:17–35; Wills, 278ff.). Further examples of the form, drawn from various Christian and Jewish sources, are given by Wills (see 1 Cor. 10:1–14; 2 Cor. 6:14–7:1; 1 Peter 1, 2; 1 Clement 4:1–13:1a; 37:2–40; the Epistles of Ignatius, *Testaments of the Twelve Patriarchs*, Josephus's *Jewish War*, etc.; examples from Hebrews are given below).

Although Wills correctly notes the near absence of this form in the O.T., he perhaps overestimates its uniqueness relative to

Greco-Roman rhetoric (296–298). It is quite possible to see in Acts 13:16b–41 the typical elements of a deliberative or judicial speech (e.g., exordium, v. 16b; narration, vs. 17–25; proposition, v. 26; proof, vs. 27–37; epilogue, vs. 38–41; see Black, 8–12; see *Speech (Acts)* in the Gospels and Acts section of this volume). The sermon form as Wills defines it is not inconsistent with standard rhetorical patterns and certainly can be studied through the use of rhetorical criticism. Nevertheless, Wills's definition of the form is helpful because it illustrates through various examples the strong emphasis upon scriptural and theological proof and especially exhortation in this type of rhetoric. The type of speech we would quickly recognize on Sunday morning as a sermon can also be found in first-century Jewish and Christian writings. Then, as now, the most basic ingredients were exposition and exhortation.

Hebrews (also called a "word of exhortation" by its author in 13:22) offers some of the best examples of this sermon form. In fact, much of the book is composed of smaller units that move from exposition to exhortation, with the final exhortation or paraenesis of one unit acting as a transition to the next. After the introduction (Heb. 1:1–4), vs. 5–13 form the first exposition, here grounded in the O.T. Verse 14 draws a conclusion based upon the evidence, and 2:1–4 forms a "paraenetic interlude" (Attridge, 17) that is based upon the former verses and also forms a transition to the next unit. Hebrews 2:5–3:1 repeats the cycle: vs. 5–13 are the exposition or exempla; vs. 14–18 offer a conclusion; 3:1, with its imperative mood, is an exhortation as well as a transition to the next sermonette. It is possible to see 3:1–4:16 as a somewhat longer and more involved sermon unit (with 4:14–16 as the final exhortation), although "imperative bursts" do appear within it (see 3:12, 13; 4:1, 11). Other longer units can be found in 8:1–10:25 (8:1–10:18, exposition; 10:19–21, conclusion; 10:22–25, exhortation) and 11:1–12:3 (11:4–38, exposition; 11:39–12:1a, conclusion; 12:1b–3, exhortation; Wills, 280–283).

This cyclical or repetitive use of the sermon form in a larger work is not unusual, as 1 Clement and Ignatius's *Ephesians* illustrate. It should be noted that not all of Hebrews fits neatly into one of these forms. Hebrews 7:1–28, for instance, appears to be a scriptural and theological exposition that is independent of an exhortation, unless one links ch. 7 with the unit in 8:1–10:25. Nevertheless, the presence of this form in Hebrews is hard to deny. As if to emphasize the importance of the sermon form, the author concludes his work with a long paraenetic section

(12:12–13:19), giving the reader the impression that the entire book has moved from exposition to exhortation.

The Value for Interpretation

Like the book of Revelation, Hebrews has a complex and enigmatic structure that is often the focus of scholarly discussion. One of the values of identifying the sermon form is that it facilitates the task of outlining the book. It is difficult to ignore, for instance, the three more lengthy sermons in 3:1–4:16, 8:1–10:25, and 11:1–12:3 as one tries to describe the overall train of thought of the author. (Note that the sermons in both 3:1–4:16 and 8:1–10:25 begin their conclusions with the phrase "since then we have," emphasizing the parallel structure in another way). And of course, once these sermon units are identified, the material around them that is formally distinct becomes identifiable as well, for example, the theological discussion in ch. 7 and the lengthy paraenesis in 12:12–13:19. Noteworthy also in terms of overall structure is the way the author links the individual forms together, often using the final exhortation of one sermon unit as a transition to the exposition of the next (see 2:1–4; 3:1; 4:14–16, etc.). Even scholars who may not recognize the sermon form as defined above note the alternation of exposition and exhortation as they attempt to outline the book (see Attridge, 14–21, for an overview of significant structural analyses of Hebrews).

The sermon form found in Hebrews most certainly reflects the structure of sermons preached in the early church and as such indicates its link with the world of rhetoric. This is a key issue for the interpreters. It encourages them to discover the relationship between the sermon form and types of Greek rhetoric and also to understand to what extent and how the author of Hebrews employs rhetorical elements. It has become fairly common in biblical scholarship to classify Hebrews as epideictic rhetoric (as Attridge puts it, "celebrating the significance of Christ and inculcating values that his followers ought to share," 14; see *Forms of Argumentation*) and to analyze the individual sermons accordingly. Hebrews 11:1–12:3, for example, is often called an "encomium" (a type of epideictic rhetoric). Its sophisticated listing and discussion of heroes of the faith (11:4–38) offers an ideal point of comparison with Greek encomiums (see the analysis offered by Mack, 73–77). To identify these units as sermons does not mean that they were uninfluenced by rhetorical stan-

dards of the day. Perhaps most significant for the interpreter
with little background in Greek rhetoric is the recognition of the
rhetorical style or craft used by the author of Hebrews. Notice
how, in Heb. 11:3–31, the phrase "by faith" is repeated for
emphasis. Notice the rhetorical shift in vs. 32ff. By means of the
rhetorical question (v. 32), lists, parallel clauses, and general
references (vs. 32b–38), the author is able to conclude while
giving the impression that many further examples exist. Notice
also the shift in vs. 39 and 40, where the author gains his hearer's
attention by stressing that they are the recipients of the promises
and that they perfect the faith of the heroes listed (see Cosby
for a detailed description of the rhetorical elements in ch. 11).
Few would question the homiletical effectiveness of Heb. 11:1–
12:3. Rhetorical criticism is one of the interpreter's most promis-
ing tools for the exegesis of the sermon form and its rhetorical
qualities.

Finally, the sermon form raises significant questions for the
interpreter about exposition and exhortation and their relationship. Why is the exposition authoritative for the hearers of Hebrews; that is, why can they be expected to heed the exhortation
it produces? The most obvious answer, of course, is that the
exposition is usually based upon scripture. It is the foundation
for authoritative Christian speech. Moreover, in Hebrews (as in
most places in the N.T.) this scriptural interpretation has a christological focus. Christ becomes the new context for understanding ancient texts. The nature and content of the authoritative
Christian exposition, in this case how scripture is used, is a key
concern for the interpreter. Just as important, of course, is the
nature of the exhortation offered. Exactly what are the hearers
being exhorted to do or to be? Why is exhortation the inevitable
result of the exposition instead of a simple conclusion? These are
difficult yet important questions for the interpreter. They not
only shed light on the sermon form in Hebrews but also invite
the exegete to think about the nature of the modern Christian
sermon as well.

Selected Bibliography

Attridge, Harold W. 1989. *The Epistle to the Hebrews. Hermeneia.*
    Philadelphia: Fortress Press. This commentary on Hebrews is prob-
    ably the best currently available; the introduction does a fine job of
    describing the structural issues in the book.

Black, C. Clifton, II. 1988. "The Rhetorical Form of the Hellenistic Jewish and Early Christian Sermon: A Response to Lawrence Wills." *Harvard Theological Review* 81, 1–18. Black presents a very helpful piece that goes beyond the work of Wills to show the dependence of the Jewish/Christian sermon upon Greco-Roman rhetoric.

Cosby, Michael R. 1988. *The Rhetorical Composition and Function of Hebrews 11: In Light of Example Lists in Antiquity.* Macon, Ga.: Mercer University Press. This book is helpful in comparing ch. 11 to other ancient example lists, but is particularly insightful concerning the rhetorical elements used to construct the passage.

Mack, Burton L. 1990. *Rhetoric and the New Testament.* Minneapolis: Fortress Press. Mack not only offers a fine introduction to rhetorical criticism, but also gives a rhetorical analysis of Heb. 11:1–12:3 and 12:5–17.

Swetnam, James. 1969. "On the Literary Genre of the 'Epistle' to the Hebrews." *Novum Testamentum* 11, 261–269. This article is valuable mainly in that Swetnam gives a summary and evaluation of the work of Hartwig Thyen, *Der Stil der jüdisch-hellenistischen Homilie.*

Wills, Lawrence. 1984. "The Form of the Sermon in Hellenistic Judaism and Early Christianity." *Harvard Theological Review* 77, 277–299. This is a key work in terms of defining the sermon form, showing its occurrence in Christian writings, and wrestling with its origins in Greek rhetoric.

TOPOI AND ADMONITIONS: JAMES

Definition of the Forms

The reader of James soon notices the large number of imperative verbs (almost half) and the formal parallels to the paraenetical sections in Paul's letters (see 1 Thess. 4, 5; Rom. 12–14). Although there is some debate about the literary form of James as a whole, it is clear that the content of the book is mostly paraenesis and that it contains typical paraenetical forms (see *Paraenesis/Topoi*). Two of these forms, "topoi" and what may be called "admonitions," are the focus of our study here.

Topoi (plural of the Greek topos: "place" or "theme")

Topoi are extended paraenetical statements dealing with particular (and often traditional) themes. Hellenistic writers discuss in their topoi such typical issues as sexual conduct or civic responsibility (see Malherbe, 144–161). Paul's topoi deal with duty to the state (Rom. 13:1–7), the eating of certain foods (Rom. 14:1–23), the Christian life relative to the eschaton (1 Thess. 5:1–12), and so forth. The topoi most easily identified in James are the three that occur in the center of the book: 2:1–13, "partiality"; 2:14–26, "faith and works"; 3:1–12, "Christian speech." These three are particularly interesting because they are short argumentative essays that employ a number of rhetorical features, including aspects of the diatribe (rhetorical questions, 2:4, 6, 7, 14–16, 20, etc.; objections anticipated and answered, 2:14, 18ff.). Terence Mullins's (542f.) suggestion that Paul's topoi exhibit the common rhetorical structure of *injunction, reason,* and *discussion* (see *Paraenesis/Topoi*) may be applicable in James as well. In James 2:1–13, for example, there appears to be a well-defined rhetorical structure: 2:1, injunction; 2:2–4, reason; 2:5–7, discussion; 2:8–11, refutation of anticipated objection (also a common feature, according to Mullins); 2:12–13, conclusion.

James also contains a slightly different kind of topos. In 3:13–18, 4:1–6, 13–17, and 5:1–6, for instance, there are extended statements on particular moral issues, but here they appear to be organized around paraenetical sayings rather than based upon an argument or a rhetorical structure. Notice the number of proverblike sayings, many of which have been borrowed from the Christian or larger Hellenistic tradition and from scripture: 3:13b, 14, 16–17, 18; 4:2–3, 4b, 5b, 6b, 14b, 15, 17; 5:2, 3, 4, 5b. Martin Dibelius (1) labels these topoi "groups of sayings."

Admonitions

The word "admonitions" serves to label the form that consists of paraenetical sayings strung together loosely. Admonitions differ from topoi in that they are not organized under a certain theme and appear to lack rhetorical structure. This "scattergun" approach to paraenesis is not unusual in Jewish or Hellenistic literature and can be found in Paul as well (see Rom. 12:9–21; 1 Thess. 5:12–22; Gal. 6:1–10). In James, admonitions occur in 1:2–27 and 5:7–20. Notice how some of the individual paraenetical sayings have been expanded (1:9–11, 19–21, 22–25) and how some are connected simply on the basis of catchwords, a common device in first-century admonitions ("lack" in 1:4 and 5; "tempted" in 1:12 and 13; "religion" in 1:26 and 27; "patient" in 5:7 and 8, etc.; see Dibelius, 7ff., for numerous examples of catchwords in first-century literature).

The Value for Interpretation

The three topoi at the center of James appear to follow typical rhetorical structures and invite the interpreter to analyze the author's train of thought. In these topoi, the author's hand is evident as he carefully constructs his paraenetical treatises. But it is really a lack of helpful structure that characterizes the other topoi and the admonitions in James. Like much of the paraenetical literature of the first century, they consist primarily of a listing of traditional ethical sayings, whether they are organized under certain themes or not. The interpreter who is aware of these loosely structured paraenetical forms in James will inevitably ask how they are related to the outline or progression of thought in the larger book. This is a key yet difficult question. The same lack of tight rhetorical structure in the admonitions appears to characterize the way in which the topoi and admonitions are strung together. Even the three central topoi (2:1–13; 2:14–26; 3:1–12) have no obvious links to one another. Many solutions to the problem of the outline of James have been offered, and limitations of space do not allow a discussion of them here (see Davids, 22–29, and Dibelius, 6, n. 22, for analysis and bibliography). Nevertheless, the exegetical issue is an important one. Are the individual literary forms in James to be interpreted as being part of a larger outline, or are they to be understood as being independent of any literary context?

The paraenetical forms in James raise the question of historical setting as well. As one might expect, first-century Christian paraenesis is often traditional. It reflects general Christian teaching and even that of the larger Hellenistic world (see *Paraenesis/Topoi, Vice and Virtue Lists, The Household Code*). The inevitable question is this: Are the paraenetical forms in James being directed toward ethical issues in specific communities, or are they to be understood as general statements, widely applicable in the early church? Here the form of the larger book becomes an issue. Note that James begins as a letter, with a statement of sender/recipient and a greeting. But the recipient statement is general (cf. 1 Peter 1:1), and there is no typical thanksgiving and no closing. It has often been suggested that James is an encyclical letter, intended to be passed among several churches. On the other hand, the letter format could be simply a literary device used to introduce a general ethical or philosophical discussion, common in the Hellenistic world (Malherbe, 79f.). Ultimately, the issue must be decided on the basis of whether the paraenesis involved, the content of the "letter," is specific or general, but even here the evidence invites debate. Dibelius (22f.) argues that the paraenetical forms, including the three central arguments obviously constructed by the author, show no relationship to a specific situation, whereas Adamson (110ff.) sees such relationships everywhere, comparing James to 1 Corinthians and calling it a pastoral letter. Again, space limitations prevent a full discussion of this issue. The exegete must be aware of the fact that the paraenetical forms in James and how they are used point to significant issues in the area of historical setting.

Selected Bibliography

Adamson, James B. 1989. *James: The Man and His Message.* Grand Rapids: Wm. B. Eerdmans. Adams offers a strong commentary with a succinct review of the formal aspects of James.

Davids, Peter H. 1982. *The Epistle of James: The New International Greek Testament Commentary,* 22–29. Grand Rapids: Wm. B. Eerdmans. See especially the author's proposed outline for James.

Dibelius, Martin. 1976. *James: A Commentary on the Epistle of James,* 1–61. Revised by Heinrich Greeven; translated by Michael A. Williams. *Hermeneia.* Philadelphia: Fortress Press. This work is still the best commentary on James; Dibelius's discussion of the paraenetical forms in James is the most helpful anywhere.

Malherbe, Abraham J. 1986. *Moral Exhortation: A Greco-Roman Sourcebook.* Philadelphia: Westminster Press. This book is an invaluable resource for Hellenistic parallels to N.T. ethical exhortation.

Mullins, Terence Y. 1980. "Topos as a New Testament Form." *Journal of Biblical Literature* 99, 541–547. Mullins gives a very helpful analysis of the structure of the topos from a rhetorical perspective.

GENERAL LETTERS: JAMES; 1, 2 PETER; JUDE

Definition of the Form

Paul uses the format of the Hellenistic letter and writes correspondence that is "situational"; it responds to specific situations and indicates a personal relationship with the churches addressed. Several later New Testament writers pen what are often called general or universal (catholic) letters. They appear to have been written for general distribution in the early church. What is interesting is that there is usually a significant formal difference between Paul's situational letters and these general letters. Paul employs the three parts of the typical Hellenistic letter (opening, body, closing) and through them illustrates his personal relationship with the addressees; that is, through expansion of sender, recipient, and thanksgiving statements in the opening, through autobiographical remarks and travel plans in the body, and through greetings in the closing (see *The Pauline Letter*). The general letters, on the other hand, omit parts typically found in Paul's letters, and the parts they do include function more as literary devices than as indicators of personal correspondence.

The book of James does have a statement of sender/recipient and a greeting, but the recipients named (the twelve tribes of the dispersion, James 1:1; cf. 1 Peter 1:1) are a metaphor for all Christians and most certainly do not point to a specific church. None of the other parts of the letter appear in James. After the opening, the book consists entirely of paraenetical admonitions and topoi that would have been widely applicable in the early church (see *Topoi and Admonitions*). First Peter also has a statement of sender/recipient and a salutation, but, as in James, the recipients named are fairly general—here the churches in Asia Minor (1:1). The book contains no thanksgiving (in Paul, a place for personal remarks to his readers); and the body of the letter, composed of a baptismal sermon (1:2–4:11) and paraenesis (4:12–5:11), gives no indication that it was written for a specific community. First Peter does have a closing with personal greetings, but the pseudonymity of the letter and the general nature of its content warn the reader not to take these final comments at face value (vs. 12–14 might also be a later addition; cf. v. 11 with the final verse of 2 Peter). Like James, 2 Peter displays only the opening of a letter. It lacks specific recipients, a thanksgiving, a closing, and a body that indicates personal correspondence. Jude appears to be an apocalyptic tract. It lacks a statement of specific recipients, a thanksgiving, and personal greetings in the closing.

Other N.T. books display similarities to the general letters. Hebrews has closing comments reminiscent of Paul's letters (ch. 13: see *The Sermon*). Revelation has a letter opening (1:4) and seven short letters that may reflect actual situations in churches addressed (chs. 2, 3), although it does not have the typical body or closing (see *Apocalypse*). The Pastorals represent a somewhat different category. They follow the form of the personal letter, but if they are pseudonymous (as many scholars believe), that form may be deceptive in terms of their setting and function (see *The Pauline Letter*).

The general letters use parts of the letter to introduce or frame various types of material (in James, paraenesis; in 1 Peter, a baptismal sermon; in Jude, an apocalyptic tract) written for wide distribution. Although it is possible that this borrowing of the letter form stems from the popularity of Paul's letters, it is more probable that it simply reflects the Hellenistic custom of framing literary essays and moral and philosophical treatises with components of the letter (see Aune, 165–170; Malherbe, 79–85).

The Value for Interpretation

Above all, the abbreviated or omitted letter parts in the general letters inform the interpreter that these are not personal or "real" letters, letters responding to issues in specific Christian communities. The authors of these documents are addressing issues in the wider church, as they perceive them. It is appropriate that Paul's letters are named for the communities addressed, whereas the general letters are named for the supposed authors. The authors' perception of the contemporary ecclesiastical situation must be an important exegetical concern. In most cases, evidence of dialogue between writer and addressees is missing in the general letters.

The components of the letter used in these general letters have the interesting function of pointing away from themselves and toward the essential content of the document. They introduce or frame what is most important. Often the central part of the general letters assumes a literary form that is quite unlike the forms usually found in the bodies of personal letters. The interpreter must be able to identify these forms. Indeed, it could be argued that such identification is more important than identifying the parts of the letter used to frame them. The interpreter must realize, for instance, that James is composed primarily of paraenetical forms, that most of 1 Peter could be called a sermon, that Jude is an apocalyptic tract, and so forth. Simply to label any of these as "general letters" without recognizing the forms that are framed by the parts of the letter is to invite misinterpretation.

Also, interpreters must not devalue the general letters simply because they are not "real" letters. They must not assume that Paul's relationship with his communities and his use of the letter form should be the standard by which the general letters are to be evaluated. Essays and treaties framed by components of the letter were very common in literary circles in the Hellenistic world. The general letter found in the N.T. is a form that was widely understood and accepted and one that indicates the willingness of the church to speak in ways that were palatable to its contemporary world.

Selected Bibliography

Aune, David E. 1987. *The New Testament in Its Literary Environment*, 158–225. Philadelphia: Westminster Press. Aune presents an excellent and readable introduction.

Doty, William G. 1973. *Letters in Primitive Christianity*. Philadelphia: Fortress Press. This older book is still perhaps the best introduction to the letter form.

Malherbe, Abraham J. 1986. *Moral Exhortation: A Greco-Roman Sourcebook*, 79–85. Philadelphia: Westminster Press. Malherbe offers examples of the various types of letters in the Hellenistic world.

Stowers, Stanley K. 1986. *Letter Writing in the Greco-Roman World*. Philadelphia: Westminster Press. This book is a scholarly and broadranging introduction with helpful references to current scholarship.

APOCALYPSE: THE BOOK OF REVELATION

Definition of the Form

During the past two decades, a significant amount of attention has been focused on the task of defining the genre "apocalypse."

The apocalypse is properly seen as a genre because it is a broad literary category that must be defined with reference to content and function as well as form. The definition offered by the Society of Biblical Literature Apocalypse Group (and revised on the basis of the International Colloquium on Apocalypticism; see Collins 1979, 9; Collins 1986, 7) is helpful:

> Apocalypse is a genre of revelatory literature with a narrative framework, in which a revelation is mediated by an otherworldly being to a human recipient, disclosing a transcendent reality which is both temporal, insofar as it envisages eschatological salvation, and spatial insofar as it involves another supernatural world, intended to interpret present earthly circumstances in light of the supernatural world and of the future, and to influence both the understanding and the behavior of the audience by means of divine authority.

The book of Revelation fits this definition well. Most of the book consists of the author's narration of visions he has received from a divine mediator, whether it be an angel (Rev. 1:1) or Jesus Christ (1:17–20). These revelations speak of eschatological salvation and judgment (20:11–15, passim) and relate the coming of a new heaven and a new earth (ch. 21). In terms of function, the visions in Revelation encourage a persecuted community (see 1:9; 21:3–4) to stand firm as Christians in anticipation of the new divine order.

This description of the genre is valuable in that it helps distinguish apocalypses from Jewish prophetic literature, revelatory literature in the Greco-Roman world, and even from other apocalyptic literature that may lack one or more of the essential characteristics. The definition also helps students of the genre become aware of variations found in apocalypses. For example, although all apocalypses have a revelation mediated by an otherworldly being, in some cases the human recipient receives visions, whereas in others he is taken on an otherworldly journey (in Revelation visions predominate, but see the heavenly journey in 4:11ff.).

As important and necessary as the above definition of apocalypse is, however, one must also realize its limitations relative to an understanding of the book of Revelation. The definition indicates significant ways in which Revelation is like other apocalypses, but it is so general that it offers little help in understanding the specific exegetical issues in Revelation, and it has little to say about literary form. Revelation is extremely diverse in terms of the subforms it contains, many of which are not constituent to the apocalypse genre. Along with the more typical prophetic oracles (1:7, 8; 14:13; 16:15; 21:5–8, etc.; see Aune 1983, 274–287), commissioning visions (1:12–20; 10:1–11:2), dirges (18:1–24), and accounts of the inauguration of the new age (ch. 20), Revelation contains such forms as hymns of various sorts (4:8; 5:9–10; 11:17–18; 19:1–2, 6–8; etc.), vice and virtue lists (9:20–21; 14:4–5; 21:8, 27), and even the letter (see 1:4f.; chs. 2, 3). The exegete is called upon to recognize the uniqueness of these forms in Revelation and to understand how they relate to the apocalypse genre. In terms of its overall literary form, Revelation is rightly labeled "narrative" (as the definition indicates), but it is the uniqueness of Revelation's narrative form that poses many key exegetical questions. The way in which the author connects his visions into a larger framework or story is of vital significance for the interpreter.

In the case of Revelation, it is perhaps less helpful to ask how knowledge of the genre facilitates interpretation of the book than to ask how the unique issues of literary form in Revelation illumine both the genre and the book. In the following section, we will discuss three such issues: (1) the narrative structure in Revelation, (2) the presence of the letter form, and (3) the use of symbolic language.

The Value for Interpretation

The Narrative Structure

One unique aspect of Revelation as an apocalypse is its complex and enigmatic structure. Most of the book consists of a narration of individual visions interwoven in a sophisticated way. The author repeats phrases and symbols throughout the book to give Revelation a sense of literary unity (e.g., "white," "smoke," "the Lamb," "beast," "fire," "I saw," "I heard," etc.). Obvious also is the use of numerical structures (the seven messages, seals, trumpets, bowls; the two witnesses, scroll commissionings; the twelve tribes, gates, apostles, etc.). These numerical structures unify the book as well; but they also, especially in the case of the three septets of plagues, lend an interesting cyclical flavor to an otherwise linear, eschatological narrative (see Fiorenza, 171). Interludes, hymns that temporarily interrupt the flow of the narrative and usually bring a message of eschatological comfort (see 11:15–19; 14:1–5; 19:1–9,

etc.), are often used to link visions of woe with the hope of final
victory. Intercalations are insertions used by John to interlock
visions. In Rev. 8:1–5, for instance, vs. 1–2 introduce the seventh
seal, which, when opened, reveals the seven angels with trumpets (a vision that continues in vs. 6ff.). But 8:3–5 has been
intercalated before the vision of the trumpets; vs. 3 and 4, with
their reference to the saints, guide the hearer back to the fifth
seal (6:9–11); while v. 5, with its images of destruction, points
forward to the first four trumpets (vs. 7–12). The effect of 8:1–5
is to link more completely the vision of the seven seals with that
of the seven trumpets. As further examples of intercalations,
note how the interlude before the seventh trumpet (10:1–11:14)
links that section with chs. 12–14 through the beast image (11:7),
and how 15:2–4, the last of the seven visions given in 12:1–15:4,
is narrated after the seven bowl plagues are introduced (15:1),
thus interlocking 12:1–15:4 with 15:1–16:21 (see Fiorenza, 170–
173, and Collins 1976, 16–19, on the interweaving techniques
used in Revelation).

This sophisticated interweaving of narrative units indicates
why it has been so difficult to ascertain the overall outline or
design of the book. Almost as many outlines exist as commentaries and monographs on Revelation. Adela Yarbro Collins, for
instance, bases her outline on what she sees as six septets and
the two scroll commissionings (ch. 1, emphasized in ch. 5, and ch.
10). According to her, Revelation is composed of two cycles of
visions, 1:9–11:19 and 12:1–22:5. The first cycle includes three
septets (the seven messages, 1:9–3:22; the seven seals, 4:1–8:5;
the seven trumpets, 8:2–11:19) that are governed by the commissionings in 1:9ff. and ch. 5. The second cycle also contains
three septets (seven unnumbered visions, 12:1–15:4; the seven
bowls, 15:1–16:21; seven more unnumbered visions, 19:11–
21:8), this time governed by the scroll commissioning in ch. 10.
Because ch. 10 is in the first cycle, it represents an interlocking
device as well. These two cycles of visions are important in
Collins's understanding of Revelation because she sees them as
structurally and thematically parallel, the second cycle
"recapitulating" and clarifying the content of the first (Collins
1976, 17–44).

The outline offered by Elisabeth Schüssler Fiorenza is informed by the septets and scroll commissionings as well, but it
is especially based upon what she sees as the A B A′ structure
of John's intercalation technique. She outlines the book as
follows:

A. 1:1–8
B. 1:9–3:22
C. 4:1–9:21 and 11:15–19
D. 10:1–15:4
C'. 15:1, 5–19:10
B'. 19:11–22:9
A'. 22:10–22:21

As seen in a chiasm, Fiorenza sees a relationship between the similarly designated parts (A, A'; B, B', etc.) and sees the central section (D) as reflecting the main function of the book, "the prophetic interpretation of the situation of the community" (Fiorenza, 175). Obviously, Collins and Fiorenza represent only two of many possibilities for outlining Revelation.

Our discussion of Revelation's interlocking structure and its overall outline indicates the complexity of the task. In spite of the difficulties involved in understanding Revelation structurally, structure remains a key exegetical issue. It is hard to think of another N.T. book in which an awareness of structural issues is so important. How the visions are joined in Revelation and what their overall design is vitally influence how the book functions as an apocalypse. To say that Revelation is a narrative is of little help unless one wrestles with the unique nature of that narrative. How does a particular vision relate to the one that precedes it and follows it? How does it function in the larger design of the book? Why does John interlock and relate visions, and how does this interweaving affect the narrative flow? Gaining an understanding of the structural issues in Revelation is the first task for a person beginning interpretation. This task of analyzing the flow of the narrative in Revelation may not be easy, but without the effort one cannot begin to understand this enigmatic book.

Apocalypse or Letter?

Although apocalypses may be prefaced with other types of material (e.g., the legends in Dan. 1–6), Revelation is the only known apocalypse to be enclosed in a letter framework (1:4–8; 22:6–21). The prescript (1:4–8) includes elements found in Paul's letters: a statement of sender and recipient (v. 4a), a grace and peace salutation (vs. 4b–5), and a doxology (vs. 5b–6; cf. Gal. 1:5), to which are appended two independent prophetic sayings (vs. 7, 8). The closing includes a series of independent

sayings about the authority and sufficiency of the revelation
(21:6–19), an entreaty for Christ to come (v. 20; cf. v. 17; 1 Cor.
16:22), and the typical benediction (v. 21). The letter form is
further emphasized by the addresses to seven churches in chs. 2
and 3. Even though these addresses have a formalized structure—(1) address and command to write; (2) a description of the
authoritative words of the divine speaker; (3) an "I know" section in which the congregation is exhorted or censured; (4) the
statement "he who has an ear, let him hear"—they appear to
address specific situations John is aware of and may indicate that
the book was passed between the churches as a circular letter.

How do these elements of the letter relate to the genre apocalypse in Revelation? It must be emphasized that the letter
framework in Revelation does not transform the book into a
letter. The author tells his readers at the very beginning that
what follows is a revelation of Jesus Christ (1:1), and he even
relates the circumstances of his vision (1:9). The seven addresses
are products of this revelation (see 1:11), and of course the bulk
of Revelation (chs. 4–21) is a series of visions, unlike the body of
a typical letter. The vision motif, a central element in apocalypses, remains preeminent.

One significant reason for John's use of the letter form in
Revelation has to do with his desire to exhort his hearers. Even
more than their Jewish counterparts, Christian apocalypses
and apocalyptic material often contain paraenesis. In the apocalyptic discourses in Mark and I Thessalonians, for instance, the
authors readily incorporate paraenetical sections (Mark 13:5, 6,
21–23, 28ff.; 1 Thess. 5:4ff.). John uses the prescript and closing,
and especially the seven "letters" to the churches (chs. 2, 3),
because they are a natural format for exhortation directed to
specific situations. Yet these "letters" do not detract from the
larger apocalypse genre. Even the seven letters have been given
in a vision (1:11)! The use of the letter format in Revelation
is a creative way of emphasizing the paraenetical within an
apocalypse.

Just as important is the way letter relates to apocalypse in
terms of the nature of authoritative revelation. On one level, the
letter format gives authority to the apocalypse because Paul's
letters would have been widely recognized as authoritative.
Even more, one must understand the power of *written* revelation in the Jewish tradition. Sometimes the written word of God,
as in the case of the tablets given to Moses or the scroll given to
Ezekiel (cf. Rev. 10:9), has special power (see Collins 1976, 7).

John emphasizes that he has been told in his revelation to *write* his vision in a book and send it to the churches (1:11; see also the word "write" in 2:1, 8, 12, 18; 3:1, 7, 14). Part of the authority of the book lies in this command to put the revelation down in writing. In Revelation, the letter format emphasizes the authority already inherent in the apocalypse's vision accounts by providing a natural way to speak of the written word of God.

Of course, the letter is just one of many subforms found in John's apocalypse, but it represents a significant exegetical issue. How do the various literary forms used in Revelation (some of which are uncommon in apocalypses) relate to the genre and the interpretation of the book? Why, for instance, is a hymn found in the middle of the vision narration in ch. 12 (vs. 10–12), and how does it affect the interpretation of the chapter? Why does John use prophetic oracles in 1:7, 8 immediately after the doxology and before the description of himself and his revelation (1:9ff.)? Why are the vice lists employed in ch. 21 (21:8, 27), and how do they affect this vision of the new Jerusalem? This awareness of the numerous subforms found in the larger narrative of Revelation must always be on the interpreter's mind.

Symbolism

Revelation is unique among apocalypses because of its extensive use of symbolism and apocalyptic imagery. Such imagery, drawn from the Christian tradition, Jewish apocalypticism, and especially the Hebrew scriptures, contributes greatly both to the appeal and the ambiguity of the book. From one point of view, it might be possible to see Revelation as poetry because of its use of symbolic language in combination with what is often a rhythmic or repetitive structure (see *Poetry and Hymn*). At the very least, one must recognize the poetic impact of the many hymns and their imagery (see 5:9b–10; 7:15–17; 11:17–18; 15:3–4; 19:1b–2, etc.). It is crucial for the modern reader to attempt to understand the evocative power these symbols would have had as Revelation was read aloud in early Christian communities.

John uses symbols in various ways and on several levels. At times he interprets the symbols in a specific way (see the seven lampstands and stars, 1:12, 16, interpreted in 1:20; those in the white robes, 7:13, 14; the dragon, 12:7–9) to make sure the hearer grasps his intended meaning. Often the symbols employed are ones commonly found in Jewish and Christian literature; they would have been readily understood by the hearer (the Lamb, Babylon, the new Jerusalem, etc.). More difficult to interpret is the imagery John uses to describe heavenly or future scenes (see 4:1–11; 21:9–21). Are these visions intended to detail the actual appearance of heavenly scenes, or are the various images intended to symbolize a reality that is beyond human comprehension? Perhaps the highest level of interpretive skill is necessary to understand the visions that treat symbolically the plight and future of the church (especially 11:1–13; 12:1–17; 13:1–18). The symbols there are open-ended and ambiguous (the two witnesses, 11:3ff.; the woman, 12:1ff.; six hundred sixty-six, 13:18, etc.), and, together with the symbolic stories in which they are found, evoke various creative responses.

Symbolism in Revelation is important in its own right, but it is also related to issues of structure in that the symbolism often reflects the mythic structure of the book. John's universe is a place of conflict between the forces of chaos and the forces of good (reflected, for example, in the images of beast or dragon and Lamb), between the wicked and the righteous (see 21:6–8). Throughout the book symbols are used that point to this dualism and hence suggest structural shifts. In the vision of the seven seals, for instance (6:1–8:1), John contrasts images of destruction and persecution (the four horsemen, 6:2–8; the altar of the persecuted, 6:9–11; the earthquake, 6:12–17) with images of salvation and hope (angels, 7:1; the seal of the righteous, 7:3; the 144,000, 7:4; the Lamb and the white robes, 7:9). The symbolism involved, especially in contrast to that which is found in 6:1–17, is a major indicator that 7:1–17 represents a structural shift.

In some cases this conflict-motif in Revelation issues forth in the typical structure of what is called the combat myth, a Near Eastern mythological pattern that usually contains (1) a rebellion of the evil forces, (2) the temporary rule of chaos, and (3) final victory for the forces of good. Notice how many of the symbols in Rev. 12:1–10 point to this combat-myth structure. The red dragon symbolizes the forces of Satan in rebellion, chaos is symbolized by the dragon's tail sweeping down the stars and by the pursuit of the woman (vs. 4–6), and victory is indicated by vs. 7–12, especially the hymn in vs. 10–12. Adela Yarbro Collins, who has especially emphasized the significance of the combat myth for Revelation, goes so far as to conclude that the symbols in the last five sections in Revelation (excluding the seven messages section) reflect this combat-myth structure. Each section shows a movement from persecution of the faithful to punishment of the nations to salvation for the faithful (Collins 1976, 32–44). Obviously, the symbols employed play a key role in signaling this combat-myth structure in Revelation.

One might expect symbolic language in a genre that attempts to speak about a "transcendent reality" (see above definition of apocalypse), but the extent of this language in Revelation makes it a key exegetical issue. The interpreter must attempt not only to understand the symbols, but also to grasp their evocative power. Just as important, the interpreter must recognize the mythological structure that they reflect and attempt to see how that structure has affected the composition of Revelation.

In a real sense, Revelation represents one of the frontiers in the N.T. for the student of literary form. The above discussions of structure, the letter subform and symbolism point to three key areas for investigation, but there are certainly many others. The book of Revelation is exciting because, in spite of many obvious literary characteristics, it remains enigmatic and difficult to define, a point hopefully communicated above. Understanding the formal characteristics of Revelation is not easy, but it is a necessary and rewarding exegetical task.

Selected Bibliography

Aune, David E. 1983. *Prophecy in Early Christianity and the Ancient Mediterranean World.* Grand Rapids: Wm. B. Eerdmans. Aune illustrates clearly the use of prophetic forms in Revelation.

———. 1986. "The Apocalypse of John and the Problem of Genre." *Semeia* 36, 65–96. This article is a very helpful analysis of current definitions of the genre apocalypse.

Beardslee, William A. 1970. *Literary Criticism of the New Testament,* 53–63. Philadelphia: Fortress Press. This section is one of the finest short introductions to the genre.

Collins, Adela Yarbro. 1976. *The Combat Myth in the Book of Revelation.* Missoula, Mont.: Scholars Press.

———. 1984. *Crises and Catharsis: The Power of the Apocalypse.* Philadelphia: Westminster Press.

———. 1986. "Introduction: Early Christian Apocalypticism." *Semeia* 36, 1–12.

The 1976 volume discusses the combat myth in Revelation, the 1984 text provides an excellent introduction to Revelation, and the 1986 article provides a quick overview relative to the definition of apocalypse. All are highly readable.

Collins, John J. 1979. "Introduction: Towards the Morphology of a Genre." *Semeia* 14, 1–20. This article is helpful in defining key terms and in setting the ground rules for understanding apocalypse.

Fiorenza, Elisabeth Schüssler. 1985. *The Book of Revelation: Justice and Judgement*, 159–180. Philadelphia: Fortress Press. This series of articles covers a variety of literary and historical issues; see especially the section "The Composition and Structure of Revelation."

Rowland, Christopher. 1982. *The Open Heaven: A Study of Apocalyptic in Judaism and Early Christianity*. New York: Crossroad. This wide-ranging study focuses on various Jewish and Christian apocalyptic material.

INDEX OF
SCRIPTURE REFERENCES